The Abolition of Slavery and
the Aftermath of Emancipation
in Brazil

The Abolition of Slavery and the Aftermath of Emancipation in Brazil

REBECCA J. SCOTT

SEYMOUR DRESCHER

HEBE MARIA MATTOS DE CASTRO

GEORGE REID ANDREWS

ROBERT M. LEVINE

Duke University Press
Durham and London 1988

The text of this book was originally published without the present introduction or the index as Volume 68, Number 3 (August 1988) of the *Hispanic American Historical Review*.

© 1988, Duke University Press
All rights reserved
Printed in the United States of America
on acid-free paper ∞
Third impression, 1995

Library of Congress Cataloging-in-Publication Data
Abolition of slavery in Brazil / Rebecca J. Scott . . . [et al.].
Includes index.
ISBN 0-8223-0888-6
1. Slavery—Brazil—Emancipation.   I. Scott, Rebecca J.
(Rebecca Jarvis), 1950–
HT 1128.A63 1988
326'.0981—dc1988-21921

Contents

A Note of Introduction

In May 1888 the Brazilian parliament passed, and Princess Isabel (acting for her father Emperor Pedro II) signed, the Lei Aúrea, or "Golden Law," providing for the total abolition of slavery. Brazil thus became the "last civilized nation," or "last Christian nation" as it was alternatively put, to decree the end of slavery as a legal institution. In 1988 the event was observed in Brazil with numerous historical congresses and other commemorations. And, just as the approach of the Columbus quincentennial has already sparked protests from some Native Americans and others who insist that Columbus's achievement is to be deplored rather than celebrated, there were counterobservances in Brazil by descendants of slaves who argue that despite legal emancipation they are trapped even today in a situation of cruel inequality.

In both cases those who wish to celebrate and those who deplore do agree on at least one thing: that the event in question was important. The freeing of slaves in Brazil, as in other countries, may not have fulfilled the hopes of improvement that it aroused, but the former slaves certainly did not call for restoration of their previous condition, and the final act of abolition is one of the defining landmarks of Brazilian history. The editors of the *Hispanic American Historical Review* therefore decided to dedicate one entire issue, in August 1988, to mark this anniversary; the resulting essays are reprinted for a wider audience in this volume. The authors represent a broad range of scholarly backgrounds and perspectives. There is one Brazilian historian, Hebe Maria de Castro, and a U.S. historian, Seymour Drescher, whose primary specialty is the history of European abolitionism. The other three authors, Rebecca Scott, George Reid Andrews, and Robert Levine, are well-known U.S. specialists in Latin American history. Only Drescher's essay deals strictly with the abolition process. However, that process and its aftermath occurred within a larger context of Brazilian history, which both affected and was affected by the decision of the parliamentary majority and Princess Isabel. It thus seems perfectly appropriate to observe the centennial of abolition with a collection of essays concerning Brazil in the age (liberally interpreted) of abolition. The scope is broad enough to cover developments from the mid-nineteenth to the early twentieth centuries, whose interconnections may not always be apparent at first glance. At second glance, however, the reader will see that all the contributions touch, to varying degrees, on certain common themes of Brazilian society during the period that was bisected by the formal abolition of slavery.

David Bushnell
Managing Editor, HAHR

Exploring the Meaning of Freedom: Postemancipation Societies in Comparative Perspective

REBECCA J. SCOTT

THE centennial of the final abolition of slavery in Cuba and Brazil has occasioned an exceptional burst of scholarly interest, perhaps in part owing to the moral weight that the questions of slavery and freedom continue to carry.[1] Integrating a moral vision into scholarship on this subject, however, has remained problematic. The old notion of slave emancipation as a purifying, redemptive triumph of moral rightness over self-interest has receded, sometimes to be replaced by a more jaundiced view of emancipation as the trading of one master for another, or the relinquishing of explicit coercion and explicit protection for implicit coercion and no protection at all. The best recent work on emancipation has challenged these polarities, emphasizing the complexity of former slaves' initiatives in the context of the constraints placed on them.[2]

*I would like to thank George Reid Andrews, Seymour Drescher, Neil Foley, Josep Fradera, Thomas Holt, Robert Levine, Sidney Mintz, Louis A. Pérez, Jr., Peter Railton, Leslie Rowland, and Anne Scott for their very helpful comments on earlier drafts of this essay.

1. Several conferences were held in 1986 to commemorate Cuban abolition. See the proceedings of meetings in Paris in the *Anuario de Estudios Americanos*, 43 (1986). Recent Cuban essays appear in Academia de Ciencias de Cuba, *La esclavitud en Cuba* (Havana, 1986); recent Spanish essays in Francisco de Solano, ed., *Estudios sobre la abolición de la esclavitud* (Madrid, 1986); and work in Catalan in a special number of *L'avenç* (Barcelona), 101 (Feb. 1987). See also the essay by Manuel Moreno Fraginals, "La esclavitud: A cien años del fin," *Revolución y Cultura* (Havana), 8 (Aug. 1986), 2–11. Brazilian abolition will be discussed at conferences in 1988 at the University of São Paulo and the University of Campinas, among others; an interesting set of short essays has already appeared in the *Folhetim* of the *Folha de São Paulo*, May 8, 1987.

2. Willie Lee Rose, in a 1976 essay, responded to the swing toward a negative view of the achievements of Reconstruction and warned of the risk of "wrongly outflanking the significance of emancipation for the freedmen themselves," of ignoring "their perceptions of the great event, their hopes and fears for the future." See her "Jubilee and Beyond: What Was Freedom?" in *What Was Freedom's Price?*, David G. Sansing, ed. (Jackson, MS, 1978), 5. For the development of an interactive perspective, see in particular Frederick Cooper, *From Slaves to Squatters: Plantation Labor and Agriculture in Zanzibar and Coastal Kenya, 1890–1925* (New Haven, 1980); Barbara Jeanne Fields, *Slavery and Freedom*

As one attempts to formulate a research design for work on the aftermath of emancipation, the question arises: what exactly should one do with this insight about behavior, this realization that slave emancipation was neither a transcendent liberation nor a complete swindle, but rather an occasion for reshaping—within limits—social, economic, and political relationships? It is one thing to invoke the concept of multiple options and multiple constraints; it is quite another to show with any precision what processes and outcomes resulted from the interaction of initiative and context.

In this essay I will first discuss certain ways in which the articles that follow expand our understanding of emancipation and postemancipation society. My focus will be on questions that can be raised for a range of societies in the Americas, with particular attention to Brazil, Cuba, and the United States. I will then try to suggest several new directions in which inquiry might go, focusing on sources, methodology, and interpretation. In some instances, I will draw on work from the very different, but conceptually related, field of Latin American colonial history. Analyses of the transformation of indigenous societies in the aftermath of conquest can, on occasion, provide both practical and theoretical insights into the study of relations between former masters and former slaves.[3]

The larger purpose of the essay is to suggest ways of studying the meaning of freedom. A comparative approach to emancipation has certain obvious advantages for the highlighting of crucial differences and the testing of hypotheses. Perhaps less obvious is the value of comparison in raising new questions and reshaping old ones. For comparison can juxtapose not only selected "cases," but also very different historiographies, each with a set of analytic presuppositions and accompanying questions. Out of the clash of those presuppositions and the careful application of some of the questions from one historical tradition to the evidence of another, new frameworks for analysis may emerge. Thus, for example, a

---

on the Middle Ground: Maryland during the Nineteenth Century (New Haven, 1985); and the volumes of Freedom: A Documentary History of Emancipation, 1861–1867, Ira Berlin, Joseph P. Reidy, Leslie S. Rowland et al., eds. (New York, 1982–). For a discussion of several recent works, see Rebecca J. Scott, "Comparing Emancipations: A Review Essay," Journal of Social History, 20:3 (Spring 1987), 565–584.

3. Portions of this essay began as a reflection on the work of Charles Gibson, presented at the 1986 American Historical Association meeting under the title, "Stress and Resilience in Relations of Subordination: Extending the Logic of The Aztecs Under Spanish Rule." In recasting the ideas of that essay, I have relinquished the explicit discussion of the ways in which an analysis of Aztecs can shape an interpretation of both methodology and theoretical questions to be asked, retaining only a few general references to the parallels that might be drawn between the study of colonial Indian communities and the study of postemancipation societies. My debt to Gibson's work, however, remains undiminished. For references to other works in colonial history, see n. 38 below.

close examination of several societies after slavery can pose a challenge to the conventional dichotomy of dependence versus autonomy for the former slave. At the same time, such a comparison may encourage us to expand our focus to encompass a wider range of social groupings, rather than attempting to isolate the interactions of former masters and former slaves.

Hebe Castro's essay, "Beyond Masters and Slaves," provides a précis of her larger work on the community of Capivary in the province of Rio de Janeiro during the nineteenth century. Her study is a model of the way in which the systematic exploration of new sources in a local context can force a reframing of central questions about the national experience.[4] Three features of this work might be highlighted. First, Castro's study illuminates the lives of poor rural Brazilians, not as individuals "marginal" to a dominant society, but as participants in a lively economy complementary to both urban society and the coffee-growing activities undertaken by more prosperous residents of the region. Second, her portrait of Capivary adds to the complexity of our image of Brazilian slavery. Like Stuart Schwartz, Castro emphasizes the dispersed character of Brazilian slaveholding, and the small size of the units on which many slaves resided, even in the context of a highly concentrated pattern of formal landowning.[5] Third, her work implicitly rejects a unilinear concept of proletarianization as the inevitable outcome of emancipation and the expansion of commercial agriculture. Whatever the aims of legislators and large-scale landowners, the poor of Capivary were not fully denied access to land. By retaining such access, they were able to escape transformation into a mere "rural work force."

Capivary, with its mixed population cultivating coffee for the internal market and manioc for consumption and for sale to the city, provides more than a simple community study. The presence of dispersed, small-scale, partially slave-based subsistence and commercial agriculture—characteristic not only of Capivary but of significant portions of the province of Rio de Janeiro—raises a question of crucial importance for the understanding of abolition.[6] The question is: how does the precise class structure of a given slaveholding society affect the transition to free labor, both in terms of changing patterns of labor use and in terms of the development of pro- and antiabolition movements? Coincidentally, the same question emerges

4. See Hebe Maria Mattos de Castro, *Ao sul da história: Lavradores pobres na crise do trabalho escravo* (São Paulo, 1987).

5. See Stuart B. Schwartz, *Sugar Plantations in the Formation of Brazilian Society: Bahia, 1550–1835* (New York, 1985), especially chap. 16.

6. On the provincial dimensions of this phenomenon, see Castro, *Ao sul da história*, 30.

in Seymour Drescher's analysis from the opposite perspective—from the vantage point of a transnational comparison of the course of abolition.

Drescher's study, "Brazilian Abolition in Comparative Perspective," explores the dramatic regional variations in the significance of slavery within Brazil that emerged after the termination of the transatlantic slave trade, and explores the consequences for the development of abolitionism and antiabolitionism. He draws parallels with similar regional disparities —North/South and East/West—in the United States and Cuba, and notes the political risks to slaveholders of such divergence. In both the United States and Brazil, there seems also to have been a concentration of slave-holding within regions in the decades before abolition, as large-scale rural owners came to hold an increasing fraction of all slaves and the proportion of farmers owning no slaves grew.[7]

The political outcomes in the United States and in Brazil, however, were very different. While planters in the U.S. South managed to forge a regional coalition to oppose abolition, planters in Rio de Janeiro and São Paulo seem to have had only limited success in mobilizing opposition to the steps that were taken toward gradual emancipation in the 1870s and 1880s. Drescher comments on Brazil: "The historian of North Atlantic abolitions is . . . struck by the absence of a united front of the major slaveholding provinces against the gradual termination of the institution."

There are many possible explanations for this contrast. Regional and intraregional variations in the degree of commitment to slavery itself constitute the factor most often cited. The slaveholders of different producing zones within Brazil varied radically in the markets they faced and the labor supply they could draw on and thus in their visions of the risks and benefits of abolition.[8] One might still wonder at the failure to organize widespread resistance to abolition in key regions of Rio and São Paulo, where the institution of slavery remained strong. The point here is not to imply that planters acquiesced early on to abolition; they did not. The question is why they did not choose to mount a broad-ranging offensive against the erosion of one basis of their livelihood. Drescher cites elite

7. Some of this concentration resulted from a relative decline of slavery in the cities. On cities in the U.S. South, see the references in Drescher's essay and Fields, *Slavery and Freedom*, chap. 3. Concentration can also be identified within rural areas. Gavin Wright, *The Political Economy of the Cotton South: Households, Markets, and Wealth in the Nineteenth Century* (New York, 1978), 34–36, points out the increase in the percentage of farm operations in the U.S. South with no slaves. For Capivary, in the period 1850–88, Castro has documented the predominance of sales of slaves from owners of small properties to owners of large properties. See Castro, *Ao sul da história*, 38–55.

8. Such differences, and accompanying cultural and ideological divergences, figure in the analyses of both Robert E. Conrad, *The Destruction of Brazilian Slavery, 1850–1888* (Berkeley, 1972) and Robert Brent Toplin, *The Abolition of Slavery in Brazil* (New York, 1971).

fear of the consequences of mobilization among a racially heterogeneous free population. Others have pointed to the ideological ambivalence and defensiveness of Brazilian planters in the face of a growing European and North American ideology of free labor.[9]

One should perhaps recall that the unity created by slaveholders in the southern United States was itself both incomplete and precarious, resting on regional identity, political concessions, ideological maneuvers, and a longstanding tradition of racism at all social levels. The costs of a cross-class white "racial" coalition were high, and its survival during wartime was uncertain.[10] The feat was perhaps hardly likely to be replicated in the very different environment of Brazil decades later.

Castro's work suggests that one should also seek a partial answer in the dynamics of relationships at the local level. From her analysis, it appears that free small-scale cultivators were often the "clients" of large landowners, but were not entirely the creatures of the elite. If we compare them to the small farmers of the southern United States, we find that they were bound to larger planters by ties of debt and credit, and perhaps by a need for protection, but not necessarily by a shared "racial" identity, and certainly not by a democratic electoral practice. The implications of this pattern for the dependence or autonomy of such individuals are ambiguous. As victims of the "clientelism" for which Brazil remains famous, the poor of Capivary acted at times to support the political power of specific patrons, and had virtually none of the political rights of their counterparts in the white population of the U.S. South. But it was the self-consciously "independent" poor southerners, not the "dependent" Brazilians, who were persuaded to join forces in a war to defend slave society. The interplay of shared and conflicting interests, culture, and ideology that brought about this contrast remains to be explored comparatively.

Drescher poses the intriguing question: "Was the relationship between

9. See, most recently, David Brion Davis, *Slavery and Human Progress* (New York, 1984), 298, as well as the voluminous literature on Brazilian abolitionism.

10. For differing analyses of the political basis of power in the antebellum South, see, among other studies, J. Mills Thornton, III, *Politics and Power in a Slave Society: Alabama, 1800–1860* (Baton Rouge, 1978), esp. 160–162 and 442–461; Eugene Genovese, "Yeoman Farmers in a Slaveholders' Democracy," in *Fruits of Merchant Capital: Slavery and Bourgeois Property in the Rise and Expansion of Capitalism*, Elizabeth Fox-Genovese and Eugene D. Genovese, eds. (New York, 1983); and Harry L. Watson, "Conflict and Collaboration: Yeomen, Slaveholders, and Politics in the Antebellum South," *Social History*, 10 (Oct. 1985), 273–297. On yeoman farmers, see also Steven Hahn, *The Roots of Southern Populism: Yeoman Farmers and the Transformation of the Georgia Upcountry, 1850–1890* (New York, 1983). On the breakdown of unity during the war, see Paul D. Escott, *After Secession: Jefferson Davis and the Failure of Confederate Nationalism* (Baton Rouge, 1978), chap. 4. I am grateful to Leslie Rowland for sharing with me her unpublished comments from the session "Class Conflict in the Confederacy," Southern Historical Association meeting, Louisville, Nov. 1984.

slaves and free people in the rural areas different in Brazil because of the cumulative effect of manumissions and the consequent existence of bonds which did not exist in the racially more polarized U.S. South?" The question, however, could quickly become even more complex. What were the implications for cross-racial social relations of a pattern of slave-holding in Brazil so widespread that people who were indisputably poor —whether white, black, or mulatto—often owned a slave or two? While frequent manumission might provide the basis for a multiracial "plebeian subculture," selective but extensive slaveownership among the poor could also create tensions that would divide free and slave.[11] More detailed comparison would seem to be necessary here. Further systematic analyses of specific regions should enable us to move beyond the stereotypes of a politically "democratic" but racially exclusionary South and an oligarchic Brazilian society with a large racially integrated marginal population.

Answers to these questions, as they emerge, will have important implications not only for the classic question of the causes of abolition, but also for the evolution of postemancipation society. Each region's social structure on the eve of abolition shaped the balance of forces with which former slaves would have to contend. Patterns of debt, credit, marketing, access to land, and social relations formed the backdrop to the transformations wrought by the ending of slavery, and the existing free rural population was generally the milieu into which former slaves would at least initially move.

Drescher emphasizes the evaporation of the Brazilian abolitionist movement after the ending of slavery and the lack of organized programs to aid the freed people. But equally significant, surely, is the relative absence of the violence and vengeance so characteristic of white southerners' responses, not only to emancipation but to the mere mention of "social equality." To what extent does the lack of white violence directed at former slaves in Brazil reflect an acceptance of social change, and to what extent does it instead reflect the containment of such change through other mechanisms?[12]

---

11. See the penetrating discussion of social relations in Manuela Carneiro da Cunha, *Negros, estrangeiros: Os escravos libertos e sua volta à África* (São Paulo, 1985). I am grateful to Judith Lee Allen, who is currently conducting research on the free population of the Bahian Recôncavo, for her discussion of "plebeian subculture" in this context. See also Allen, "Tailors, Soldiers, and Slaves: The Social Anatomy of a Conspiracy" (M.A.thesis, University of Wisconsin, Madison, 1987).

12. This observation is not meant to downplay the significance of violence and repression in Brazilian society, but merely to emphasize that such repression was rarely framed in terms of the maintenance of a "racial" order. Emília Viotti da Costa and others have argued that the strength of class rule and clientelism in Brazil blunted the need for an explicitly "racial" ideology and practice of domination. See da Costa, *The Brazilian Empire: Myths and Histories* (Chicago, 1985), esp. chap. 9.

Though the image of oligarchic continuity can be overdrawn, it seems clear that in some regions, such as the Northeast, the incorporation of former slaves into existing patron-client relations diminished the probability of direct confrontation. Peter Eisenberg, for example, has argued that former slaves working on the sugar plantations of Pernambuco continued in a position of dependency. They moved into established roles in the agricultural economy, becoming part of a longstanding free, but impoverished, work force.[13] But what of areas such as São Paulo, where former slaves were not smoothly incorporated into the evolving pattern of agricultural production?

Reid Andrews, in "Black and White Workers: São Paulo, Brazil, 1888–1928," cautiously uses the category of "marginality," rejected by Castro, to describe the role of Afro-Brazilians within the growing rural and urban economy. One strength of his analysis is that his use of the concept is time dependent, contextual, and specific. He disputes Florestan Fernandes's emphasis on the importance of a slave "heritage" in handicapping Afro-Brazilians in the postemancipation labor market, focusing instead on the specific choices and bargains that former slaves attempted to make, and on the context in which they had to negotiate.

In Andrews's view, it was planters, in alliance with the state, who took the initiative in excluding Afro-Brazilians by flooding the São Paulo labor market with subsidized immigrants once abolition was underway. But at the same time, the values on which *libertos* insisted put them repeatedly at a disadvantage in competition with immigrant laborers. *Libertos'* desire to be treated with respect, to escape the direct coercion of plantation overseers, and to construct a new family division of labor conflicted with planters' preferences. Employers generally sought subjugated laborers who were prepared to put all members of the family to work in the fields or factory. The image of the "marginal" Afro-Brazilian thus ceases to be one of an incapable worker and becomes one of an individual unwilling to submit to unreasonable exigencies for inadequate pay, particularly in the face of employers who explicitly disparaged his or her capacities.

Instead of attributing fixed patterns of behavior to immigrants and

13. Peter L. Eisenberg also sees a general decline in the standard of living for rural workers. See Eisenberg, *The Sugar Industry in Pernambuco: Modernization Without Change, 1840–1910* (Berkeley, 1974), esp. chap. 8. Jaime Reis, by contrast, points out the pitfalls of constructing a pessimistic portrait of the fate of sugar workers in the postslavery world. He points out that the descendants of slaveholders on whose memoirs such a portrait partially relies may have shaped their evidence to defend the conduct of an old elite against the depredations of a new one. See Reis, "From *Banguê* to *Usina*: Social Aspects of Growth and Modernization in the Sugar Industry of Pernambuco (1850–1920)," in *Land and Labour in Latin America: Essays on the Development of Agrarian Capitalism in the Nineteenth and Twentieth Centuries*, Kenneth Duncan and Ian Rutledge, eds. (Cambridge, 1977), 369–396.

libertos, Andrews shows how the demands and bargains of each group evolved. As the immigrants gained a footing, they too balked at low wages and direct control. When factory jobs opened up for Afro-Brazilians with the ending of subsidized European immigration, the composition of the labor force changed, and elite portraits of the descendants of slaves altered swiftly to revalue the "national worker." One might draw a parallel here to Walter Rodney's analysis of the Guyanese working population, in which he contrasts the experiences and behavior of Afro-Guyanese Creoles and East Indian immigrants, but carefully avoids the classic stereotype of "submissive" indentured immigrant workers.[14]

One could perhaps take this analysis a step further and emphasize the highly relational character of contemporary portraits of different groups of workers. In São Paulo, former slaves were juxtaposed with Italian immigrants, and planters characterized the former slaves as excessively demanding and sensitive to violations of their dignity. In Bahia, on the other hand, observers in the early twentieth century contrasted the *moradores* resident on plantations, often descendants of slaves, to the *catingueiros* who came in seasonally from the back country to work on the sugar estates. The stereotypes and attributed attitudes were suddenly reversed: the *morador* was portrayed as a good and reliable worker, the *catingueiro* as strong but haughty and proud.[15]

Obviously, substantive differences between Bahia and São Paulo shaped the behavior of former slaves in each area after emancipation. But the variability of the stereotypes invoked should alert one to the need for extensive direct evidence of actual beliefs and behaviors against which to measure attributed "attitudes." Scholars have become sensitive to the malleability of elite views concerning the aptitudes of different ethnic groups for different kinds of work. As Andrews points out, these tended to shift with changing labor markets, and cannot be taken as descriptions of reality.[16] But equal caution may be called for in using indirect

14. Walter Rodney, A *History of the Guyanese Working People, 1881–1905* (Baltimore, 1981). An important earlier discussion of Afro-Brazilians in the rural labor force in São Paulo is Warren Dean, *Rio Claro: A Brazilian Plantation System, 1820–1920* (Stanford, 1976).

15. See the observation by S. Fróes Abreu in *Alguns aspectos da Bahia* (Rio de Janeiro, 1926), 72. He writes that the *catingueiro* is not a bad worker, but notes, "Tem, entretanto, grandes defeitos; é altivo demais e não se sujeita muito á condição de servilidade, como o negro."

16. Fields is a forceful proponent of the view that both "race" and racism are variable and contextual, and that elite descriptions of the capacities and incapacities of Afro-Americans were not only descriptively inaccurate, but also should not be seen as reified "racist attitudes" capable on their own of determining behavior. Instead, such descriptions shifted with changing social and economic circumstances, and were part of the larger "ideology of race." See, for example, Fields, "Race and Ideology in American History," in *Region, Race, and Reconstruction: Essays in Honor of C. Vann Woodward*, J. Morgan Kousser and James McPherson, eds. (New York, 1982), 143–177. See also Lawrence N. Powell, *New*

evidence of the attitudes of the former slaves themselves. Contemporary accounts of prideful former slaves may seem less obviously biased than accounts of lazy ones, but in both cases the descriptive terms should themselves be subject to critical scrutiny.

Robert Levine's essay, "'Mud-Hut Jerusalem': Canudos Revisited," also addresses the question of the goals of rural Brazilians, but from a very different angle. While Castro traces the structure of rural society and Andrews analyzes the evolution of the labor market, Levine examines a specific social movement that cut across the line dividing former slaves and long-free rural folk. Perhaps most intriguing in Levine's portrait of the followers of Antônio Conselheiro is his emphasis on their common vision of self-sufficiency, a desire to achieve a degree of insulation from the demands of large landholders and government authorities. While discussing the conjunctural political factors that shaped elite responses to Canudos at both the national and the state levels, Levine also discerns an economic and social vision within the religious vision of the community. The goal of self-sufficiency expressed by the followers of Conselheiro, though a frequent feature of religious secessionist movements, could also constitute a significant challenge to the economic power of dominant groups, if it were realized on a large scale.

One might draw a parallel with the exodus of Afro-American families to Kansas from the rural South in the late 1870s. There, too, religious figures and a degree of apparent unrealism marked the sudden mobilization of population. At least some of the participants in each of the two movements shared a millenarian vision, but one resting on a concrete experience of the intolerable hardship of existing conditions in the countryside, heightened in the Brazilian Northeast by drought and in the southern United States by systematic white violence. In both instances, the protagonists shared a dream of access to land and of mutual responsibility for sufficiency. In both northeastern Brazil and the southern United States, landholders were frustrated by the real or potential loss of labor, and by the threatened disruption of labor and social relations. Government responses to the two movements differed sharply, with authorities opting for state-directed repression in Brazil, and national neglect, combined with a degree of local repression, in the United States. While the followers of Conselheiro were virtually exterminated, some of the Kansas migrants became relatively successful. But neither movement became a sustained solution, and for most of the rural poor the dream of self-sufficiency had to be postponed or redirected.[17]

Masters: Northern Planters During the Civil War and Reconstruction (New Haven, 1980), esp. chap. 6.

17. A classic account of the "Kansas fever" and its antecedents is Nell Irvin Painter,

In a sense, these studies can be seen as contributing a partial answer to the question: how did former slaves give meaning to their freedom? What did they seek when they had achieved a modicum of economic power, or even just the capacity to move freely? What were the consequences of this striving, given the constraints imposed by direct coercion, by limited employment opportunities, by immigration, and so forth? By examining Capivary, São Paulo, and Canudos the authors have challenged any uniform portrait of postemancipation societies, while suggesting multiple ways to explore the initiatives of former slaves. With these examples in mind, we might consider two additional strategies for exploring the reshaping of society after slavery.

The first involves the notion of mapping as a way of capturing the consequences of the physical mobility that accompanied the end of slavery. A model here might be the work of Charles Gibson on the Valley of Mexico, in which by mapping encomiendas, *cabeceras, sujetos,* and parishes he discerned the degree of overlap between Spanish and indigenous systems of administration, and the differential significance of that overlap in the realms of church activity, private holdings, and governmental authority. In the case of postslavery societies, one needs to choose a geographical unit small enough to be explored in detail, but large enough to encompass a degree of movement by former slaves. One can then undertake a mapping of settlements, churches, and places of employment as a means of identifying patterns of continuity and transformation across the period of transition.

To begin with, one might ask whether former slave plantations remained nuclei of population, or whether individuals and families dispersed beyond their boundaries. It may make a significant difference to family autonomy, for example, whether a worker's spouse and children continued to live in barracks on the estate, or the worker simply came to the plantation week by week from a nearby town or settlement.[18] At an even smaller scale, moving to dispersed cabins throughout the property, as opposed to remaining in the old quarters, could influence not only a family's relationship with the employer, but also its relations with other families and the

---

Exodusters: Black Migration to Kansas after Reconstruction (New York, 1977). In chaps. 9 and 10 Painter analyzes the role of the figure of Benjamin "Pap" Singleton and his vision of a God-given mission to lead Afro-Americans to Kansas. On Conselheiro, see, in addition to Levine's essay in this volume, Ralph della Cava's very suggestive account, "Brazilian Messianism and National Institutions: A Reappraisal of Canudos and Joaseiro," *HAHR*, 48:3 (Aug. 1968), 402–420. Della Cava sees a degree of cooperation between Conselheiro and local landowners in the early phase of the movement.

18. I have discussed this phenomenon briefly in the Cuban context. See Scott, *Slave Emancipation in Cuba: The Transition to Free Labor, 1860–1899* (Princeton, 1985), chap. 10.

possibilities for collective action.[19] Conversely, there may be cases where the nuclei of former estates remained population centers even when the estate itself had broken up or gone bankrupt—and such continuity might have significant implications for the development of community institutions such as churches and mutual-aid societies.

If new clusters of population did emerge, where were they located? Did former slaves, for example, tend to migrate toward areas with access to local markets, as the recent work of Thomas Holt suggests for Jamaica?[20] In those areas where slaveholding was more widespread than in the classic plantation pattern, what became of those who had previously resided on small slaveholdings? Does the dispersed slaveholding pattern identified by Schwartz and Castro translate into a dispersed population pattern for former slaves after slavery; and, if so, what were the implications for collective action? Geographical mobility was one component of freedom, and we need to examine how it was used and how it was constrained. Potentially, this "physical" measure can tell us a significant amount about the experiences of former slaves, the options they faced, and the social relations in which they participated.

One function of such mapping would be to help determine the incidence and shape of patterns of postemancipation experiences whose diversity is already apparent from other sources. It is clear that freedom could have a different meaning for an urban artisan and a rural field laborer, for an elderly African and a young creole, for a mother of three and an adolescent male, and so forth. By tracing the consequences on the ground of identifiable trends such as the extensive migration eastward in Cuba after slavery, the shift away from the estates in Jamaica, the increase in seasonal migration in Louisiana, and the shift toward cities and the frontier in Brazil, we can begin to suggest the options and priorities of different groups of former slaves.

A second component of freedom was a new form of legal personhood

19. Such dispersal is commented on in São Paulo and in cotton-growing regions of the U.S. In sugar regions of Louisiana, by contrast, there was often a continuity of residence in the old quarters. On rural São Paulo, see Andrews, "Black and White Workers," in this volume. On the gradual development of family sharecropping in the South, see Gerald David Jaynes, *Branches Without Roots: Genesis of the Black Working Class in the American South, 1862–1882* (New York, 1986). On the development of a dispersed pattern of residence see David C. Barrow, Jr., "A Georgia Plantation," *Scribner's Monthly*, 21 (Apr. 1881), 830–836. On Louisiana, see the contemporary account of J. Bradford Laws, "The Negroes of Cinclare Central Factory and Calumet Plantation, Louisiana," *Bulletin of the U.S. Department of Labor*, 38 (Jan. 1902), 95–111.

20. Thomas C. Holt has uncovered a tendency on the part of former slaves to gravitate toward regions that were at a distance from, but not entirely isolated from, plantations, and that provided reasonable access to local population centers. See Holt, *The Problem of Freedom: Race, Labor, and Politics in Jamaica and Britain, 1832–1932* (forthcoming).

for those who had been slaves, and thus a new set of relations to other legal persons and to the legal process. This implies at least the possibility of a second research strategy: the close examination of postemancipation legal records. Overt violence, intimidation, poverty, and illiteracy could, in practice, drastically constrain access to legal processes, but legal records still remain a crucial source. Land disputes and other civil and criminal cases provide evidence of the continuing injustices to which former slaves were subject, but they are also a means for identifying some of the forms of striving those former slaves displayed, as well as helping to show how they conceived of themselves and their status. Of necessity, such records place a disproportionate emphasis on overt conflict, but interesting patterns may emerge in the frequency, the content, and even the language of disputes. These, in turn, may reveal shifts in the locus and terms of significant conflict, even if the records themselves tend to mislead us about the basic frequency of conflict. At the same time, one can indirectly trace the effects of changes in laws regarding access to land, the control of crops, and the ability to shift employment.

The records of the Freedmen's Bureau in the United States, the Stipendiary Magistrates in the British West Indies, and the Juntas de Patronato in Cuba all provide raw material for understanding the goals of slaves, "apprentices," and masters during the transition to free labor, and scholars have begun to explore the strategies and values reflected in them. As one moves away from the period of slavery, however, the task of exploring legal sources becomes very difficult, for there are no longer centralized records that juxtapose two sets of protagonists, former slaves and former masters, in the presence of an intervening or mediating state. The records of the Cuban Juntas end with final abolition; those of the Freedmen's Bureau end a few years after emancipation. Once they are gone, disputes are dealt with elsewhere. We must turn to the huge body of criminal records, civil records, and land records, involving citizens who may or may not be identified as former slaves.[21]

21. The records of the Brazilian emancipation boards are less rich than those of the Cuban Juntas de Patronato, but their proceedings may nonetheless yield qualitative evidence on social relations, in addition to the quantitative evidence that has already been extracted from them for the study of abolition itself. Like the Juntas, however, their role in supervising the new labor system was much reduced compared to that of the Freedmen's Bureau in the United States.

In those instances where a branch of the state continued to be identified as a potential ally of former slaves, correspondence that was directed to specific government agencies can be revealing. (Scholars of the U.S. South, for example, have located letters describing contemporary conditions in the files of the Department of Justice for the 1870s and 1880s. See Painter, *Exodusters*, esp. chaps. 2 and 3.) For somewhat different reasons, the *relatórios* of Brazilian state governors and the ministers of agriculture on occasion contain detailed evidence on trends and incidents.

Few scholars of postemancipation society have tried to deal with this mass of disparate sources. Land disputes, for example, quickly draw one into a web of detail and dissimulation. Yet they may provide the best access we will find into the actual patterns of ownership, tenancy, and squatting. Castro's work, which rests heavily on notarial archives, demonstrates the usefulness of these sources in outlining patterns of landholding, slaveholding, property transfer, and lending. Where notarial archives or their equivalent are available, it should be possible to explore patterns of land sale and acquisition; where these can be complemented by land registers and inventories, the possibilities expand still further. Indeed, Castro's work demonstrates the importance of using the two kinds of evidence together, since land registers may present a misleading picture of landholding based on formal claims of ownership, thus concealing a more complex pattern of smallholding and squatting.[22]

The inquiry should go beyond the search for individual "responses" to freedom, and look for group behaviors as well, exploring what kinds of collective action emerged, and under what circumstances such action crossed perceived racial lines. Louisiana provides a particularly significant area for study because of the experiences of unionization in the cane fields and the short-lived cross-racial populist coalitions.[23] But even in areas where unionization was blocked, as in colonial Cuba, conflict continued in other domains. Records of the expulsion of squatters are particularly revealing, as are disputes over the forms of payment and the terms of work.[24]

Other legal records offer similar possibilities. Recent scholarship, for

22. Castro, *Ao sul da história*, esp. 132–157. Stanley J. Stein's classic *Vassouras: A Brazilian Coffee County, 1850–1900* (Cambridge, MA, 1957) and Dean's *Rio Claro* use notarial records very effectively. A new generation of Brazilian researchers has been systematically analyzing local legal documents for the light they may throw on economic structures and social relations in a variety of regions. See, for example, Sidney Chaloub, *Trabalho, lar e botequim: O cotidiano dos trabalhadores no Rio de Janeiro da Belle Époque* (São Paulo, 1986) and Sílvia Hunold Lara, "Campos da violência: Estudo sobre a relação senhor-escravo na capitania do Rio de Janeiro, 1750–1808" (doctoral thesis, University of São Paulo, 1986).

23. See Jeffrey Gould, "The Strike of 1887: Louisiana Sugar War," *Southern Exposure*, 12:6 (Nov.–Dec. 1984), 45–55; Thomas Becnel, *Labor, Church, and the Sugar Establishment: Louisiana, 1887–1976* (Baton Rouge, 1980), 7–8; and William Ivy Hair, *Bourbonism and Agrarian Protest: Louisiana Politics, 1877–1900* (Baton Rouge, 1969).

24. On various forms of collective action in late nineteenth-century Cuba, see Scott, "Studying Social Change and Social Movements: New Directions in Cuban History," *Proceedings of the Thirty-Second Annual Meeting of the Seminar on the Acquisition of Latin American Library Materials, University of Miami, May 1987* (forthcoming). For a perceptive discussion of the expulsion of squatters and smallholders, and popular responses to it, see Louis A. Pérez, Jr., "Politics, Peasants, and People of Color: The 1912 'Race War' in Cuba Reconsidered," *HAHR*, 66:3 (Aug. 1986), 509–539. For an analysis linking social conditions, the role of the state, and collective action in the U.S. South, see Eric Foner, *Nothing But Freedom: Emancipation and Its Legacy* (Baton Rouge, 1983).

example, has raised questions about our commonsense interpretation of debt as an index of dependence.[25] Through examining wills and inventories, we can explore the lines of debt and credit that were found in regions whose economy had previously rested on slavery, and ask whether debt was or was not a significant mechanism for the constraint of agricultural labor in this context. Castro's work on Capivary calls attention to the function of debt as a mechanism not simply of labor coercion but of establishment of lines of clientage. The picture in some cases may turn out to be an even more complex one, since sharecropping and share wage systems rest not simply on the extension of credit to the worker by the landowner for supplies, but also on the implicit extension of credit *by* the worker to the landowner in the form of deferred wages.[26]

Scholars have long recognized the utility of private plantation records, and studies of individual estates have portrayed the evolution of the employment of slaves and former slaves over time.[27] But we still need middle-range studies that examine work patterns over a rural area larger than a single estate. With those in hand, we could begin to trace the network of connections between large plantations, small commercial farms, and subsistence agriculture.[28] Where plantation employment records survive (as they do, for example, for the U.S. South and Cuba), they can be used to trace the range of job opportunities, the level and form of payment of wages, and the seasonal pattern of work.[29] If used in conjunction with land

25. Gibson made several early suggestions along these lines. See *The Aztecs Under Spanish Rule: A History of the Indians of the Valley of Mexico, 1519–1810* (Stanford, 1964), 249–256. For a general discussion, see Arnold J. Bauer, "Rural Workers in Spanish America: Problems of Peonage and Oppression," *HAHR*, 59:1 (Feb. 1979), 34–63.

26. This is, of course, true of any system in which wages are deferred. A detailed discussion of forms of payment of wages in the U.S. South after slavery may be found in Jaynes, *Branches Without Roots*.

27. See, for example, Michael Craton, *Searching for the Invisible Man: Slaves and Plantation Life in Jamaica* (Cambridge, MA, 1978) and Teresita Martínez Vergne, "New Patterns for Puerto Rico's Sugar Workers: Abolition and Centralization at San Vicente, 1873–92," *HAHR*, 68:1 (Feb. 1988), 45–74, among others.

28. Schwartz, in *Sugar Plantations*, undertakes such an analysis, but for an earlier period. The significance of linkages between the peasant and plantation sectors has long been acknowledged by scholars of Caribbean peasantries. See, for example, Richard Frucht's important article, "A Caribbean Social Type: Neither 'Peasant' nor 'Proletarian,'" *Social and Economic Studies*, 16 (Sept. 1967), 295–300 and the work of Sidney W. Mintz, especially *Caribbean Transformations* (Chicago, 1974).

29. Employment records of several Louisiana plantations, for example, may be found in various repositories and in the papers of the Freedmen's Bureau. See, among others, the Henry Clay Warmoth Papers, Southern Historical Collection, University of North Carolina; the Lemann Family Papers, Manuscript Division, Tulane University Library; and the plantation inspection reports from various parishes of Louisiana in papers of the Louisiana Assistant Commissioner, Bureau of Refugees, Freedmen and Abandoned Lands, RG 105, United States National Archives. Records for a few Cuban plantations after emancipation can be found in the Archivo Nacional de Cuba, the Biblioteca Nacional José Martí, and the Archivo Provincial de Sancti Spíritus. See, for example, the records of the ingenios San

records, they may yield a picture of the back-and-forth between work on small plots and employment in large-scale agriculture that we know in a general way to have been characteristic of many areas after slavery.

The challenge is to find ways to read and order these records once we no longer have the category of "slave" as an organizing principle. The fact that the members of the category of "former slave" are often much harder to identify poses not only an enormous practical problem but also an important interpretive one: to what extent can we reasonably expect to analyze the situation of former slaves without continual reference to former free persons of color, poor native whites, and immigrants? Indeed, the entire concept of postemancipation society necessarily expands beyond the counterpoint of former master and former slave to a world of employers and employees, patrons and clients, planters and smallholders, in which these cross-cutting pairs do not strictly correspond to the older division of master and slave.

In northeastern Brazil, for example, from the point of view of the written records, former slaves nearly vanish into a large free poor rural population. To cope with this, we have to develop not only new research strategies, but also new definitions of the questions. We need to ask, for example, whether this blurring of categories in the records corresponds to an actual reduction of barriers to alliances across lines that previously seemed rigid, or whether distinctions that disappear from the written records remained firm in the minds of those who had always been free and those who had once been slaves. Levine's analysis of the Canudos experiment is tantalizing in this respect, since former slaves can be identified as participants but seem to have been closely allied with those who had never been enslaved. Similar alliances may be discerned among the rebels of eastern Cuba in the last years of Spanish rule.

These suggested strategies, all contingent on intense archival research into conditions in relatively limited geographical areas, may seem at once too ambitious and too modest to accomplish our goal of understanding the character of postemancipation societies. They are ambitious in that they require great feats of record linkage and detailed mapping; they are modest in that they focus on the discernible facts of employment, mobility, and legal proceedings. But it may be useful to recognize that even if the ultimate goal is to capture the "meaning of freedom," the initial questions we pose need not, perhaps, deal directly with the elusive

---

Fernando and Natividad, leg. 24, Fondo Valle-Iznaga, Archivo Provincial de Sancti Spíritus. Relatively few Brazilian plantation records appear to be available in public repositories, though there are important documents from state-subsidized central sugar mills in file IA[8], 1–4, Arquivo Nacional do Brasil, Rio de Janeiro.

phenomenology of freedom. We can commence with recorded behavior and hope to move toward lived experience, in part through the addition of records of religious activity, musical expression, and other aspects of popular culture.[30]

As we try to understand the relative degrees of dependence and autonomy, mobility and immobility, cultural expression and cultural repression, among former slaves, we may have to set about our work in a somewhat literal-minded way. For example, we can explore the presence or absence of sharecropping contracts, which can reveal specific strategies adopted by both parties and may be relatively easy to identify from legal records.[31] Harold Woodman's work on the U.S. South has demonstrated how much agricultural history can be extracted from a close examination of contract law; in Cuba, Brazil, and the United States, contracts and discussions of contract law have survived and can be explored comparatively.[32] Establishing the character of contracts for service and for land, and examining their enforcement or nonenforcement, can be a first step toward understanding patterns of dependency and the limits of autonomy.

At the same time, such inquiries will require new interpretive strategies if we are to make the shift from the tangible evidence of contracts to the intangible inference of subordination or resistance. We can explore the degree of physical mobility and the transformed legal status of former slaves, and we may look to their behavior in these respects to tell us about their dependency or autonomy. But detailed investigation may also lead us to rethink what we mean by dependency and autonomy, and, in some cases, perhaps, to abandon the dichotomous formulation altogether. In-

---

30. By way of parallel, *The Aztecs under Spanish Rule*, for all of its innovations of method and interpretation, is organized along quite conventional lines, with chapters titled "Tribes," "Towns," "Encomienda and Corregimiento," "Labor," "Land," and so forth. Gibson was exploring what we might now describe as different forms of collapse and resilience on the part of Indian communities under the stress of Spanish rule, but he approached those questions in a very matter-of-fact way.

31. Clearly, if many such contracts in a given region were oral it will be more difficult to obtain a representative sample. But some trace even of oral contracts probably remains in legal records, either as the result of disputes, or in the lists of debts and property in wills and inventories, or possibly in tax registers. In cases where such arrangements were entirely customary, without even the formality of an oral contract, we may be forced to rely on memoirs, observers' reports, and ancillary testimony in criminal and civil cases.

32. See Harold Woodman, "Post-Civil War Agriculture and the Law," *Agricultural History*, 53:1 (Jan. 1979), 319–337. Extensive discussions of Cuban agricultural contracts appear in the depositions filed with the Spanish Treaty Claims Commission in the U.S. National Archives. For the sugar regions of Brazil, the Arquivo Nacional contains records of contracts made with the short-lived *engenhos centrais*. Throughout Hispanic America, of course, evidence of various kinds of contracts appears in notarial archives and in wills and inventories. For the United States, there are contracts in the Freedmen's Bureau papers, as well as the materials that may survive in ordinary court records.

deed, the category of "autonomy" itself is culturally variable and may at times be an anachronistic imposition.[33]

First, it is already clear that former slaves often placed goals of family and community above the assertion of simple individual autonomy. An entire literature on emancipation in the United States has emphasized the importance to former slaves of reconstituting families and pursuing collective aims.[34] Moreover, family welfare and individual well-being were frequently intertwined, making the concept of individual autonomy misleading. While the notion of autonomy might at least initially apply, for example, to single males engaged in seasonal migration in search of work, it is somewhat less useful in evaluating the situation of a widow with several children attempting to remain on plantation land in the face of new demands for the payment of rent.[35]

Second, in looking at former slaves, we need to explore the ways in which protection was sought, along with autonomy. In some cases, the establishment and modification of reciprocal ties may have been as significant as the achievement of a degree of independence. In others, the struggle for a collective political voice was a prerequisite for individual physical security. The point here is not to downplay individual struggles for autonomy, but to examine the existing patterns of clientelism and the strategies former slaves developed for dealing with what was often a very narrow range of choices.

On these questions, northeastern Brazil offers several challenges: it is seemingly the *locus classicus* of continued dependency on the part of former slaves. But by asserting a simple continuity of domination, scholars may have inadvertently avoided the exploration of what actually went into

33. Orlando Patterson has made this argument in a different context in *Slavery and Social Death: A Comparative Study* (Cambridge, MA, 1982).

34. See, for example, Herbert G. Gutman, *The Black Family in Slavery and Freedom, 1750–1925* (New York, 1976) and Jacqueline Jones, *Labor of Love, Labor of Sorrow: Black Women, Work, and the Family from Slavery to the Present* (New York, 1985). Andrews calls attention to family-oriented goals through his emphasis on the withdrawal of women and children from wage-paid field labor in São Paulo; Holt has discussed community goals in his work on Jamaica; and I have emphasized the changing family division of labor in Cuba.

35. An explicit attention to the role of age and gender within family strategies should also be incorporated into such analyses. We need to ask how the socially constructed roles of men and women were transformed during and after emancipation, and to analyze the links between these transformations and the parallel struggles over forms of labor. Most discussions of the "withdrawal" of women's labor tend to blur the question of choice and decision, leaving it unclear just who initiated the reallocation of work time, at what point, and in what directions. For some initial suggestions on the labor of former slave women in the U.S., see Jones, *Labor of Love, Labor of Sorrow*. For a brief discussion of women in the rural labor force in Cuba, with particular attention to their participation in harvest labor, see Scott, *Slave Emancipation*, 242–243.

patron-client relations.[36] Within Brazilian historiography, the emphasis on oligarchical control has been a logical reaction against romanticized claims of paternalism. Nonetheless, we still need to explore what *kinds* of reciprocal or pseudoreciprocal relations were established, and with whom. What did former slaves give up when they entered into such relations, and what, if anything, did they gain? Was there a degree of choice among patrons; if so, how was it manipulated? Only in this way can we begin to delineate the actual meaning of domination, and explore the ways in which options were shaped and limited by established patterns of social relations.[37]

Perhaps the most striking feature of scholarship on slavery in the last decades is the way in which it has broken the association of subordination with stasis and passivity. (In this, it parallels recent work on early colonial society, in which indigenous resistance and adaptations are highlighted within a framework of colonial domination.[38]) Scholars have found numerous ways to examine slave initiatives without denying oppression, to explore the creation of oppositional belief systems in the context of attempted ideological domination, to delineate the slave community while acknowledging the continual efforts at repression of many of its essential features. In postemancipation studies we are seeing a similar development, as monolithic portraits of peonage or marginalization are superseded by accounts that emphasize negotiation, initiative, and choice, though in a situation of extreme constraint and, often, violence. By way of conclusion, we might identify three features of this evolving reevaluation.

36. On patron-client relations in general, see S. N. Eisenstadt and Louis Roniger, "Patron-Client Relations as a Model of Structuring Social Exchange," *Comparative Studies in Society and History,* 22:1 (Jan. 1980), 42–77.

37. Allen Johnson writes, in a review of Shepard Forman's work on rural Brazil, "A landlord's political power rests to a considerable degree on the loyalty of his dependent workers, and Forman is wrong in not seeing this 'personalism' as a form of influence on the peasant's part (however much we might despise the form)." (See Johnson, "Essays and Polemics: Latin American Society from Diverse Perspectives. A Review Article," *Comparative Studies in Society and History*, 22:3 [July 1980], 478–484.) It is not yet clear, however, to what extent such "influence" can be attributed to poverty-stricken rural wage earners of the Northeast in the late nineteenth century, where suffrage was highly limited and economic options were few.

38. This reevaluation within colonial history might be seen as beginning with Gibson and developing through the work of many subsequent scholars, including Nancy Farriss, Karen Spalding, Steve Stern, and William Taylor, among others. See Nancy M. Farriss, *Maya Society Under Colonial Rule: The Collective Enterprise of Survival* (Princeton, 1984); Karen Spalding, *Huarochirí: An Andean Society Under Inca and Spanish Rule* (Stanford, 1984); Steve J. Stern, *Peru's Indian Peoples and the Challenge of Spanish Conquest: Huamanga to 1640* (Madison, 1982); and William B. Taylor, *Drinking, Homicide and Rebellion in Colonial Mexican Villages* (Stanford, 1979). Indeed, such a perspective could be said to characterize a large portion of contemporary scholarship on the social history of subordinate groups in a wide range of contexts.

The first is an emphasis on change over time. There was often a period of uncertainty immediately after the end of slavery in which various methods of labor control were tried, and relationships were tested, before a uniform pattern of subordination was reestablished.[39] Examining how that uncertainty was resolved provides a clue to the aims of each group, to the important relations of power involved, and to the various constraints —such as the lack of capital, or the pressure of population growth—that ultimately made themselves felt. Andrews's work on employment patterns provides an example of a new interpretation that rests on a close attention to change over time. He emphasizes the rapidity of the initial adjustment in São Paulo, but also argues that it was subject to renegotiation once conditions altered. Similarly, Levine's analysis of Canudos takes as its context not simply the continuing poverty of northeastern Brazil, but a specific period of drought and economic depression that triggered the search for new solutions. In these and other cases, we are moving toward a more complex picture of the interlinked shifts in economic opportunities, levels of violence, and rationales of domination.

The second emphasis is on particular geographical and environmental patterns. At one level, this is so obvious that it goes without saying. Any good historical analysis pays attention to place. But in the case of slave emancipation, there is a particular significance to changes in the physical location and environment of residence and employment, precisely because of the constraints that slavery had placed on physical movement. The enforced isolation of slaves on estates was often a key component of social control. Attempts to maintain that isolation, and attempts to break it, thus became elements in the struggle over the meaning of freedom. Change could take the form of permanent relocation, daily travel, or seasonal migration. In each case, these forms of movement shifted the patterns of communication and experience, while expanding the awareness of options.

Charles Gibson wrote of colonial villages in the Valley of Mexico:

> The patterns of subordination, however uniform in their abstract characteristics, were locally bounded. Cabecera jurisdictions, encomiendas, and haciendas were discrete manifestations of localism effectively preventing a consolidation of Indian interests. All native conduct was so confined. No two towns were ever capable of unit-

---

39. The work of Fields emphasizes this initial uncertainty, particularly over the meaning of "free labor" and the character of each party's obligations to the other. Jaynes traces the wide range of labor forms attempted in the first years after abolition, before family-based sharecropping emerged as the dominant form in the cotton South. See Fields, *Slavery and Freedom on the Middle Ground* and Jaynes, *Branches Without Roots.*

ing in organized resistance. The common qualities of Indian towns were insufficient bases for concerted action.[40]

It is difficult to say whether the subordination of slavery was similarly felt as something which took place on an individual estate, or in an individual household, thus dampening the possibilities for concerted action. There is evidence both of isolation and of alliances in spite of isolation. But one can ask to what extent juridical freedom, and the physical mobility that accompanied it, helped to make broader alliances possible. In Cuba, former slaves joined in a socially radical, cross-class, anticolonial insurrection just nine years after abolition. The vitality of that movement, with its deep roots in the racially mixed population of eastern Cuba, suggests that in at least some cases juridical freedom, however constrained, did open the way for broader communication, alliance, and struggle. The mixed character of the Canudos experiment, though it ended in destruction, might suggest the same.

Third, there has been an increasing effort to distinguish the relative importance of different components of subordination, and, in turn, of different elements of freedom. Slavery obviously involved multiple constraints on human freedom, some of which were lifted with legal emancipation and some of which were not. One could list in general terms the goals that former slaves in many societies sought and in some cases enunciated explicitly: access to land, freedom from violence, political voice, respect for individual dignity, integrity of their families, education for their children. But we are still a long way from identifying the relative importance of these different goals in different societies and contexts. Freedom was, in Barbara Fields's phrase, "a constantly moving target."[41] But it was not everywhere an identical target.

The purpose of an exploration of the elements of continued oppression and successful challenge is not the academic exercise of asking whose misery was more severe, of measuring the physical terror of racist violence in the U.S. South against the crushing poverty of the Brazilian Northeast or the colonial tyranny of Cuba. It can instead be part of an effort to comprehend the goals of different individuals and groups in order to comprehend choices and actions. To return to the case of Cuba: thousands of former slaves and their descendants were prepared to join in a long, bloody struggle to achieve political independence from Spain. They put aside the immediate pursuit of land or education and took enormous risks as part of a nationalist movement that was also a movement for social change. The study of the "meaning of freedom" for Cuban slaves thus exceeds

40. Gibson, *Aztecs*, 405.
41. Fields, *Slavery and Freedom on the Middle Ground*, 193.

the limits of the immediate postemancipation adjustments, encompassing a series of larger questions about political and social mobilization and participation. We will better understand the choices those rebels made to the extent that we can comprehend their own perception of the forms of their oppression, and the resultant selection of targets for resistance.[42]

Perhaps some of the research strategies outlined here can begin to provide detailed portraits of economic and social options and constraints faced by former slaves, and thus illuminate the patterns of their individual and collective behavior. At the same time, we will need to listen for the faint echoes of the voices of the participants themselves. One might recall that it was Gibson's close reading of Indian *títulos*, in conjunction with his study of the evolution of property in the Valley of Mexico, that convinced him that land encroachment was the primary preoccupation and grievance of the indigenous population.[43] We need, I think, to continue to seek out similar kinds of documentation for postemancipation societies, and similar ways of reading such documentation.[44] A reading of those documents that reflect the voices of the participants may help us carry out the task of determining which elements of subordination weighed most heavily on former slaves, and which they could successfully resist or turn to their own use.

It is perhaps appropriate, then, to give the last word to a slave woman from rural Matanzas, in Cuba. She worked on the Ingenio Mercedes and was known to the master as Elvira, though the other slaves called her Paloma. On the morning of April 21, 1879, in the tumultuous final year of formal slavery in Cuba, the overseer roused her and told her to begin work piling dry cane stalks.[45] On that day, two other slaves of the estate

42. On the 1895–98 conflict, see, among other studies, Pérez, *Cuba Between Empires, 1878–1902* (Pittsburgh, 1983). In "Politics, Peasants, and People of Color," Pérez uses an analysis of targets as a means for reevaluating the goals of events in 1912 that have generally been characterized as a "race war."

43. Gibson, *Aztecs*, 405.

44. Two concerted efforts to locate such material for the U.S. South are Leon F. Litwack, *Been in the Storm So Long: The Aftermath of Slavery* (New York, 1979) and the volumes of Berlin et al., *Freedom: A Documentary History of Emancipation*. The WPA slave narratives are also a classic source. Very little material of this kind has been located for Brazil, though Reis makes some interesting suggestions in "From *Banguê* to *Usina*." The richness of the evidence in Mary C. Karasch, *Slave Life in Rio de Janeiro, 1808–1850* (Princeton, 1987) suggests that documents on Afro-Brazilian brotherhoods and religious organizations might be particularly valuable for the postslavery period. Some parallel material on Cuban cabildos is available in the Cuban national archives. (See Scott, *Slave Emancipation*, 265–268.) *Liberto* appeals for passports to travel to Africa appear in the archives in Bahia, in northeastern Brazil, and might be read for the light they cast on *libertos'* perceptions of conditions in the province itself. See Arquivo Provincial do Estado da Bahia, Seção Histórica, maços 6346, 6347.

45. Slavery was legally abolished in Cuba in 1880, but was replaced by a form of

were being held in stocks, bound by leg irons. Paloma's response to the overseer reflected a mixture of exhaustion and determination. She said to him

> that he was always in a hurry, that here justice ordered blacks into the stocks to die of hunger, that that was what they knew how to do, and to this the overseer said to her: be silent, *negra;* Elvira answered that she was within her rights to speak and that no one could take that away from her. The overseer said again that she should be silent; and she answered him that she did not wish to and that no one could silence her. . . .

The overseer slapped Paloma; she came back at him; he whipped her; she fled; he pursued her on horseback and returned her to the estate. The incident exploded into a near-revolt as the overseer attempted to put Paloma in chains and other slaves came to her defense, threatening to take to the hills. Paloma was released; the "riot" was suppressed; the slaves grudgingly returned to their work "refunfuñándose más o menos entre dientes."[46]

The challenge of postemancipation studies, in effect, is to follow Paloma and her companions. In 1879, she was concerned with the pace of work, with hunger, and with justice and punishment. At the same time, she already phrased her own entitlement to speak her mind as a claim of *right.* In the years that followed, how would she judge the society that emerged, along these multiple dimensions of work, hunger, and justice? And how would she choose to act when her evidently indomitable spirit was again moved by exhaustion, by frustration, or by an emboldening claim of right?

"apprenticeship" that obliged former slaves to continue to labor for their former masters. Apprenticeship was abolished in 1886.

46. The account of this incident appears in leg. 20/34, Fondo de Esclavos, Archivo Histórico Provincial de Matanzas. I am very much indebted to Professor Juan Francisco González, of the Instituto Superior Pedagógico de Matanzas, for providing me with a transcription of it.

Brazilian Abolition in Comparative Perspective

SEYMOUR DRESCHER

O N the eve of the age of abolition, even intellectuals who were morally opposed to slavery were far more impressed by its power and durability than by its weaknesses. Adam Smith reminded his students that only a small portion of the earth was being worked by free labor, and that it was unlikely that slavery would ever be totally abandoned. Across the channel, the Abbé Raynal could envision the end of New World slavery only through a fortuitous conjuncture of philosopher-kings in Europe or the appearance of a heroic Spartacus in the Americas. No historical trend toward general emancipation could be assumed.[1]

Little more than a century later, the passage of the "Golden Law" through the Brazilian legislature—to the accompaniment of music, public demonstrations, and street festivities at every stage—was regarded as only a belated provincial rendezvous with progress. Until then, Brazilians had been humiliated by condescending references to their country as the last Christian nation that tolerated slavery, on a level with "backward" African and Asiatic slaveholding societies.[2] Brazilian emancipation was hailed as

*I would like to thank George Reid Andrews, Stanley L. Engerman, Frederic C. Jaher, and Rebecca J. Scott for their helpful suggestions.

1. Adam Smith, *Lectures on Jurisprudence*, R. L. Meek, D. D. Raphael, and P. G. Stein, eds. (Oxford, 1978), 181; G. T. F. Raynal, *Histoire philosophique et politique des établissements et du commerce des européens dans les deux Indes*, 7 vols. (Geneva, 1780).

2. David Brion Davis, *Slavery and Human Progress* (New York, 1984), 298; Robert E. Conrad, *The Destruction of Brazilian Slavery, 1850–1888* (Berkeley, 1972), 71. It was, of course, European-oriented members of Brazil's elite who felt most strongly that their country was humiliated by slavery and that it was a nation which played no role in building civilization or prosperity. See Joaquim Nabuco, *Abolitionism: The Brazilian Antislavery Struggle*, Conrad, trans. (Urbana, 1977), 4, 108, 117–118. On the influence of European and U.S. models on Brazilian concepts of progress and slavery, see Richard Graham, *Britain and the Onset of Modernization in Brazil, 1850–1914* (Cambridge, 1968), esp. chaps. 6 and 10, and "Causes for the Abolition of Negro Slavery in Brazil: An Interpretive Essay," *HAHR*, 46:2 (May 1966), 123–137; and E. Bradford Burns, *The Poverty of Progress: Latin America in the Nineteenth Century* (Berkeley, 1980), chap. 2.

opening a new stage in the "civilizing" of Africa and Asia. Counting from the formation of the first abolitionist societies in the late 1780s, the Brazilian action almost precisely marked a "century of progress."

Perhaps because it occurred so late in a world dominated by a concept of libertarian progress, Brazilian abolition received relatively little attention from those who wrote general histories of slavery.[3] The demise of Brazilian slavery seemed to follow a path roughly prescribed by a dozen predecessors in the Americas and Europe. This impression may have been due in part to the fact that until recently there were few extensive analyses of the Brazilian case,[4] a lack which was compounded by the "North Atlantic" or even national orientation of most North American and European historians of slavery. Moreover, when Brazilian slavery has been treated in comparative perspective, the contrast is almost invariably with the U.S. South.[5] In this study, I shall expand the range of cases to include a number of emancipations in areas which were subject to European polities during the nineteenth century.

3. For good general syntheses which treat Brazilian abolition primarily as a mopping-up operation by modernizers, see C. Duncan Rice, *The Rise and Fall of Black Slavery* (London, 1975), 370–381; and Edward Reynolds, *Stand the Storm: A History of the Atlantic Slave Trade* (London/New York, 1985), 90–92. The historiography of Brazilian abolition is sometimes elaborated within a broader model of social progress in which the inherent inefficiencies or "contradictions" of slave labor utilization converge with other causes of technological and economic retardation. For a good example of this "convergence" thesis, see Emília Viotti da Costa, *The Brazilian Empire: Myths and Histories* (Chicago, 1985), 148–171 and *Da senzala à colônia* (São Paulo, 1966), chap. 5. The issue of the efficiency of slave labor is sometimes not distinguished from the issue of technological progress in general. See the perceptive discussion in Peter L. Eisenberg, *The Sugar Industry in Pernambuco: Modernization Without Change, 1840–1910* (Berkeley, 1974), chap. 3 and n. 18, below.

4. But recently, see da Costa, *Brazilian Empire*, chap. 6; Robert Brent Toplin, *The Abolition of Slavery in Brazil* (New York, 1972); and Conrad, *Destruction*. The pervasive structural foundations of Brazilian slavery are presented in greatest detail by Stuart B. Schwartz, *Sugar Plantations in the Formation of Brazilian Society: Bahia, 1550–1835* (Cambridge, 1985), esp. chap. 16 and Robert Wayne Slenes, "The Demography and Economics of Brazilian Slavery: 1850–1888" (Ph.D. diss., Stanford University, 1975).

5. Carl Degler, *Neither Black nor White: Slavery and Race Relations in Brazil and the United States* (Madison, 1986); Frank Tannenbaum, *Slave and Citizen: The Negro in the Americas* (New York, 1947); Stanley Elkins, *Slavery, a Problem in American Institutional and Intellectual Life* (Chicago, 1959); Arnold Sio, "Interpretations of Slavery: The Slave Status in the Americas," *Comparative Studies in Society and History*, 7:3 (Apr. 1965), 289–308; Davis, *The Problem of Slavery in Western Culture* (Ithaca, 1966), chaps. 8 and 9. Even Rebecca J. Scott who analyzes Cuba, the other late emancipation in Latin America, makes only a passing reference to Brazil (*Slave Emancipation in Cuba: The Transition to Free Labor 1860–1899* [Princeton, 1985], 284). However, Scott recognizes the comparative opportunities afforded by the Cuban and Brazilian cases in her comments on Eric Foner, *Nothing But Freedom: Emancipation and Its Legacy* (Baton Rouge, 1983), in "Comparing Emancipations: A Review Essay," *Journal of Social History* 20:3 (Spring 1987), 565–583, esp. 574–575. See also Davis, *Slavery and Human Progress*, 294–297. For U.S.-Brazilian comparisons, see also Eugene D. Genovese, *The World the Slaveholders Made: Two Essays in Interpretation* (New York, 1969), part one.

Historians of abolition usually approach causal discussions along a range of analytical categories: demographic, economic, social, ideological, and political. The historiography of abolition in Brazil, as elsewhere, is usually embedded in implicit or explicit theories about the relative weight to be assigned to each of these facets of social development and to their long- or short-term significance in the outcome. This essay will address two major elements of Brazilian abolition in comparative perspective— the demographics and economics of late Brazilian slavery, and the peculiar characteristics of Brazilian abolitionism and its opposition. I should say at the outset that I am entirely dependent on the existing historiography for the details of Brazilian development.

Demographic Dependency and Economic Viability

Slave Trade Abolition

As elsewhere in the New World, Brazilian slavery was stimulated by a shortage of labor relative to opportunities for rapid expansion in specialized commodity production. Like that of the Caribbean slave systems, the relative decline of the institution in Brazil was initially a consequence of external political pressures for the restriction of slave recruitment.[6] Exactly as in Cuba, Brazilian imports of African slaves had actually reached an all-time peak just before the enforcement of abolition in 1851.[7]

The impact of slave trade abolition on Brazil was similar to West Indian terminations in two other ways. Insofar as Brazil continued to expand its staple production, it increasingly had to rely on some combination of free and slave labor and a redistribution of its diminishing slave labor. The slave population inevitably declined, as a percentage both of the total labor force and of Brazilian capital. After 1851, that trend was inexorable and predictable.

Moreover, market pressures alone assured that, as in the British colonies and Cuba after ending slave importation from Africa, slave labor would be concentrated toward commodity production which could optimize the output from that form of labor. Certain economic sectors had to become less dependent on slavery. Without such inhibiting political

---

6. Leslie Bethell, *The Abolition of the Brazilian Slave Trade: Britain, Brazil, and the Slave Trade Question, 1807–1869* (Cambridge, 1970), 385; Conrad, *Destruction*, 65–69. On the U.S. linkage between abolition of the trade and decline of slavery, see n. 14 and 25, below. For a summary of economic models used to explain the rise and continuation of the slave trade, see Robert W. Fogel, *Without Consent or Contract: The Rise and Fall of American Slavery* (forthcoming), chap. 1.

7. David Eltis, *Economic Growth and the Ending of the Transatlantic Slave Trade* (New York, 1987), app. A.

restrictions on the flow of slave labor as occurred between islands of the British Caribbean in the decades after slave trade abolition in 1807,[8] there was a shift of Brazilian slaves from the city to the countryside in expanding frontier regions. This type of redistribution occurred even in the U.S. South, where there was a positive and high rate of postabolition natural increase.[9]

In Brazil, local expansions of the slave labor force could come only from redistribution. Shortly after African migration ended, the northeastern provinces which were losing slaves vainly attempted to follow the "British" model by prohibiting the interprovincial slave trade. As the northeasterners noted, the interprovincial flow of slaves created growing differentials of dependency on, and commitment to, slavery.[10] But, by the time political fear became more important than economic interest to the importing south-central region (in the early 1880s), it was too late. By 1884, fewer than half the provinces of Brazil had populations of more than 10 percent slaves, and more than one-fourth of the provinces (mostly northern and northeastern) were even below 5 percent, the level at which many northern U.S. states had opted for immediate emancipation.[11]

8. Eltis, "The Traffic in Slaves between the British West India Colonies, 1807–1833," *Economic History Review*, 25:1 (Feb. 1972), 55–64. For the urban decline in the British West Indies after 1807, see B. W. Higman, *Slave Populations of the British Caribbean, 1807–1834* (Baltimore, 1984), 92–99; for the urban decline in Brazilian slavery, see Mary C. Karasch, *Slave Life in Rio de Janeiro, 1808–1850* (Princeton, 1987), 61, table 3.1.

9. Compare the percentage reductions in numbers of slaves in Ceará, Pernambuco, Bahia, and Sergipe in Brazil's Northeast from 1864 to 1884 with those in the northern tier of U.S. slave states—Maryland, Virginia, Kentucky, and Missouri—from 1840 to 1860. Also compare Conrad, *Destruction*, app. 3 with Bureau of the Census, *Negro Population in the United States, 1790–1915* (New York, 1968), 57, table 6. On the general shift of slave labor toward the South-Center, see also da Costa, *Da senzala*, 132–137. For the impact of slave trade constriction and concentration of ownership in Cuba, see Jordi Maluquer de Motes, "Abolicionismo y resistencia a la abolición en la España del siglo XIX," *Anuario de Estudios Americanos*, 43 (1986), 311–331, esp. 323–324.

10. Conrad, *Destruction*, 65–69. According to Conrad, the nonimporting areas of the Northeast might have begun to consider the potential increase of prices for their slaves even before abolition of the trade in 1850–51. The antiabolitionist "Barbacena Project" of 1848 was opposed by some representatives of the northern provinces. See Conrad, "The Struggle for the Abolition of the Brazilian Slave Trade: 1808–1853" (Ph.D. diss., Columbia University, 1967), 289–303. Some indication of the impact of slave trade abolition on the northeastern planters is the fact that, circa 1850, slaves normally outnumbered free laborers on Pernambuco sugar plantations by more than 3:1. But "by 1872 free workers outnumbered slaves in all occupational categories, from 14:1 in unskilled labor and 5:1 in agricultural labor, to 3:1 in domestic labor." See Eisenberg, *Sugar Industry*, 180.

11. Conrad, *Destruction*. Just ten years earlier, in 1874, 14 of the 21 provinces of Brazil had slave populations of more than 10 percent, and only 2 had levels of under 5 percent. In the declining regional economy of the Northeast slavery became a relatively more urban phenomenon. See Thomas W. Merrick and Douglas H. Graham, *Population and Economic Development in Brazil, 1800 to the Present* (Baltimore, 1979), 69–71.

By the last quarter of the nineteenth century, the free population of the Northeast had grown sufficiently to facilitate the transition to free labor in that less dynamic region. Within southern Brazil itself, a new regional differentiation developed in the mid-1880s. As foreign immigration to São Paulo increased rapidly, the Paulista planters joined the ranks of the abolitionists, leaving the slaveowners of Rio de Janeiro and Minas Gerais in isolation.[12]

Two comparative demographic points can be emphasized. The regional divisions in Brazil developed over a much shorter period than in the southern United States, because of the different reproduction rates in the two slave societies. Also, free immigrants were few compared to those of the antebellum United States. As an alternative agricultural labor force they seem to have played a last-minute role, relieving the labor crisis of the Paulista planters, and helping to convert them to abolition in 1887–88. It would thus appear that highly organized foreign labor recruitment was more a response to the prospect of imminent abolition in the mid-1880s than a long-term causal variable.[13] For the generation after abolition of the slave trade, free mass immigration was an uncertain potential rather than an actuality.

Brazil's situation resembled the Caribbean model more than that of the United States in that abolition of the African slave trade condemned slavery to a speedy relative decline. The political significance of redistribution seems to have been dramatically borne out in only one generation. It reduced urban interest in the system and it stimulated higher slave prices and concentration of ownership. The frequently remarked Brazilian planters' acceptance of the "inevitability" of slavery's decline (even when used as a political argument against the need for further abolitionist legislation) was based on a logical assessment of the data and an accurate reading of Caribbean history.[14]

12. Slenes, "Demography," chaps. 6–8. See also Merrick and Graham, *Population*, 82–83.

13. Toplin, *Abolition*, 162.

14. The relative demographic decline of U.S. slavery was different from that of Brazil and the Caribbean area primarily in that it was drawn out over a longer period because of a high rate of natural reproduction. Without African imports to match free European migration in the half century before 1860, that decline became progressively more apparent. Peter Kolchin's recent comparison of U.S. and Russian masters interestingly concludes that the U.S. slaveowners were both more entrepreneurial and more paternalistic than their absentee and rentier-minded counterparts among the Russian nobility. The decisive division of slaveowner "mentalities" therefore occurs between the capitalist-paternalist masters of the U.S. South, on the one hand, and the capitalist-rentier lords of Russia, on the other. In Brazil, too, entrepreneurial and paternalistic characteristics are arguably combined. Kolchin, *Unfree Labor: American Slavery and Russian Serfdom* (Cambridge, MA, 1987), 126–156, 357–361; Slenes, "Demography," chap. 11.

A glance at the Cuban example reinforces both the general causal weight assigned to the ending of the slave trade and the political significance of regional differentiation resulting from its termination. The constriction of the African slave supply was a more drawn out and fluctuating process in Cuba than it was in Brazil. Cuban import flows were generally more volatile.[15] Cuban slave prices rose about as rapidly as Brazil's between the 1830s and 1860, but Cuban prices were always higher, and the total value of its staple exports grew faster. This indicates that market pressures for finding alternative sources of labor were felt more keenly in Cuba than in Brazil, and may explain Cuba's earlier recourse to non-African labor. In regional terms, Cuba's poorer eastern provinces were less able to afford either slave or Asiatic labor, and as in Brazil's Northeast, those Cuban provinces produced movements more willing to add elements of abolitionism to their political agenda in the 1860s and 1870s.[16]

Everywhere in the Euro-American bound labor systems except the southern United States, recruitment from without played a crucial role. For centuries, expansion had been effected via the transoceanic slave trade, as in the case of Afro-Caribbean slavery; by binding the native population, as with Russian peasants; or by combining both methods, as in the Brazilian recruitment of both Indians and Africans. During the nineteenth century, Brazil followed the circum-Caribbean pattern which required transoceanic transfers of Africans for expansion.[17] Without such recruitment, all the systems (with the one exception noted) faced deteriorating active population ratios, as well as a variety of other difficulties. If, as David Eltis cogently argues, the "natural limits" of slavery (in

15. One can measure the comparative volatility of these two most important slave-importing areas of the Americas during the last generation of the transatlantic slave trade. During the period 1826–50, Brazil's average quinquennial importation of slaves was 192,500. The widest deviations from this mean were a low of 93,700 (or 49 percent of the average) in 1831–35, and a high of 257,500 (or 139 percent) in 1846–50. By contrast, Cuba's quinquennial average importation in the period 1836–60 was 53,500 slaves. The widest deviations from this mean were a low of 15,400 (or 29 percent) in 1846–50 and a high of 95,700 (or 179 percent) in 1836–40. Three of Cuba's five quinquennia fell outside the Brazilian extremes. The same general conclusion holds if the time span is doubled. During the 50 years between 1801 and 1850, Brazil's highest quinquennial average importation (1846–50) was 2.75 times greater than its lowest (1831–35). During the 50 years between 1811 and 1860, Cuba's highest quinquennial average (1816–20) was 8.3 times greater than its lowest (1846–50). My calculations are derived from figures in Eltis, *Economic Growth*, 243–244, tables A.1 and A.2.

16. Between 1862 and 1877, the slave populations of Cuba's eastern provinces declined by 77 percent, while in the great sugar provinces of the West the decline was only 31 percent. The differential impact of the Ten Years War had much to do with this contrast. As in Brazil, however, where the staple prospered, slavery persisted. See Scott, *Slave Emancipation*, 87.

17. Eltis, *Economic Growth*, part two. As late as 1830, Brazilians turned toward interior recruitment of Indian labor when British pressure seemed to threaten importations from Africa. See Conrad, "The Struggle for the Abolition of the Brazilian Slave Trade," 216–217.

terms of changing technology, decreasing land-labor ratios, management techniques, lower profits from slave labor, or potential slave supply) were nowhere in sight at any point in the nineteenth century, many of the supposed contradictions and stresses observed within slave economies are primarily consequences of slave trade abolition, rather than contradictions between slavery and economic growth.[18]

Economic Growth

The degree of dependence of New World slave societies on external recruitment probably constitutes their most important socioeconomic characteristic from start to finish. As agricultural and extractive frontiers, they also tended to be more dependent for technological innovation and even for much of their cultural self-definition on the increasingly "free" metropolises. Only rarely was one or another of these slave societies able to imagine itself as an autonomous economic and political actor,[19] and Brazil alone developed a domestically based slave trade with Africa well before the beginning of interventionist British abolitionist diplomacy. This stood Brazil's slaveowners in good stead during the semiclandestine stage of the slave trade after Waterloo. However, before restriction of the African labor supply, almost all slave economies were probably expanding faster in population and wealth than the metropolitan societies which dominated them politically. Even the roughest statistical approximations would have led one to conclude that Brazil in particular was more than

18. Eltis, *Economic Growth*, 14. In the cases of the British West Indies, the U.S. South, and Cuba the claims of a contradiction between slavery and technology, or slavery and productivity, are challenged by recent economic analysis. For Cuba, see Scott, *Slave Emancipation*, 26–28; for the British West Indies, see R. Keith Aufhauser, "Slavery and Technological Change," *The Journal of Economic History*, 34:1 (Mar. 1974), 34–50; for the United States, see Stanley L. Engerman, *Time on the Cross: The Economics of American Negro Slavery*, 2 vols. (Boston, 1974), I, chap. 6 and Fogel, *Without Consent or Contract: The Rise and Fall of American Slavery* (forthcoming), chap. 3. The discussion of Brazilian slavery within a historiographical framework of rise, prosperity, and decline is well illustrated in Stanley J. Stein's excellent *Vassouras: A Brazilian Coffee County, 1850–1900: The Roles of Planter and Slave in a Plantation Society*, reprint ed. (Princeton, 1985), part 4. This approach was recently challenged by Slenes, "Grandeza ou decadência? O mercado de escravos e a economia cafeeira da Província do Rio de Janeiro, 1850–1888," in *Brasil: História econômica e demográfica*, Iraci del Nero da Costa, ed. (São Paulo, 1986), 103–155. Free labor, however constricted, was a second best alternative among the most entrepreneurial Paulistas. See Verena Stolcke and Michael M. Hall, "The Introduction of Free Labour on São Paulo Coffee Plantations," *Journal of Peasant Studies*, 10:2 (Jan. 1983), 170–200. The Paulista planters of Rio Claro continued to buy slaves until the eve of abolition. See Warren Dean, *Rio Claro: A Brazilian Plantation System, 1820–1920* (Stanford, 1976), 52.

19. Perhaps those who came closest to independence were the U.S. southern elites in 1776 and 1860, and the Brazilian planters at the time of national independence. Only the 1860 southerners, however, explicitly claimed that their peculiar institution might operate indefinitely against the free labor trend in the Western world.

matching Portugal in total population growth, growth of the value of exports, and with regard to other similar indicators during the period before independence.

By most of the usual criteria of economic development, Brazilians were unlikely to have been impressed by the "progress" of Portugal at the beginning of the nineteenth century. With a population of only 2,000,000 in 1700, between 300,000 and 500,000 Portuguese departed for Brazil over the course of the eighteenth century. On the eve of its own movement for independence, Brazilian agricultural growth contrasted markedly with relative Portuguese industrial and agricultural stagnation, and Brazilian reexports largely accounted for Portugal's trade surplus with England.[20]

In the second half of the nineteenth century, Brazilians, especially those who traveled abroad, increasingly measured themselves against a broader West, in which the long-term weaknesses of their society became more manifest with each passing decade. In this respect, the significant comparisons were not those of the marketplace such as crop output, productivity, profits, the net worth of slaveholders, or the aggregate wealth of the nation. What was important was Brazil's relative dearth of railroads, canals, towns, factories, schools, and books. The echoes of Alexis de Tocqueville's contrast between the bustle of free societies and the stagnation of slave societies in the United States resonated among the Brazilian elite.[21] Long before 1850, it was clear that Brazil's demographic dependency on

20. See the essays by Maria Luiza Marcílio and Dauril Alden, in *The Cambridge History of Latin America*, Bethell, ed. (Cambridge, 1984–), II, 37–63 and 602–660, esp. 602–612 and 649–653. The abolition of slavery in Portugal in 1773 had no visible impact on its economic growth. Even at the end of the age of Brazilian slavery, Portugal remained "backward by any contemporary standard," and "only the eye of faith could detect much in the way of economic development there." Eric J. Hobsbawm, *The Age of Empire 1875–1914* (New York, 1987), 18.

21. See Alexis de Tocqueville, *Democracy in America*, 2 vols., J. P. Mayer, ed. (Garden City, NY, 1969), 345–348. It should be noted that in per capita terms the railroad milage of the U.S. South was almost equal to that of the North just before secession. See Fogel and Engerman, *Time on the Cross*, I, 254–255. Graham argues that, compared with Brazil, the slave South of the United States was far from being economically underdeveloped. See "Slavery and Economic Development: Brazil and the United States South in the Nineteenth Century," *Comparative Studies in Society and History*, 23:4 (Oct. 1981), 620–655. On the development of railway building in the south-central provinces of Brazil, see C. F. van Delden Laerne, *Brazil and Java: Report on Coffee-Culture* (London/The Hague, 1885), chap. 8. In 1889, the provinces of Rio de Janeiro, São Paulo, and Minas Gerais had 65 percent of Brazil's total railroad milage. See Mircea Buescu, "Regional Inequalities in Brazil During the Second Half of the Nineteenth Century," *Disparities in Economic Development Since the Industrial Revolution*, Paul Bairoch and Maurice Levy-Leboyer, eds. (London, 1981/1985), 349–358. For an interpretation of Brazilian slave trade abolition tied closely to the political economy of transportation development, see Luiz-Felipe de Alencastro, "Répercussions de la suppression de la traite des noirs au Brésil," delivered at the Colloque International sur la Traite des Noirs, Nantes, 1985 (forthcoming).

Africa was the most critical ingredient in slavery's viability as an economic system.

Brazil also contributes to the labor "flexibility" debate in slavery historiography. The argument has often been made that slaves were "immobilized" labor compared with wage laborers.[22] Whether or not slaveowners in the South proved to be more market responsive than entrepreneurs using free labor in the North in the antebellum United States, Brazilian slavery seems to have been as flexible and fluid as that of the U.S. South in the redistribution of labor in the generation after slave trade abolition. Comparing the interregional slave migrations within the U.S. South and Brazil, Robert Slenes concludes that, in proportion to the populations of the respective exporting regions, "the two migration currents were about the same size."[23] In regional terms, it would appear that the "exporting" Brazilian slave areas were divesting at a faster rate than those in the upper South of the United States during the generation before their respective emancipations.

As can be seen in the cases of the British West Indies, the United States, Cuba, and Brazil, all of the dynamic plantation economies produced a variety of crops so long as the traffic with Africa remained unimpeded. In the British Caribbean and the U.S. South, that situation ended in 1808. Thereafter, the former moved toward a concentration on sugar and the latter toward cotton. In Cuba, the trend was toward expansion of all produce into the 1830s. With increasing constriction in the 1840s the slave labor force began to concentrate on sugar production and to increase its productivity. After full prohibition of the African labor supply and the beginning of gradual emancipation in 1870, the convergence of slavery and sugar became even more pronounced. In 1862, the major sugar zones of Cuba (Matanzas and Santa Clara) had 46 percent of Cuba's slave population; by 1877 they had 57 percent. A "ruralization" of slavery, similar to that of the U.S. cotton zone and the Brazilian coffee zone, occurred in Cuba.[24]

Of course, this demographic/economic flexibility came at the cost of regional political divergence. Contrary to convergence models of abolition, we confront the paradox that Brazilian economic and political variables operated against each other in some respects. Economic winners hastened their institution's political decline, while the economic losers for

22. See Genovese, *The Political Economy of Slavery: Studies in the Economy and Society of the Slave South* (New York, 1965), 227.

23. Slenes, "Demography," 145, ff. See also Anyda Marchant, *Viscount Maúa and the Empire of Brazil* (Berkeley, 1965), 269.

24. On Cuban slave concentration, consult Eltis, *Economic Growth*, 190–193 and Scott, *Slave Emancipation in Cuba*, 86–90.

TABLE I: Distribution of Foreigners, United States and Brazil

United States 1860	% of all foreigners	% of total population	Brazil 1872	% of all foreigners	% of total population
Free states and western territories	86.5	17.5	Provinces with the lowest proportion of slaves[a]	13.2	1.2
Slave states	13.5	3.5	Provinces with the greatest proportion of slaves[b]	86.8	2.9

Sources: *The Statistical History of the United States, From Colonial Times to the Present* (Stanford, 1965), 11–12; *Population of the United States in 1860* (Washington, 1864), 300; *Recenseamento da População do Imperio do Brasil . . . agosto de 1872*, Quadros geraes.

Notes: On the eve of secession in 1860, there were four million foreigners in the United States. Indeed, there were more foreigners in the southern slave states in 1860 than in all of Brazil at the time of the Rio Branco law. However, insofar as attracting free European immigration was concerned, the northern United States already contained more than four times as many foreigners in 1860 as the South of 1860 and Brazil of 1872 combined. Whether measured by total migrations or in per capita terms, the flow of European free migration was clearly toward the free labor zone of North America.

a. Includes 11 provinces at, or below, the median proportion of slaves.

b. Includes 9 provinces and the Município Neutro (Rio de Janeiro) above the median.

a time futilely attempted to retard slave labor flexibility by warning of political divergence.[25] Eventually Ceará, the most distressed province in preemancipation Brazil (where the only transferable capital left by 1880 was in slaves), became the pioneer province in emancipation. Moreover, the trend toward free labor in the Brazilian Northeast after 1850 was not associated with industrialization as in the U.S. Northeast: industry did not come first to Ceará or to Amazonas as it did to Massachusetts. After 1850, urbanization proceeded more swiftly in the cities located adjacent to the principal slave holding and slave-importing provinces of the South-Center than those in the slave-exporting Northeast. European immigration also flowed primarily to just those areas that were among the last to be converted to abolition in 1887–88. Many of the indicators of "progress" rhetorically used to demonstrate the greater dynamism of the northern United States in the analysis of antebellum slavery (industrialization, transporta-

25. Conrad, *Destruction*, 65–69. In the case of the United States, the movement of slaves toward the frontier initially strengthened the institution by providing for the entrance of new slave states to match the free labor settlement to the north. Later, the movement of slaves out of some border states aroused anxiety about a declining political commitment to slavery in those areas. I designate as convergence theories of abolition those which assume that all or most of the major economic variables (labor, credit, technology, productivity, profitability) combined with each other to induce the abolition process. For a recent elaboration of the general case against such a role for economic growth in slave zones of the nineteenth-century Americas, see Eltis, *Economic Growth*, passim.

tion, urbanization, immigration) seemed to favor the more dynamic slave regions of Brazil.[26]

The Brazilian case therefore suggests that the enterprises, urban areas, and provinces least involved in economic growth and modernization were the first to turn against slavery. This is consistent with Eltis's conclusion that the burgeoning of nineteenth-century European and North American capitalism fueled the general expansion of slavery in terms of investment, consumer demand, and technological innovation.[27] However, there was no area of Brazil, before the mid-1800s, which could assume the role of a "free labor" abolitionist zone, as in the Anglo-American (i.e., British and United States) case. Until late in the emancipation process, "pressure from without" came predominantly from beyond the Brazilian polity.

Political Abolition

Comparative analysis of the politics of Brazilian emancipation might begin with any one of a number of salient criteria. One can distinguish between violence and nonviolence in the process;[28] between abolitions which came from "above" (Russia, the Netherlands, etc.) and those which came from "below" (Haiti);[29] between gradual and partial abolitions (Pennsylvania, Argentina, Venezuela) and simultaneous and total abolitions (France,

26. See Temperley, "Capitalism, Slavery, and Ideology," *Past and Present*, 75 (May 1977), 94–118. See Davis, *Slavery and Human Progress*, 110, for the classic Emersonian comparison of freedom and slavery. It should be noted that even the antebellum South compared favorably with Europe on a number of indexes of "progress." See Fogel and Engerman, *Time on the Cross*, I, 256 and II, 163–164.

Regional comparisons indicate that immigrant flows could hardly have played the same role in Brazil as they did in the United States after 1850. At the time that Brazil passed its gradual emancipation law, the overwhelming proportion of its foreigners resided in those provinces with the highest percentage of slaves—exactly the inverse of the situation in the United States on the eve of its Civil War (see Table I).

Regarding urban areas, a relatively high level of slave labor (either within urban areas or in the adjacent province) does not appear to have been a major deterrent to those foreigners who located themselves in Brazil. Four major cities with substantial foreign populations had substantial slave populations. They were also located in provinces with above median slave populations (see Table II).

27. Regarding manufacturing, slaves in Rio de Janeiro were beginning to be incorporated into nineteenth-century factory employment when the abolition of the slave trade and the coffee boom drained slaves from the cities to the plantation areas. See Eulália M. Lachmeyer Lobo, "A história do Rio de Janeiro" (Rio de Janeiro, 1975), mimeograph, as summarized in Merrick and Graham, *Population*, 51; see also Karasch, "From Porterage to Proprietorship: African Occupations in Rio de Janeiro 1808–1850," in *Race and Slavery in the Western Hemisphere: Quantitative Studies*, Engerman and Genovese, eds. (Princeton, 1975), 369–393. This is consistent with Claudia Dale Goldin's conclusion that slaves in the U.S. South were drawn out of urban areas by strong agricultural demand (*Urban Slavery in the American South, 1820–1860: A Quantitative History* [Chicago, 1976], conclusion).

28. Genovese, *World*, part one.

29. Kolchin, *Unfree Labor*, 49–51.

TABLE II: Percentage of the Labor Force in Selected Urban Areas

Area	Slaves	Foreigners	Slaves in province
Rio de Janeiro	21.1	34.7	45.2 (Rio de Janeiro)
Pôrto Alegre	23.4	13.9	18.7 (Rio Grande do Sul)
São Paulo	15.0	9.9	21.6 (São Paulo)
Recife	16.7	10.1	14.3 (Pernambuco)
Brazil			11.9 (provincial median)

Sources: For the percentage of the labor force in the four largest cities, Merrick and Graham, *Population and Economic Development*, 73; for the median provincial percentages, Table I, above.

Massachusetts); or between compensated emancipations (Britain, France, Denmark) and uncompensated emancipations (the United States, Brazil). Some of these taxonomies seem designed to engender terminological disputes. For example, if we include all legislative acts, from minor restrictions on further recruitment to complete and immediate freedom of contract for all labor, all abolitions, including even the Haitian revolutionary case, were gradual. Similarly, there is simply no case in the plantation Americas in which slaveholders prostrated themselves before economic forces and consensually agreed to initiate abolition.[30] From the historical point of view, all emancipations in the plantation Americas were initiated by exogenous pressures on the planter class.[31]

In formal terms, Brazilian slavery was gradually brought to an end by parliamentary legislation. Abolition occurred in three major political stages: the effective prohibition of the African slave trade in 1851; the passage of the "free birth" (Rio Branco) law in 1871; and the passage of the "Golden Law" of emancipation in 1888. The first stage virtually terminated transatlantic recruitment of slaves. The second deprived the slave system of its means of endogenous reproduction. The third registered the accelerating impact of the extraparliamentary demolition of chattel slavery.

Considering all three stages as part of a single historical development, how can one best view this process in comparative terms? In a study of British and French antislavery in the period between 1780 and the end of the U.S. Civil War, I suggested a contrast between an Anglo-American

30. Genovese, *World*, 14.
31. For the first wave of abolition see Davis, *The Problem of Slavery in the Age of Revolution, 1770–1823* (Ithaca, 1975), chaps. 1 and 2. For Haiti, see C. L. R. James, *The Black Jacobins: Toussaint L'Ouverture and the San Domingo Revolution* (London, 1938). For the Spanish Caribbean, see, inter alia, Arthur F. Corwin, *Spain and the Abolition of Slavery in Cuba, 1817–1886* (Austin, 1967).

and a continental European model of abolitionism.[32] The distinguishing characteristics of the Anglo-American variants were their relatively broad appeal and long duration. Citizens in Great Britain and the United States attempted to bring public pressure to bear on reluctant or hostile economic interests and hesitant agencies of the state. They used mass propaganda, petitions, newspapers, public meetings, lawsuits, and boycotts, presenting ever more radical antislavery action as a moral and political imperative. They achieved, at least occasionally, a reputation for fanaticism. Organizationally, this form of abolitionism tended to be decentralized in structure, and rooted in widely dispersed local communities. Anglo-Americans usually aimed at inclusiveness, welcoming participants who were otherwise excluded from the ordinary political process by reason of gender, religion, race, or class.

The "continental" variants usually had different tendencies. Their leaders were reluctant or unable to seek mass recruitment. They concentrated on plans of abolition (submitted to, or commissioned by, the central government) containing elaborate provisions for postemancipation labor control and planter compensation. They often attempted to act as brokers between external pressure groups (including British abolitionists) and their own slaveowners. Public discussion was restricted to the capital or the chief commercial center. Continental abolitionists, in other words, preferred to work quietly from within and from above. They almost never were considered as fanatics, even by their adversaries. Continental variants also tended to be limited in duration. A small movement would typically form in response to an external (usually British) stimulus. It would last only until the abolition of its nation's own slave trade or slave system. Continental abolitionist societies remained satellites of their British counterpart, and failed to capture any mass following on their own soil.

French abolition was a partly anomalous case. During the Great French Revolution, the source of collective mobilization for emancipation was the slaves in the French Caribbean. Even so, during most of France's age of abolition (1788–1848), the movement was a continental variant—a discontinuous series of elite groupings, unable and usually unwilling to stimulate mass appeals. French slave emancipation occurred in two surges (1793–94 and 1848), with an intervening restoration of slav-

---

32. Seymour Drescher, "Two Variants of Antislavery: Religious Organization and Social Mobilization in Britain and France, 1780–1870," in *Anti-Slavery, Religion, and Reform: Essays in Memory of Roger Anstey*, Christine Bolt and Drescher, eds. (Folkestone, UK/Hamden, CT, 1980), 43–63.

ery under Napoleon wherever his military forces prevailed. Every major French abolitionist thrust (1794, 1815, 1831, and 1848) came in the wake of a revolution, with little abolitionist mobilization in the metropolis; France was a case of abolition without mass abolitionism.[33]

In the Spanish empire, abolition was generally contingent on the fate of colonial mobilizations for national independence. The process on the American continent extended over half a century until the 1860s. Some areas with relatively small slave systems enacted total emancipation in one legal step, in the immediate aftermath of political independence. Others, like Venezuela, Peru, and Argentina, began the process during the independence struggle but moved through slow stages with frequent retrenchments. Cuba, however, was Spain's most important New World slave colony, and its nineteenth-century path to abolition clearly reveals the significance of the absence of strong metropolitan antislavery mobilization. Cuba's dependency on Spain imposed few ideological or political constraints on its slave system for the first two-thirds of the century. On the contrary, Spain was the most extreme example of the "continental" variant of abolitionism; not even a nominal movement existed before the U.S. Civil War. Until southern secession, the United States also provided a formidable counterweight to British abolitionist diplomacy, and was undoubtedly decisive in permitting Africans to reach Cuba for more than a decade after the Brazilian slave trade crisis of 1850. Even after the northern victory in 1865 and the emergence of political abolitionism in Spain, much of the initiative for abolition within the Spanish empire came from foreign countries and the colonial periphery (Cuba and Puerto Rico).[34]

Brazil appears to have shared some characteristics of both major variants of abolitionism. Before the late 1860s, Brazil conformed pretty closely to the continental European model. During the final phase, in the 1880s,

33. Drescher, *Capitalism and Antislavery: British Mobilization in Comparative Perspective* (London/New York, 1987), chap. 3; Davis, *The Problem of Slavery in the Age of Revolution,* 137–148.

34. On Spanish American abolition in general see Leslie B. Rout, *The African Experience in Spanish America, 1502 to the Present Day* (New York, 1976); Herbert S. Klein, *African Slavery in Latin America and the Caribbean* (New York, 1986), chap. 11. For Venezuela, see John V. Lombardi, *The Decline and Abolition of Negro Slavery in Venezuela, 1820–1854* (Westport, 1971). For Argentina, see George Reid Andrews, *The Afro-Argentines of Buenos Aires, 1800–1900* (Madison, 1980). For Cuba and Puerto Rico, see Corwin, *Spain,* esp. chaps. 6–15 and David R. Murray, *Odious Commerce: Britain, Spain and the Abolition of the Cuban Slave Trade* (Cambridge, 1980). Maluquer characterizes Spanish policy toward Cuban slavery and the slave trade before 1860 as a politics of silence and inaction. See "Abolicionismo," 312–322. A shadowy abolitionist society appears to have been formed in Madrid in 1835 (ibid., 315–316). As with its more public Parisian counterpart, the probable stimulus was the implementation of British slave emancipation in the West Indies in 1834. See Drescher, *Dilemmas of Democracy: Tocqueville and Modernization* (Pittsburgh, 1968), 155–166.

it came to more closely resemble the Anglo-American variant, and developed its own original characteristics of popular mobilization.

For almost 60 years, from the Anglo-Portuguese treaty of 1810 to the end of the U.S. Civil War, Brazil conformed to the European pattern in the sense that exogenous forces played a far greater role than endogenous ones in the timing of moves toward abolition. Great Britain's role was preponderant in linking the achievement of independence with formal abolition treaties. Britain also intervened in Brazilian domestic slavery over *emancipado* issues, i.e., over the treatment of ostensibly free Africans who had been rescued from illegal slaving ships. Even more blatantly than in the European context, moreover, the British government "colonized" abolitionism in Brazil through secret subsidies and covert agents.[35]

If slave trade abolition was the first and most important step in the destruction process, it is instructive to consider the Brazilian case in comparative political perspective. Throughout the tropical Americas, the abolition of the slave trade was opposed by expanding plantation areas before such legislation was passed, and was massively evaded afterward for as long the enforcing polity was willing to connive at large-scale smuggling. A huge proportion of Brazil's slave labor force in the second third of the nineteenth century entered the country after the first prohibition in 1831.[36] Given the economic incentive for expansion, however, it is noteworthy that nowhere in the Americas did slaveowners attempt to resist slave trade abolition with military force. The U.S. South was clearly the most acquiescent, with a majority of southern legislators willing to abolish imports at the first constitutional opportunity, in 1807. (Indeed, even those states that originally made constitutional postponement of the abolition question a prerequisite of entry into the union did not make perpetuation a sine qua non of union). Even in secession, the Confederacy did not move to reopen the slave trade. Elsewhere (as in the British case) the majority of slaveowners engaged in protracted lobbying efforts against prohibition.[37] Yet a minority of planters readily acquiesced, and in no case did ending of the trade cause a major internal upheaval in slave societies.

The Brazilian case is especially interesting in political terms. Brazil—along with Cuba—was one of the last two slave societies in the Americas to effectively prohibit African recruitment. Despite other similarities to the U.S. South, there had been relatively little endogenous political activity in Brazil against the illegal traffic during the generation before 1850,

35. Bethell, *Abolition*, 313; Eltis, *Economic Growth*, 114–119, 140–141, 214–216.
36. Eltis, *Economic Growth*, 243–244, table A.1.
37. See Drescher, *Econocide: British Slavery in the Era of Abolition* (Pittsburgh, 1977), 181.

certainly nothing comparable in scale to British agitation in favor of abolition. The major push for Brazilian abolition of the trade thus came from
outside the nation—in a virtual *casus belli*, in June of 1850. When the
British navy mounted an attack on slave ships within Brazilian territorial
waters, a number of remarkable results ensued. Unlike the localized impact of naval interventions on the coast of Africa, the entire slave trade to
Brazil was brought to a precipitous end.[38] The only nominally independent
slave society in the Americas acquiesced in the total elimination of what
had been its major source of plantation labor recruitment for centuries.
Since the Brazilian elite's commitment to slavery was a primary source of
common loyalty,[39] such rapid enforcement and the inaction of the traders,
slaveowners, and potential slaveowners are indeed striking, although not
out of line with developments elsewhere.

From the perspective of established slaveowners, a general restriction
on their long-run powers of expansion was an obvious setback, but its
acceptance both spared them the short-term trade losses entailed in a
British naval blockade and, as in the U.S. South, offered the medium-term
gains of a rise in slave prices flowing from abolition. The immediate losers
were outsiders on the verge of becoming slaveholders. The acquiescing
planters were mortgaging their political future.

A second important observation concerns the absence of attempts to
use public opinion or mass demonstrations, either against the British vio-
lators by proslavers or against the Portuguese slavers by supporters of the
British demands. The political decision was made behind closed doors, in
secret session. Popular opinion might have been welcome after the Chamber had acted, but it was not incorporated into the decision-making process itself either for resistance or for acquiescence.[40]

Sectoral Divisions

Comparative analysis also seems to support those interpretations of
Brazilian abolition which emphasize the significance of regional and sec-
toral differentiation without the need for recourse to sociopsychological
divisions of the planter class along progressive-bourgeois and traditionalist-
paternalist lines.[41] The demographic decline of slaves produced by ter-

38. Bethell, *Abolition*, 380–383.
39. A. J. R. Russell-Wood, ed., "Preconditions and Precipitants of the Independence
Movement in Portuguese America," *From Colony to Nation: Essays on the Independence of
Brazil* (Baltimore, 1975), 38.
40. Bethell, *Abolition*, 335–341. Eisenberg, *Sugar Industry*, 152, speaks of the British
action as an "unreturnable insult." On the other hand, there was agitation in the late antebellum South to reopen the slave trade, in order to diffuse ownership and support for slavery.
41. See Toplin, *Abolition*, chap. 1; Genovese, *World*, 75–93; Elizabeth Fox-Genovese

mination of the slave trade, combined with the differential expansion of
the slave-based economy, produced an accelerated emptying of certain
economic sectors which had still been tied into slavery under the lower
labor costs of the African slave trade. The same regional erosion occurred
in the United States, but over a much longer period. Some of the southern
calculations about the need for secession in 1860 were based on perceived
trends of slavery's decline in the border states.[42]

The British West Indian case offers an interesting exception to regional erosion that supports the general model. Despite the slave price
gap which opened up between the developed and the frontier colonies
between British slave trade abolition in 1807 and emancipation in 1833,
none of the British slave colonies broke ranks before 1833 in the manner
of Amazonas and Ceará in Brazil. The ability of British slaveowners to
transfer slaves to high-price areas was legally curtailed. Consequently, the
process of regional divestment could not occur.[43] Redistribution of labor
occurred only between crops or within separate island labor markets. One
of the principal advantages of the use of slave labor over free workers was
thus reversed in the British case during the interregnum between slave
trade abolition and emancipation.[44]

As already mentioned, by the time the political consequences of the
free market in slaves clearly outweighed the economic advantages to slaveowners in Brazil, it was far too late. The social consensus in favor of slavery
at the time of independence had dissolved. The relationship between abolition and the increasing economic concentration of slavery seems as clear
as in the case of geographical redistribution. It has been shown that for
the U.S. South there was "a striking increase in the percentage of farm
operations with no slaves," from less than 40 percent in 1850 to approximately 50 percent in 1860. Not only was the percentage of southerners in
the total U.S. population falling, but the percentage of southern families
who owned slaves was also steadily dropping in the generation before

---

and Eugene D. Genovese, in *Fruits of Merchant Capital: Slavery and Bourgeois Property
in the Rise and Expansion of Capitalism* (New York, 1983), 47–48, reiterate their emphasis
on the basically seigneurial labor relationships of northeastern Brazil, but their conclusion
(pp. 394–395) places all slaveholders within the same antimodern category. For a discussion
of alternative models of planter behavior, see Slenes, "Demography," chap. 1.

42. Compare Slenes, "Demography," chap. 11 and Gavin Wright, *The Political Economy of the Cotton South: Households, Markets, and Wealth in the Nineteenth Century* (New
York, 1978), 37, and n. 9, above.

43. Peter F. Dixon, "The Politics of Emancipation: The Movement for the Abolition of
Slavery in the British West Indies, 1807–1833" (D. Phil. thesis, Oxford University, 1971);
Eltis, *Economic Growth*, 8–9.

44. Higman, *Slave Populations of the British Caribbean 1870–1834* (Baltimore, 1984),
67–69.

1860. The rising proportion of slaveless white families was probably more significant politically than any distinction between large and small slaveholders, because a southerner who owned just two slaves and *nothing else* was as rich as the average antebellum northerner. The need to maintain the loyalty of the nonslaveholding backbone of the electorate was the major task of the dominant party in the South.[45]

In addition to the effects of regional redistribution, rising Brazilian slave prices after 1850 must have prevented more and more Brazilians from entering into slaveowning altogether. Aspirations to ownership and a stake in the future of the system receded, as the free population increased more rapidly than the slave. I have found no figures on the percentage growth of slavelessness in Brazil after 1850, but the available analyses of slave redistribution, price trends, and slave/free population ratios after 1850 all point in the direction of a parallel to the antebellum South. The short-term benefits to existing owners of capital may conceivably have weakened their resolve to oppose abolition of the slave trade in 1850, but thereafter the same factors weakened the potential appeal of slavery to nonowners, eroding the consensual base of slavery.

The Politics of the Planters

The early historiographical focus on planters in Brazilian abolition appears to be quite reasonable, in view of their general dominance and cohesiveness in imperial Brazilian society. Since the abolitionist process was, from the slaveowners' perspective, first initiated from without, the Brazilian case can perhaps be most fruitfully examined within the comparative context of responses to abolitionist threats.

There were certain similarities between the slaveowners' situations in Brazil and the U.S. South on the eve of the external threats to their respective slaveries. Plantation profits were generally increasing in both economies during the first half of the nineteenth century, which should have encouraged counterabolitionist action. The same upward trend was true of long-term demand for their staples.[46]

45. Wright, *Political Economy*, 34–35. On southern fears of a class division between slaveholders and "no-property men," see Michael F. Holt, *The Political Crisis of the 1850s* (New York, 1978), 225–226, 246–247. See also Paul D. Escott, *Many Excellent People: Power and Privilege in North Carolina, 1850–1900* (Chapel Hill, 1985), chap. 2.

46. For the United States, see Fogel and Engerman, *Time on the Cross*, 92–94; for Brazil, see Eltis, *Economic Growth*, 186. Slave prices in Pernambuco almost doubled during the 1850s, and reached an all-time peak in 1879 (Eisenberg, *Sugar Industry*, 153). "In coffee-producing Rio de Janeiro, moreover, nominal slave prices rose even higher, and reached a peak in the late 1870s at a level nearly four times that of the early 1850s. The coffee sector's greater prosperity allowed the coffee planters to outbid the sugar planters for slaves, and after 1850 Pernambuco began shipping slaves south" (ibid., 156).

But there were divergences between the two economies which made for very different outlooks in contemplating courses of action. The coffee planters of the Brazilian South-Center would have been less buoyed by the nature of their market in 1850 or in 1871 than were their U.S. counterparts. The latter might rationally have anticipated that secession would succeed without violence. Their major premise was that the South, "safely entrenched behind her cotton bags . . . can defy the civilized world—for the civilized world depends on the cotton of the South." Their optimism was supported by northern disarray and by the fears voiced in England about a cotton famine.[47]

The situation of the Brazilian planters in 1850 was quite different. They were presented at the outset with a military fait accompli which offered only the choice between preparation for war and acquiescence in the ending of the slave trade. No one was under the illusion that a British blockade of Brazilian coffee or sugar exports would quickly bring a major component of the English economy to its knees. The British public and government could always be tougher toward coffee- and sugar-producing areas than toward cotton-producing ones. Only a political regime able to dismiss short-term economic considerations could seriously have considered challenging the British navy. There is no indication that Brazilian society was remotely organized for a scorched trade policy in the mid-nineteenth century, and the Brazilian government seems to have played a continental-style mediating role between Britain and Brazil's slaveowners.

After 1865, the timing of the initial movement toward gradual emancipation in Brazil also seems to have been dominated by external events, including emancipation in the United States and the Spanish Caribbean and the Paraguayan War. Early explorations of popular channels of abolitionism (extraparliamentary organization and newspaper appeals) were confined to a very small section of the elite until the national legislation was actually presented in the form of a "free womb" emancipation bill in 1871.[48]

By 1871, the model of emancipation by birth, as Robert Conrad notes, had been among the tested formulas for emancipation for almost a century. It had most recently been employed in the Spanish colonies the year before.[49] One might, of course, emphasize the limitations of the Rio Branco Law in order to enhance the significance of the mass mobilization phase of the 1880s. It should be noted, however, that the law certainly cut down the projected duration of slavery from a multigenerational perspective to the lifespan of a slave. It definitively set the clock running on termination.

47. Wright, *Political Economy*, 146–147.
48. Conrad, *Destruction*, chap. 5.
49. Ibid., 87–90; Corwin, *Spain*, chap. 13.

Subsequent popular mobilization made a difference of perhaps 10 to 15 years in the duration of Brazilian slavery. Although abolitionists in the 1880s were quick to note that slaves born in 1870 could live for another 60 to 70 years,[50] the active slave population would have been so small and so aging a proportion of the labor force by 1900 that it is difficult to imagine further resistance to accelerated, and even compensated, immediate emancipation. Compensation based on the European model would have become far more palatable as the pool of prime, able-bodied slaves evaporated. In some other areas where gradual legislation was passed (e.g., New York State, 1799) the tendency was for acceleration of the emancipation clock as the slave labor pool shrank and aged.[51]

Brazil's was the only plantation society to peacefully enact free womb emancipation entirely from within. In 1870, Brazil was operating under far less serious direct external and internal threats than Cuba.[52] Why then did Brazil adopt a law which was so definitive about the outer time limit of its slave system, and one which did not offer a guarantee of compensation to planters against the eventuality of further accelerated emancipation?

Conrad's study indicates that during the gradual emancipation debate an area *within* Brazil—the Northeast—began to play the role of mediating the transition to a free labor system. However, the social dynamics of realignment within the Northeast are still insufficiently clear.[53] Were the northeastern deputies of still substantial slave areas responsive to slaveholders who already felt secure in their ability to make the transition to free labor over another generation? The willingness of slaveowners from Pernambuco or Bahia to support the law, when between 12 and 20 percent of their populations were still slaves, stands in stark contrast to Delaware's refusal to consider a compensated emancipation proposal by Abraham Lincoln in 1861, when that state had fewer than 2,000 remaining slaves.

The opposition to the Rio Branco Law raises equally interesting questions. It was located primarily in the dynamic South and South-Center (although São Paulo divided evenly).[54] Given the region's expanding need for interprovincial labor recruitment, why was the resistance not far greater when the Rio Branco bill was introduced? Faced with the histori-

50. See Toplin, *Abolition*, chap. 2, pp. 92–96.
51. Arthur Zilversmit, *The First Emancipation: The Abolition of Slavery in the North* (Chicago, 1967), 212–213.
52. See Corwin, *Spain*, 144–171, 294–299; Scott, *Slave Emancipation*, chaps. 2 and 3; and Murray, *Odious Commerce*, chap. 14.
53. Conrad, *Destruction*, 91–93. Even as late as 1884–85 in northeastern Brazil it was possible for small elite electorates of less than a thousand voters to nearly defeat Nabuco's candidacy for the Chamber of Deputies. Nabuco was defeated in his bid for reelection in Recife in 1886. See Carolina Nabuco, *The Life of Joaquim Nabuco* (Stanford, 1950), chaps. 11 and 13.
54. Conrad, *Destruction*, 301, table 21.

cal record, the planters could hardly have been in doubt that abolitionists, like Oliver Twist, always came back for more. Where was the cry of "no emancipation without compensation," which had unified British, French, Dutch, and Danish colonial planters before their respective emancipations, often postponing abolition for decades? The Rio Branco Law was obviously no more than a stop-gap measure for those Brazilians who wished to "catch up" with their century.

The behavior of the Brazilian slaveholders can be contrasted most dramatically with that of the southern United States after Lincoln's election climaxed a decade of escalating sectional crisis. In Brazil, there was some sectional revitalization of federalism in response to the developing emancipationism of the late 1860s and a resurgence of republicanism in reaction to gradual emancipation demands in 1870–71. But there seems to have been no serious move in the Brazilian South to either overthrow the regime or withdraw from it. For the period 1865–71, the limits of political mobilization on both sides are again evident, but those on the part of Brazil's dynamic southern slaveowners are more intriguing because it was their future which was being most compromised.

The historian of North Atlantic abolitions is therefore struck by the absence of a united front of the major slaveholding provinces against the gradual termination of the institution. Supporters of reform could argue their case before thousands in the theaters of Rio de Janeiro, a city whose hinterland was one of the three most "hard core" slave provinces, with a delegation in the Chamber of Deputies that voted by a ratio of three to one against the law.[55] (The fact that the Município Neutro deputies also voted 3 to 0 against the law indicates that as late as 1870 neither economic modernization, nor urbanization, nor slave disinvestment had yet converted the enfranchised notables of Rio.[56]) The proslavery forces did not even attempt to match the preemptive censorship against abolitionism which was so characteristic of the antebellum U.S. South. Could New Orleans have been, like Rio, the venue for the largest antislavery debates in the entire country during the Kansas-Nebraska controversy or the 1860 election?

The disunity of slaveowners at the national level circa 1870 and the weakness of civil threats at the regional level stand in contrast not only to the southern states of the United States in the late 1850s but even to Jamaica. In 1830–31, the first mass petition for immediate emancipation in Great Britain, combined with new ministerial restrictions on the planters' disciplinary powers, triggered the most vigorous proslavery

---

55. Ibid., 93.
56. Ibid., 301, table 21. As late as 1870, more than one-fifth of Rio's population was still slave. Karasch, *Slave Life*, 61, table 3.1.

countermobilization in Jamaican history. Public assemblies throughout the island threatened secession. As a result, the last round of imperial restrictions was virtually suspended. (On the other hand, planter mobilization also helped to stimulate the most widespread slave revolt in British Caribbean history a few months later.[57]) By contrast, Brazilian elite suspicion of popular mobilization, revealed in the crisis of 1850, may again have kept planter action to a low level of nonviolent opposition in 1870. A detailed consideration of the slaveowners' perceptions and actions in 1870–72 would make an important addition to the historiography of Brazilian abolition and of the demise of New World slavery.

Popular Abolitionism

In the final phase of emancipation (1880–88), Brazil became the only non-English-speaking country to develop a full-blown, Anglo-American-style variant of antislavery. Brazilian mass abolitionism was largely confined to the years just before the Golden Law of 1888.[58] As in the British case, Brazilian emancipation was enacted by the regular legislative process, and, as in the British case, the legislature lagged behind popular action.

The early phase of the Brazilian popular movement drew on Anglo-American recipes for mobilization: newspaper publicity, mass rallies, autonomous abolitionist local organizations, and the underground railroad.[59] In the final phase, however, Brazilian abolitionism was distinctive and inventive. The first public rallies in Brazil were held in theaters and concert halls rather than in the town halls, courts, churches, and chapels which formed the centers of British and U.S. abolitionist rallies. Anglo-American antislavery mobilized in the image of familiar political structures: through town meetings, formal petitions, and deputations to the legislature. Abolitionist meetings followed the rules and discourse of parliamentary procedures. At critical moments, Anglo-American electoral campaigns had to address slavery as a central national issue. Candidates were forced to take explicit positions on slavery-related questions before aroused, and ultimately decision-making, audiences.[60] Brazilian popular mobilization apparently flowed more easily from the familiar modes of public entertainment than political organization. The proportion of programs devoted

57. See Dixon, "Politics," 203; Drescher, *Capitalism*, 106–108; Mary Turner, *Slaves and Missionaries: The Disintegration of Jamaican Slave Society, 1787–1834* (Urbana, 1982), 163.
58. Conrad, *Destruction*, chap. 9; Toplin, *Abolition*, chap. 3.
59. Conrad, *Destruction*, 193 ff.; Toplin, *Abolition*, 86 ff.
60. Drescher, *Capitalism*, chap. 4.

to music and poetry at rallies would probably have surprised a veteran of the British antislavery lecture campaigns. Petitioning in particular seems to have played less of a role in Brazil than in Anglo-American abolitionism. Although petitioning was permissible in both imperial Brazil and monarchical France, in neither country was it central to the antislavery movement.[61]

Yet the inventiveness of Brazilian popular abolitionism extended far beyond the public concert and the victory carnival. Perhaps because of the inertia of its political system, Brazilian abolitionism's distinguishing characteristic was to be seen in decentralized direct action. Brazil created two new patterns of direct and nonviolent action which enabled much of the nation to dismantle its slave system without any special enabling legislation, province by province, municipality by municipality, and even city block by city block.

There are few more dramatic stories in the history of abolition than the collective liberations of Ceará, Goiás, and Paraná in the mid-1880s. For the first time in Brazilian history, "free" labor zones, analogous to the European metropolis or the U.S. North, were established in whole provinces, as well as in urban areas of all major regions in Brazil. Popular liberations were enacted entirely outside the formal political and bureaucratic channels of the central government. When local ordinances were involved, they were likely to be ratifying what had already taken place.[62] Never before in the history of Brazil had mass political agitation simultaneously extended over the whole territory of the nation or involved so many Brazilians. As with Anglo-American abolitionism, Brazilian mobilization afforded an entrée for large numbers of people who had not previously participated in the national political process. From accounts of participation in the victory celebrations, it would also appear that far more people identified with abolition in 1888 than with the establishment of the republic in 1889.[63]

A second Brazilian form of direct action was equally original in style, scale, and effectiveness. Once de facto zones of freedom were established in provincial and urban areas, the Brazilian "underground railroad" came into its own. By any measure it was the largest such network in the history

---

61. Ibid. For recourse to the theaters see, inter alia, Carolina Nabuco, *The Life of Joaquim Nabuco*, 74. The Spanish abolitionist society, like that of Brazil, initially tended to favor artistic appeals rather than conventional political rallies (Maluquer, "Abolicionismo," 324). Spanish and Cuban abolitionism also adopted petitioning as a tactic in the early 1880s. See Corwin, *Spain*, 309.

62. Conrad, *Destruction*, chap. 11.

63. Toplin, *Abolition*, 256; June E. Hahner, *Poverty and Politics: The Urban Poor in Brazil, 1870–1920* (Albuquerque, 1986), 72.

of New World slavery. The very term "underground railroad" is something of a misnomer. It defers too much to its U.S. predecessor. Fleeing slaves often used the Brazilian *overground* railway itself. More often than in the United States, flight was undertaken collectively, with whole plantations being simultaneously abandoned. Abolitionist initiatives were indeed so open and so numerous that the policing system simply broke down in entire provinces.[64] In contrast to most emancipations, Brazilian planters seem to have had to conduct their counterattacks without access to either the full panoply of official coercion or the active cooperation of the free masses.[65] At critical moments in the spread of collective flight, the cities and the armed forces proved unreliable and indeed hostile to enforcers of the law.

Although a nonviolent termination of slavery by the refusal of slaves to continue working without wages had been unsuccessfully attempted at a late stage in the British emancipation process, the inability of Brazilian officials to mobilize the coercive forces of the state was decisive in the accelerating success of the Brazilian movement. Therefore, in the late nineteenth century, Brazil came as close to demonstrating a "withering away of the estate," despite planter opposition, as any slave system in the Americas except Haiti's.

Violence was not absent from Brazilian abolition. However, given the size of its slave population and the scale of its movement, Brazilian emancipation lies at the nonviolent end of the spectrum. In recounting the bloodiest incidents, historians indicate implicitly that violence and brutality were regarded as exceptional, not normative. Bloodshed shocked the public, rather than polarizing it. The fact that one of the worst incidents of vigilante violence involved two U.S. veterans of the Confederate Army, who taunted Brazilian slaveowners for their lack of manhood and honor, is certainly illustrative. In this instance the government of one of the major slave provinces of Brazil was forced, by public opinion, to indict the participants, although the charges were not pursued to a conclusion.[66]

---

64. Toplin, *Abolition*, chap. 8; Conrad, *Destruction*, chap. 16.

65. Toplin, *Abolition*, 213. Planter organization against abolitionism in the northeastern provinces seems to have come very late, in reaction to the Ceará abolition of 1883–84, and the planters themselves were deeply divided over the question of gradualism vs. immediatism (Eisenberg, *Sugar Industry*, 166–170). The Cuban path to abolition followed the earlier Spanish American pattern. Until after the U.S. Civil War the Spanish military presence and political repression made open proslavery and nonviolent antislavery mobilization impossible. See Robert L. Paquette, *The Conspiracy of La Escalera* (forthcoming). The Ten Years War for national independence in 1868–78 opened the door to selective manumissions for military purposes and partial abolition in areas under rebel control. But if insurrection accelerated gradual abolition in the 1870s, the settlement of the conflict inhibited popular agitation in favor of the final emancipation legislation of the 1880s.

66. Toplin, *Abolition*, 212–213; Conrad, *Destruction*, 256–257. The most violent series

When the slaves engaged in violence, they seem to have directed their attacks toward overseers, and only occasionally toward masters. The fact that many surrendered themselves to the authorities immediately after such incidents indicates a substantial level of trust, at least in the non-brutality of the authorities. Virtually absent are accounts reminiscent of the horrors of St. Domingue, with slaves burning their plantations and eventually extending the repertoire of vengeance to the women and children of their owners. (Also entirely absent are the scenes of calculated terrorism as carried out by planters and public authorities both before and after the St. Domingue uprising, including all the refinements of torture.) Even the British West Indies had experienced the largest slave uprising in their history less than two years before emancipation. The Brazilian slaves, by contrast, appear to have concluded that neither bloody insurrections nor guerrilla warfare were necessary or productive.[67]

Most significant, in comparative terms, was a fourth class of participants in the abolition process, the free masses, who seem to have played their major role in Brazilian abolition less as laborers than as political actors. It is not elite attitudes toward the laboring masses but attitudes of the nonslave masses toward slavery and abolition that most need further articulation by historians.[68] Slavery as an institution was ultimately dependent on those who were neither masters nor slaves. Masters required more than just passive acquiescence to support their system of domination. During the eighteenth century, British West Indians began to lose control over the slaves they brought to England when the London populace failed to cooperate in returning runaways.[69]

But the free population in Brazil did more than refuse to condone planter violence and to tolerate the formation of free towns at the edges of the cities. Nonslaveholders participated as emissaries to the countryside, encouraging large-scale flight. They made it impossible for slaveowners and their employees to deal with resistance by ordinary policing and patrol methods. The phenomenon of abolitionists fanning out into the

---

of confrontations apparently occurred in the plantation areas of Campos in Rio de Janeiro, where fazendeiro-led gangs resorted to "lynch law." Even in Campos, however, the power of the slaveowners was openly challenged by abolitionist leaders and armed defenders. See Toplin, *Abolition*, 220–222.

67. Compare James, *Black Jacobins*, with the accounts in da Costa, Toplin, and Conrad. On the Jamaica uprising in 1831–32, see Michael Craton, *Testing the Chains: Resistance to Slavery in the British West Indies* (Ithaca, 1982), chap. 22.

68. Relations between the elite and the free poor in the countryside are analyzed for one locality in Hebe Maria Mattos de Castro, *Ao sul da história* (São Paulo, 1987), but the link between those relationships and the national political process of abolition has not yet been systematically investigated.

69. Drescher, *Capitalism*, chap. 2.

countryside with relative impunity was novel in plantation slave societies: elsewhere, abolitionists and slaves were usually separated by thousands of miles of water or (as in the United States) by the solidarity of a very hostile free local population. How to account both for Brazilian permeability to abolitionism and for the failure of the slaveowners to sufficiently mobilize against the British ultimatum in 1850, gradual abolition in 1871, or popular abolition in the mid-1880s remains the most intriguing political question about Brazil in comparative perspective.

Racial Ideology and Abolition

The ideological mobilization of Brazilian masters was in one respect more analogous to that found in the British, French, and Russian empires than to that of the United States. The pro-slavery "positive good" argument of the U.S. South, so highly articulated in both religious and racial terms, played a relatively minor role in Brazilian political discourse. As in the Caribbean and in Russia, Brazilian planters invoked arguments based more on economic necessity, social order, and the advantages of gradual change than on slavery as a superior form of economic, racial, and social organization.[70] This occurred despite the fact that theories of innate racial superiority and social Darwinism were attaining ever-increasing respectability in Europe and the United States during the decades just before Brazilian emancipation.

In his comparative study of U.S. and Russian slavery, Peter Kolchin concludes that the extent to which bondsmen were considered to be outsiders affected the nature and vigor of the defense of servitude. Slaves in the U.S. South were regarded as alien in origin and nature. They belonged to a racial minority of "outsiders," and most members of that minority were slaves. Hence, the equation of slaves as both black and alien could be more existentially sustained. In Russia, the peasants, perceived as "natives," were the overwhelming majority of the population.[71] The formulation of a racially based mobilization of proslavery ideology was thus dependent on the degree of overlap between racial and juridical divisions. In this respect, Brazil conceived of itself as intrinsically multiracial long after whites in the United States were determined to think of theirs as a country of white people. There was no major movement in Brazil to re-

---

70. Toplin, *Abolition*, 131; Conrad, *Destruction*, 167. Spanish defenders of the status quo, like their Brazilian counterparts, stressed economic necessity or political constraints, not the intrinsic superiority of slavery. See Maluquer, "Abolicionismo," 321. Compare with the Anglo-American positive good argument in Marcus Cunliffe, *Chattel Slavery and Wage Slavery: The Anglo-American Context 1830–1960* (Athens, GA, 1979), chap. 1.

71. Kolchin, *Unfree Labor*, 170–191.

export free blacks to Africa, although some abolitionists called for racial removal in the 1830s.[72] At the very time that a movement to deport free blacks was being launched in the United States, serious proposals were still being made in Brazil to replace the threatened supply of slaves by recruiting free Africans. In Brazil, the importation of Chinese workers also continued to be seriously debated when the United States was moving to prohibit their immigration. (The unresponsiveness to Chinese immigration projects seems to have come as much from the Chinese as from the Brazilian side.[73])

In terms of race, the crucial difference between Brazil and the U.S. South as it affected the political process was not potential sources of labor recruitment but the relative proportions of slaves and free blacks. For the politics of abolition, the "degrees of freedom" were more important than the degrees of constriction. At the time of independence, the Brazilian free colored population was already almost a third as great as the slave population. A communally based mobilization in defense of unfree labor would presumably have required (among other things) a free majority racially distinguished from the slave population. In the Brazilian situation, slaveholders could not, at any point during the crisis of their system, mobilize either a credible political-military defense against external pressure or a sectional defense against internal pressures. In this they resembled Caribbean slave societies rather than the U.S. South. Caribbean planters did not have the option of mobilizing free masses in the colonial areas. The Russian situation was analogous. There were no nonserf "masses" to mobilize in defense of the existing social structure, only peasants who identified more closely with the serfs than with the lords.[74]

In Brazil and Cuba, a mass mobilization of all free people in defense of slavery would have required risking a social revolution, appealing to a racially mixed, disenfranchised rural population. The Iberian slave polities were distinctive in having developed a free sector which was racially more mixed and socially more hierarchical than that of the United States. Politically speaking, the "free" masses of Brazil and Cuba were the functional equivalents of the free masses of continental Europe, useless or worse to the planters in a long-term struggle against external abolitionism.[75] On the

---

72. Repatriationist ideologies based on racism were not absent in Brazil. Early abolitionists in particular argued for the removal of former slaves from Brazilian society. See Manuela Carneiro da Cunha, *Negros, estrangeiros: Os escravos libertos e sua volta à África* (São Paulo, 1985), 84–86. Once again, it is the lower level of collective action for these ends in Brazil compared with the United States that is striking.

73. Conrad, *Destruction*, 33–36, 133.

74. Kolchin, *Unfree Labor*, 177–183.

75. The role of the Spanish "Volunteers" as defenders of the imperial connection and

other hand, the free colored urban masses of Brazil, equally uninvolved in the national political process, were also not generally accessible to the abolitionists. Emília Viotti da Costa and June Hahner note the failure of abolitionism to attract large numbers of former slaves and free colored workers. Brazilian abolitionists were aware of this problem as late as the very eve of emancipation.[76]

Comparative analysis therefore seems to highlight the significance of political organization and demography in accounting for Brazil's path toward abolition. The planters of the U.S. South, accustomed for two generations to sharing decision making with the vast number of individuals owning few or no slaves, had forged a regional identity resting on economic and racial solidarity which Brazilian planters had never, and probably could never have, replicated in their hierarchical regime of "notables."[77] Lacking both the political and racial building blocks for a slaveowner *herrenvolk* democracy, the planters tacked cautiously within the narrow boundaries of their political system against the combined pressures of a shrinking demographic base, an expanding national economy, and a contemptuous free world. In 1830, Brazil was still one of many unenfranchised, illiterate, unindustrialized nations with a large, permanently bound labor force. Two generations later, it stood virtually alone.

---

the traditional political economy during Cuba's Ten Years War may demonstrate how ethnocultural interests could be linked to a defense of slavery. Communal or cultural loyalties could even cause slaves to reject outsiders with abolitionist agendas as they did in some British islands during the Anglo-French conflict of the 1790s. On the British Caribbean, see David Geggus, "The Enigma of Jamaica in the 1790s: New Light on the Causes of Slave Rebellions," *William and Mary Quarterly*, 44:2 (Apr. 1987), 274–299, esp. 292 and Craton, *Testing the Chains*, 180–210. In both cases, however, the planters were auxiliaries to imperial military forces.

76. Da Costa, *Da senzala*, 438. Hahner emphasizes that color-class divisions within Brazil's cities contributed to the fact that "most dark-skinned Brazilians did not participate in the formal abolitionist movement," and class divisions were evident within the movement as well (*Poverty and Politics*, 67–68).

77. A majority of Brazil's population in the early nineteenth century was deemed "marginal," both to the economy and to the polity. See Caio Prado, Jr., *The Colonial Background of Modern Brazil*, Suzette Macedo, trans. (Berkeley, 1967), 328–332; and Michael C. McBeth, "The Brazilian Recruit during the First Empire: Slave or Soldier?" in *Essays Concerning the Socioeconomic History of Brazil and Portuguese India*, Alden and Dean, eds. (Gainesville, 1977), 71–86. There appears to have been considerable ideological, as well as social, continuity of attitudes toward the *desclassificados* in the colonial period. See, e.g., Laura de Mello C. Souza, *Desclassificados do ouro: A pobreza mineira no século XVIII* (Rio de Janeiro, 1982) and Andrews, "Race and the State in Colonial Brazil," *Latin American Research Review*, 19:3 (1984), 203–216. Compare this configuration of class relations with Fletcher M. Green, *Democracy in the Old South, and Other Essays* (Nashville, 1969), chap. 3; Steven Hahn, *The Roots of Southern Populism: Yeoman Farmers and the Transformation of the Georgia Upcountry, 1850–1890* (New York, 1983), 99; Fox-Genovese and Genovese, *Fruits*, chap. 9; and John McCardell, *The Idea of a Southern Nation: Southern Nationalists and Southern Nationalism, 1830–1860* (New York, 1979), 319–335.

Regional divestment, urban-rural and crop redistributions, concentration of slave ownership, and above all Brazil's increasing divergence from the Western model of civil liberty weighed against the status quo. As conflicts of interest and outlook grew wider the consensus of slaveholders eroded. As their numbers dwindled, demoralized slaveowners faced an increasingly popular abolitionism without the potential for a racially grounded antiabolitionism.[78]

It is important to note that not all Brazilian planters subscribed to the European model of civil progress implied in the antislavery ideology. Moreover, the high price of slaves until the final wave of abolitionist mobilization indicates that Brazilian slaveowners, like their counterparts in Cuba, conducted their slave enterprises within relatively short-term time horizons, even after the implementation of gradual emancipation legislation. But three final observations about Brazilian ideology and self-identification are worth making. First, as in much of Latin America, a Europeanized social future, including the demise of slave labor, remained the dominant forecast of Brazil's destiny. Second, some of those who most vigorously rejected the model of Europeanization in other respects (for example, Sílvio Romero's *História da literatura brasileira* in 1888), emphatically supported an egalitarian and fusionistic racial destiny for Brazil.[79] And third, the "patriarchal" vision of Brazil did not fade away without many nostalgic literary evocations. However, no school arose in Brazil during the nineteenth century which successfully crystallized that diffuse counteregalitarian mentality into a cultural identification with the perpetuation of slavery. Brazilian planters remained closer to the ideological norm of the Americas than to that of the antebellum U.S. South.

Conclusion

Brazilian abolition seems to offer some intriguing contrasts with abolition in other slave societies. There was no profound revolutionary crisis in Brazil before 1888 to stimulate the extension of abolitionist appeals to broader social sectors, and not until the Paraguayan War of the 1860s did Brazil experience military problems even slightly analogous to those which accelerated moves toward abolition in much of Spanish America. At the same time, a distinctive political characteristic of the process in Brazil was the inability of planters to rally the country around the principle of slavery, and to use exogenous threats as a catalyst for effective countermobilization. The midnineteenth century was a moment when nationalism

78. On late divisions among the planters, see Toplin, *Abolition*, chap. 9 and Conrad, *Destruction*, chap. 16.
79. Burns, *The Poverty of Progress*, 62–63, 79.

was emerging throughout the West as a rallying point for intensive state-building. The U.S. South linked its bid for national independence to its "peculiar" institution. The southerners failed to achieve nationhood, but only after a massive military and political mobilization of resources. Brazil, however, never developed an interregional nationalism against the British in 1830–50, or a regional nationalism against gradual abolition in 1865–72 and immediate abolition in 1880–88. Brazilian slaveowners lacked the tradition of, or the means for, orderly popular mobilization, and they clearly hesitated to construct such mechanisms before 1850, when slavery was still a consensual institution. Even a planter-led popular mobilization entailed the risk of losing control over the political process at a time when abolitionist attacks were as yet cautious and sporadic. Much like the French *pays légal* of the 1830s and 1840s, Brazilian planters clung to a regime of notables.

Concentrating on the planters and the cities, students of Brazilian abolition have paid less attention to the rural free population. Only recently has there been a historiographical focus on small-scale cultivators which would allow historians to speculate why the free poor were never asked to defend their traditional community on a scale or intensity equal to what occurred in the southern United States. Did planters never even imagine appealing to the rural free masses in favor of slavery because of their distrust of their neighbors? Was the relationship between slaves and free people in the rural areas different in Brazil because of the cumulative effect of manumissions and the consequent existence of bonds which did not exist in the racially more polarized U.S. South? Or did southern U.S. planters play a role that had no parallel in Brazil—shielding nonslaveholders from low wages and the risks of the world market, and guaranteeing the free masses considerable comfort by contemporary world standards?[80] Although historians duly note tensions which existed between yeomen and slaveowners of the antebellum United States, the relative strength of the southern commitment to slavery remains a critical benchmark for comparisons with Brazil. The South had become politically democratic for the white male population in the half-century before the secession crisis, and the abolition of slavery was not on the southern political agenda because no substantial group of southern nonslaveholders elected men to state office who fundamentally challenged that institution. To secessionist leaders, nonslaveholders may still have posed political

80. Hahn, *The Roots of Southern Populism*, 88; Fox-Genovese and Genovese, *Fruits*, 250; Holt, *The Political Crisis of the 1850s*, chap. 8. For the relatively high wages of free laborers in the South, see Fogel, "Without Consent," 155.

problems, but in the struggle that followed far more was asked of them and given by them than the planters of Brazil requested even of themselves.

Equally significant in Brazil was the dearth of nonelectoral alternatives through which to popularize antislavery. The Catholic church, like established churches everywhere, proved very reluctant to mount any challenge to the status quo in general, and to Brazilian slavery in particular. There was no counterpart in Brazil to the dissenting denominations of early nineteenth-century Anglo-American society that facilitated local and regional abolitionist organization. As the French case also showed, a highly centralized religious authority was not easily accessible to abolitionist penetration.

Newspapers and other means of mass communication were alternative sources of mobilization. Here one could note the limitations of Brazilian literacy and a weaker national communications network compared with Anglo-America. In general, Brazil lacked the national network of voluntary associations which so impressed de Tocqueville in the nineteenth-century United States. Brazilian abolitionists therefore had to improvise along different lines. The result was to add some startling pages to the history of slavery. In the last phase, it was an extraparliamentary abolitionism, forcing a reluctant legislature and a demoralized planter elite to verify a fait accompli.

In the end, two major characteristics force themselves on our attention. Brazil presents us with an example of a planter class which, though it successfully resisted termination of the slave trade for two generations, could not after that successfully mobilize against abolitionism, even with a constitution made to order for its domination of society. Secondly, Brazil offers us the case of an urban abolitionist movement which had to effect emancipation primarily through ingenious ad hoc agitation and temporary coalitions of diverse groups largely outside the political framework. Abolitionists could dismantle slavery but could not dictate any of the terms of social change beyond that. The Golden Law, like the first French emancipation decree in 1794, was a tersely worded death warrant for a collapsing structure. The very brevity of the law revealed the limits of Brazilian abolitionism—no compensation for the slaveholders, no welfare for the slaves, no planned transition to a new order.

In this respect, it is noteworthy that the major monographs on Brazilian abolition discuss postabolition Brazil almost exclusively in terms of the fate of former masters and former slaves, and are virtually silent on the continuity and impact of antislavery. The abolitionist movement appears to have dissolved even more quickly than it had formed. There was no concerted movement to aid the freed slaves, and neither was Brazilian abolitionism an ideological and organizational exemplar for a multitude of other reform mobilizations as in Anglo-America, although it did have echoes in the *jacobinos'* agitation of the 1890s.[81] Brazil offered its slave-holders little leverage to resist external pressures for liberation, but it provided the abolitionists with little leverage to follow through after slave emancipation. Brazilian abolition seems to have lacked the means of political reproduction.

81. Brian Harrison, "A Genealogy of Reform in Modern Britain," in *Anti-Slavery*, 119–148 and *Peaceable Kingdom: Stability and Change in Modern Britain* (Oxford, 1982), chap. 8. In isolated instances, the Brazilian abolitionist mobilization did have an organizational and ideological spillover effect analogous to that of the English mass mobilizations a half century earlier. Rio typographers sought to transfer the abolitionist momentum into "a new abolition for the *free slaves*," and their intensive participation in the abolitionist victory celebration played a role in stimulating a more militant labor organization. See Hahner, *Poverty and Politics*, 86–87. Indeed, the rarity of successful social movements in Brazil may have contributed to the psychological impact of abolition among skilled workers (ibid., 87).

Beyond Masters and Slaves: Subsistence Agriculture as a Survival Strategy in Brazil During the Second Half of the Nineteenth Century

HEBE MARIA MATTOS DE CASTRO

THE accumulation of capital has been a preferred framework for choice of topics of study in Brazilian historiography. This tendency is found not only in the emphasis on regional studies that concern principal exporting areas and, later, industrial centers,[1] but also in social history. Studies involving sociohistorical analysis are concerned predominantly with the type of work force which contributed to capital accumulation: slavery until the nineteenth century, immigration during the First Republic, urban workers after 1930.

I do not intend to deny the obvious relevance of these topics of analysis, but only to emphasize that this tendency has led to neglect of the demographic variable as a fundamental factor in the historical study of any society. For example, the second half of the nineteenth century, the period of specific interest here, has been studied preferentially from the viewpoint of agricultural exportation based on slave labor, whereas free and freed people composed 41 percent of the Brazilian population by 1818, a proportion which grew to 84 percent by 1874.[2] Notwithstanding its numerical significance (comprising a majority by the second half of the past century), the poor free population in slave society has almost

* Translated, by Kathleen M. Ruppert, with the help of a grant from the Tinker Foundation.

1. The expression "accumulation of capital" is used here in a broad sense, not necessarily linked to capitalistic relations of production. In Brazilian historiography, from the now classic syntheses such as *Formação econômica do Brasil* by Celso Furtado (São Paulo, 1969) and *Formação do Brasil contemporâneo* by Caio Prado, Jr. (São Paulo, 1971) to more recent monographic studies, there has been an emphasis on study and analysis of sugar production of the Northeast during the colonial period, the mining regions of the eighteenth century, coffee in the Paraíba Valley and the West of São Paulo in the nineteenth and early twentieth centuries, and of industrialization in Rio and São Paulo in the present century.

2. Lúcio Kowarick, *Trabalho e vadiagem: A origem do trabalho livre no Brasil* (São Paulo, 1987), 69.

always been only marginally considered by scholarly literature. Classic authors such as Caio Prado Júnior and Celso Furtado have already noted the significant demographic weight of free people in Brazilian slaveholding society. Yet, at the same time, they underscored the exclusion of free people from the market economy and their personal dependence on large landowners in such a way as to endow them with only secondary social and historiographic interest.

According to Celso Furtado, free people who arrived in Brazil "as artisans, soldiers, or simply adventurers, in one way or another became dependants of the large landowning class." They engaged in subsistence agriculture of "very low productivity," almost always on land belonging to someone else, utilizing "minimal capital" and "the most primitive techniques." In some cases, however, they would have appreciable demographic importance, as, for example, in Minas Gerais after the decline of mining, where, according to Furtado, a "relatively numerous population" found "space for expansion within a subsistence regime," and came "to constitute one of the principal demographic nuclei of the country."[3] For Caio Prado, they were "the embryonic form of a middle class between the large landholders and the slaves," composed of mestizos and "degenerate whites," dedicated to a "miserable subsistence agriculture," which became the occupation of nearly 50 percent of the population of the empire.[4]

After reading the above two authors, one can have little doubt that there were many small, rural, free producers in both colony and empire, a number which continued to grow until the advent of the Golden Law. Yet, because poor free people had no clear place in the export plantation system that was held to be "dominant," they were regarded as irrelevant as a specific topic meriting further study. In the end, the reification of a structure of domination to explain the essence of the social process turns references to this social group into disconnected parenthetical comments, which contribute nothing to a comprehension of the historical developments that one is seeking to analyze.

Until a few years ago, there was one work, *Homems livres na ordem escravocrata*, by Maria Sylvia de Carvalho Franco,[5] that undertook an analysis "of the figure of the poor free man in the social system" of nineteenth-century Brazil. I disagree, however, with the classification system adopted by Franco for two basic reasons:

3. Furtado, *Análise do "modelo" brasileiro* (Rio de Janeiro, 1972), 98 and *Formação economica*, 84–85.
4. Prado, *História econômica do Brasil* (São Paulo, 1979), 42 and *Formação do Brasil contemporâneo*, 161.
5. Maria Sylvia de Carvalho Franco, *Homens livres na ordem escravocrata* (São Paulo, 1974), chap. 2.

1. Under the rubric "free poor men," her analysis includes social categories which from my point of view are quite diverse and not always clearly distinguished by "poverty." For example, *tropeiros* (muleteers), *vendeiros* (general store merchants), and *sitiantes* (small farmers) are grouped with *agregados* (rural dwellers living on property that belonged to someone else) and *camaradas* (farmhands).

2. Personal dependence on large landholders is used by Franco more than "poverty" as a unifying characteristic of the free population studied. Such dependency held quite diverse meanings for each social category on the list, and this diversity appears to be at least as important as the traits they had in common.

Referring to the term *tropeiro* (understood to be an owner and trader of livestock), it is difficult to classify him as a "poor free man" in view of the importance of supplying cattle to fazendas and cities—especially the capital. Muleteers were a significant segment of property owners. Often, in other regional settings devoted to animal husbandry, they influenced and defined political and social control.[6]

Only in the analysis of small farmers does the term "personal dominance" appear to really define the category. To be sure, according to Franco, the ongoing relationship between fazendeiros and these farmers was in many ways one among equals. "Both fazendeiros and *sitiantes* were landowners, both holding an interest in landed property ownership and living on it, which thus conferred permanence and continuity on their relationship." This formal equality was solidified in the bond of godparenthood (*compadrio*), which concealed the principle of personal dominance, manifested in the form of "economic assistance from fazendeiro to *sitiante* in exchange for political loyalty."[7] The *sitiantes* are characterized as voters and small landholders without being precisely defined in the text as to whether they were also slaveowners or what kind of agriculture they were engaged in. Instead, they are defined mainly in terms of their relationship to the large landholders. Having been recognized as equals by the fazendeiros on whom they depended economically and politically, the *sitiantes* are not easily clustered with other categories characterized most often by frequent migration, such as farmhands and *agregados*.

In the case studied by Maria Sylvia Franco, the physical dimensions of the area legally appropriated by the large slaveholders surpassed the area needed for production plus the area set apart for expansion. This, in turn, permitted the survival of the independent peasant (*caipira inde-*

6. Cf. Alcir Lenharo, *As tropas da moderação, o abastecimento da Corte na formação política do Brasil, 1808–1842* (São Paulo, 1979).

7. Franco, *Homens livres*, 80–81.

pendente) as a "resident on another's property." The same author points out, then, that the abundance of land and the spatial mobility of these poor freemen imposed limitations on the personal control exercised by the large landholders. In particular, this situation prevented large landowners from utilizing them in the regular work force "even when the demand for workers in large-scale agriculture became pressing," thereby preserving the *caipira tradicional* from being "changed into a free worker."[8] Without denying the importance that has been attributed to "favors" in exchange for "services rendered," as a regulating device in the relations among free men in nineteenth-century Brazilian society, I would argue that the fluidity of these relations needs to be more clearly emphasized, and that the role which land ownership plays as a foundation of personal domination must be challenged.

I have intentionally left for final consideration Franco's treatment of the *vendeiro*. This figure is not to be confused with the dealer of the large commercial centers, but is one of the thousands of proprietors of general stores directed toward local consumption. What deserves to be noted is not only that they remained largely independent of the fazendeiros, who were not even their customers, as Franco argues, but, principally, that their presence in the local economy reveals consumption standards and economic activity closely integrated into the world of those "free poor men" who lived at the margin of the dominant social sectors. Although Franco suggests that the *vendeiros* were a "quasi" dispensable element, their numerical presence suggests that the matter should be analyzed in greater depth.

More recently, some other studies have considered the poor free population in Brazilian slaveholding society as a topic of investigation. However, they approach the topic by turning to the discourse among elites of the period as their main source. This type of information, grounded in the negative stereotype of the "vagrant," is used almost exclusively as the empirical basis for theorization on socioeconomic dislocation.[9] For these authors, poor free people were stigmatized as a labor force in an exclusive (slaveocratic) socioeconomic system which, ironically, both denied them better work opportunities and labeled them vagrants. Thus, beginning

8. Ibid., 92.
9. See, especially, Laura de Mello e Souza, *Desclassificados do ouro: A pobreza mineira no século XVIII* (Rio de Janeiro, 1986) and Kowarick, *Trabalho e vadiagem*. From our standpoint, the dominant discourse is rich for the purpose of understanding how the elites viewed poor free people, but not for defining them as a social category. For an analysis of the mentality of the elites in relation to poor free and freed people in the nineteenth century, see Célia Maria Marinho de Azevedo, *Onda negra medo branco: O negro livre no imaginário das elites, século XIX* (Rio de Janeiro, 1987).

with the premise that only the accumulation of capital—made possible primarily within the confines of the slave system—conferred historical intelligibility on Brazilian colonial and imperial society, they sentenced anyone who lived outside that axis to a state of limbo destitute of meaning or purpose.

Taking the Paulista case as a reference point, it is still considered that slavery thoroughly degraded the notion of work for former slaves and poor free people, thereby marginalizing them as a labor force in immediate postslavery Brazil. Victims of the system, these people became a "reserve army,"[10] first to the slaves and, later, to the immigrants, temporarily passed over by the agrarian elites as a viable work force in the eyes of the agrarian elites.

In a recent study, I set out to revise this type of interpretation, seeking to consider the poor free person in the second half of the nineteenth century as a socioeconomic agent. Using empirical material that could shed some light on this group, I sought to examine the ways in which it was included (not excluded) in the dominant slaveocratic order. For this purpose, I abandoned any pretense to wider generalization in favor of the case study of a region where there was a significant presence of the free population in the second half of the last century, and where this group could be analyzed through recourse to documentary series such as notarial registers which might more directly reveal local life.[11]

The regional differentiation of Brazil in the nineteenth century must be a key factor in reevaluating the role of the poor free national in the transition away from slave labor. In the Northeast—at least in Pernambuco[12]—the older settlement of the region, which precluded anything like a moving agricultural frontier, and the hardening of clientelistic relations inherited from the colonial structure, determined the replacement of the slave by the free national long before the definitive extinction of slavery. In the south central region (Minas Gerais, Rio de Janeiro, and São Paulo with the exception of the West), the spectre of an insufficient work force, denunciations of "indolence" and "laziness" of the free and freed national, as well as laws which compelled them to work, all persisted until 1888.[13]

---

10. Mello e Souza defines them as the "reserve army of slavery" (*Desclassificados*, 73), and Kowarick theoretically bases his analysis on the idea that "the exploitation of the work force directly engaged in the productive process is related dialectically and contradictorily to the reserve army" (*Trabalho e vadiagem*, 13).

11. See Hebe Maria Mattos de Castro, *Ao sul da história: Lavradores pobres na crise do trabalho escravo* (São Paulo, 1987).

12. Peter L. Eisenberg, *Modernização sem mundança* (Rio de Janeiro/Campinas, 1977), esp. part 2.

13. See, among others, Azevedo, *Onda negra*; Emília Viotti da Costa, *Da senzala à colônia* (São Paulo, 1982), 111–112; Ana Lúcia Duarte Laura, "O café e o trabalho livre em

Paradoxically, the free population of these provinces grew during the entire second half of the nineteenth century, with a tendency to concentrate in areas where access to open land was still obtained with relative ease. The availability of free, or only nominally appropriated, lands made alternative survival strategies feasible, and, at the same time, protected poor free people from transformation into a labor force. Nossa Senhora da Lapa de Capivary, a município of the province of Rio de Janeiro, the topic of our study, was one of these areas. In this article, I set forth some of the conclusions from the investigation, and, based on them pose some questions concerning the terms which governed the utilization of both free and freed people in the rural south central region.

The Case of Capivary

At the end of the eighteenth century, the current município of Silva Jardim in the state of Rio de Janeiro formed the parish of Nossa Senhora da Lapa da Capivary in the município of Cabo Frio—an area practically devoid of inhabitants and covered by tropical vegetation.[14] An integral part of the so-called Baixada Fluminense,[15] adjoining the Serra do Mar in the present município of Nova Friburgo, Silva Jardim possesses a broken topography which rises steadily from low altitudes (40 meters) in the direction of the Serra escarpment (1,000 meters). The configuration of the land limits the amount of alluvial soil in the area suitable for the cultivation of sugar cane, which up to the end of the eighteenth century determined the nonindigenous occupation of the lowland (Baixada) region.

The expansion of coffee production in the Fluminense province in the first half of the nineteenth century would radically alter the initial appearance of the countryside. During its expansion period, coffee cultivation initially followed two roads—that of the highlands, extending all the way from Rezende and Vassouras to the Paraíba Valley, and that of the "hot lands," which began on the slopes covered with sugar cane fields in the eastern Baixada Fluminense at São Gonçalo and Itaboraí, and finally integrated into the slave economy all the part of the lowlands touched by the foothills of the Serra do Mar, i.e., Silva Jardim, Rio Bonito, Cachoeiras de Macacu.[16]

Minas Gerais—1880/1920" and Maria Lúcia Lamounier, "O trabalho sob contrato: A lei de 1879," in *Revista Brasileira de História*, 12 (1986).

14. See "Cartas topographicas da Capitania do Rio de Janeiro" (1767) and Manuel Vieyra Leão, "Carta topographica da Capitania do Rio de Janeiro" (1767), in the Mapoteca do Itamarati.

15. The Baixada Fluminense is defined as the low-lying areas of the current state of Rio de Janeiro that extend from the Serra do Mar escarpment to the Atlantic Ocean, between Itaguaí and the Campos plain.

16. Francisco José de Oliveira Vianna, "Distribuição geográfica do cafeeiro do Estado

The first occupation of the area was based on a concentrated appropriation of great expanses of available land, by producers who could count on a supply, however modest, of capital resources and slaves.[17] In the valley and the lowlands, coffee was planted by slaves on the sides of the hills, on soil originating in decomposed rock formations. Meanwhile, the fields planted in the Paraíba Valley rapidly outdistanced those of the Baixada. It was thus discovered that, for optimum production, coffee should not be planted below altitudes of 400 meters, at least where important economic enterprises were concerned. Coffee from the hotter regions designated *capitânia*[18] was for the internal market. With the rise in food prices starting in the second half of the nineteenth century,[19] producers around Capivary would diversify to include large-scale manioc flour production.

Both coffee and manioc flour were grown for commercial purposes and were initially sent to neighboring marketplaces,[20] from there to be redistributed to the markets of Rio de Janeiro and Niterói, as well as to fazendas engaged in specialized agricultural production in the eastern Paraíba Valley. At the same time, the opening up of new highways and roads, along with the slow expansion of coffee cultivation (by virtue of the limitations of the internal market in comparison with the international market), attracted growing numbers of free people who set up farms and small garden plots on uncultivated lands situated within and without the already legally appropriated lands. By 1856, Capivary, already elevated to the status of município, contained the seventh-smallest concentration of slaves in the province. Of a population numbering 15,584, 38.5 percent were slaves. The normal rule in other municipalities was that the number of slaves equaled or exceeded the free population.[21]

The relatively high numbers of free people in the population, as well

do Rio de Janeiro, in *Textos selecionados de história fluminense: O café no Rio de Janeiro*, Marcos W. Reis, comp. (Niterói, n.d.).

17. Between 1855 and 1857, 72.5 percent of the land claimed in the *registros paroquiais de terra* of the município, now located in the Arquivo Público do Estado do Rio de Janeiro (hereafter, APERJ), belonged to just 24 claimants.

18. V. D. Laerne, *Le Brésil et Java, rapport sur la culture du café en Amérique, Asie et Afrique* (Paris, 1885), chap. 10.

19. See Sebastião Ferreira Soares, *Notas estatísticas sobre a produção agrícola e carestia dos gêneros alimentícios no Império do Brasil* (Rio de Janeiro, 1860) and Costa, *Da senzala*, 77–123.

20. Before the advent of the railroad, especially the river ports of Porto das Caixas and Barra de São João. See entries referring to Capivary in *Almanack Laemmert* (i.e., *Almanaque agrícola e comercial da Província do Rio de Janeiro* [hereafter *AL*]), 1851/52/54/56/58/60/ 62/64/66/68/70/76/78/80/82.

21. In the majority of the municípios of the eastern Paraíba Valley, the slave population was more than two times that of free people. "Recenseamento da População dos Municípios da Província do Rio de Janeiro (1850/56)," Relatórios do Presidente da Província do Rio de Janeiro, 1851/58, APERJ.

as the continued decrease in Capivary's stock of slaves,[22] initially appeared
to indicate a precocious deterioration of the local slaveholding structure,
as Capivary became a supplier of slaves to more dynamic areas after 1850.
According to slave transactions registered in local notarial records for the
entire period under study (1850–88), more than half (56.8 percent) cor-
responded to the sale of slaves destined for areas outside the town.[23] The
importance of this participation in the so-called "intraprovincial slave traffic"[24] can only be fully appreciated, however, when it is placed within the
context of the social stratification of local agricultural producers and patterns of slave ownership existing up to that point. In order to establish the
stratification I shall use as a reference the list of agricultural producers'
register in the *Almanack Laemmert*[25] as an indication of the inclusion of
local producers in a wider commercial circuit. Those who paid to have
their names cited in the publication could not have been the producers
dedicated to subsistence agriculture.

A second look at notarial records concerning the buying and selling
of slaves reveals that of the total number of slaveowners listed as sellers
to destinations outside the municipality, 63.2 percent were slaveowners
not appearing in the classified lists in *Laemmert*. In the local transactions,
74.0 percent of the sellers do not appear in *Laemmert*, 12.3 percent of
them being residents of adjoining towns (Araruama, Rio Bonito) which
also appear among the areas that purchased slaves. At the same time,
more than half of the buyers involved in transactions inside the municipality (58.4 percent) are classified in the almanac as coffee fazendeiros and
"larger" ("mais fortes") producers (see Table I).

The slave labor force initially appears to be widely spread throughout the local socioeconomic structure. Until at least the mid-1860s, the
presence of one or two slaves is registered even in the smallest units of
production. Nevertheless, many of these enterprises do not seem to have
assumed strictly commercial status, being limited to the exchange of a
small, unpredictable surplus at the local marketplace for a few consumer
goods. And, with time, the increase in slave prices tended to concentrate
ownership in the local agricultural society.[26]

22. The variation of slave population in Capivary between the 1856 census as cited
above and the data for the município in the general census of 1872 (*Recenseamento da
população do Império do Brasil . . . 1872*) is − 0.02 per annum.

23. See records of purchase and sale of slaves in the Livros de Registro de Escrituras
dos Cartórios de Silva Jardim (1° e 2° Ofício de Notas, Cartório de Correntezas e Cartório
de Gaviões).

24. Imênia Lima Martins, "Problemas da extinção do tráfico africano na Província do
Rio de Janeiro" (Doctoral thesis, Universidade de São Paulo, 1972).

25. *AL*, lists for the município of Capivary, 1851/52/54/56/58/60/62/64/66/68/70/76/
80/82.

26. This topic will be discussed further in the second half of the article.

TABLE I: Sales of Slaves Recorded in the Local Registry

Slaves traded[a]	256	
Destined inside municipality	106	(41.4% of slaves traded)
Destined outside municipality	150	(58.6% of slaves traded)
Transactions	206	
With slaves destined inside municipality	89	(43.2% of transactions)
With buyers listed in *Almanack Laemmert*	52	(58.4% of buyers)
With buyers not listed in *Almanack L.*	37	(41.6% of buyers)
With sellers listed in *Almanack L.*	23	(25.8% of sellers)
With sellers not listed in *Almanack L.*	55	(61.8% of sellers)
With sellers from outside municipality	11	(12.3% of sellers)
With slaves destined outside municipality	150	(58.6% of transactions)
Sellers listed in *Almanack L.*	43	(36.7% of sellers)
Sellers not listed in *Almanack L.*	74	(63.2% of sellers)

Source: Livros de Escrituras do 1°, 2° e 3° Ofícios de Notas de Silva Jardim.
a. Not including free-born children.

Taking as our source the postmortem inventories of property of deceased persons found in the local Segundo Ofício de Notas do Cartório, we can describe the social stratification more precisely.[27] Of the 230 documents under consideration, 99 described agricultural enterprises whose proprietors appeared in the classified lists of the *Almanack Laemmert* as "fazendeiros, lavradores e proprietários mais fortes." All the individuals listed in the inventories as owning more than ten slaves also appeared in the *Almanack*. I further subdivided the agricultural proprietors as owners of (1) fazendas and (2) "commercial farms" (*sitios comerciais*). Both were market oriented and owned slaves, but they were nevertheless differentiated in regard to their position within the socioeconomic hierarchy of the community.

In order to understand exactly what is meant by "fazenda" within the local agrarian setting, we must first take into account that various agricultural enterprises were given this classification in more than one of the sources analyzed, their owners being known as fazendeiros. The identification by name of some of these owners made it possible to select a sample of inventories of fazendeiros. The sample is too small for quantitative analysis, but it suggests some common characteristics capable of providing coherence to the analysis that follows.

The first point of fundamental importance that identified members of the sample is the number of slaves they owned—all had more than 20 in the inventories, in addition to other common traits in such matters as standard of living, amount of wealth, and size of producing units. On the other

27. For this research I used all extant inventories in the Cartório do 2° Ofício de Notas do Forum de Silva Jardim. The Cartório do 1° Ofício also had pertinent records in its archives, which unfortunately were not organized, making it impossible to consult them.

hand, many owners of relatively small amounts of land, but with numbers of slaves in excess of 15 showed similar characteristics; productive units possessing between 15 and 20 formed a transition group between fazendas and commercial farms. With the social concentration of slave ownership which occurred in the region in the second half of the nineteenth century, that transitional group tended to disappear, and those who owned that number of slaves came to rank as more and more "prosperous" in relative terms. Therefore, all productive agricultural units with more than 15 declared slaves (42 documents) will be considered fazendas. Likewise, agricultural enterprises with less than 15 slaves whose owners were nevertheless listed in the *Almanack Laemmert* will be considered commercial farms (57 documents).

When we use the term "fazendeiros," we are very far from any real resemblance to the large coffee planters of the Paraíba Valley. If, in coffee cultivation generally, the scale of producing units was already much less in terms of land, slaves, and other comparisons with the model of the large-scale sugar plantation of the Northeast, the "rich" producers of Capivary could assume pretensions as large producers only in relation to their small local universe. If we take into consideration the parameters normally used to characterize the large landholdings in the Paraíba Valley, it is evident that in Capivary we are dealing with small units of production. References for Paraíba to more than 200 *alqueires* of land, 100,000 coffee plants, or 60 slaves[28] have no resonance for the area under examination here. In concrete terms, many of the agricultural enterprises described in this study actually are closer in many aspects to the productive units of *sitiantes* and *agregados* described by other authors for regions where the cultivation of coffee was synonymous with prosperity.[29]

However, it appears that the key element for comprehending the dynamics of the community and its relationship to the surrounding society is not to be found in the actual productive capacity of the agricultural enterprises. The political and economic importance of "localism" in the Brazilian society of the period determined the composition of local or regional hierarchies in the configuration of political power and forms of social control. "Small large-scale farmers" became fazendeiros in Capivary simply by being the wealthiest group of local slaveholding producers, thereby giving credence to their claim of political and social control over the municipality.[30]

28. João Luís Fragoso, "Sistemas agrários em Paraíba do Sul" (Master's thesis, Universidade Federal do Rio de Janeiro, 1983).

29. See Laerne, *Le Brésil et Java*, chap. 10.

30. The political and social control of the community by its wealthier producers, though

TABLE II: Percentage of Coffee Trees More Than 16 Years Old on Capivary Fazendas, 1855–88

Period	Percent
1855–64	27.3
1865–74	27.3
1876–88	22.3

Source: Inventários *post-morten* do 2° Ofício de Notas de Silva Jardim (1855–88) (42 cases).

TABLE III: Manioc Farming in Capivary Fazendas, 1855–88

Period	Average number of plants per productive unit
1855–64	3,888.1
1865–74	5,077.8
1875–88	10,362.2

Source: Same as Table II (42 cases).

In spite of the low income generated by their enterprises in comparison with other producing areas, these farmers succeeded in resupplying their establishments with slave labor until the 1880s, partly to the detriment of the other local producers. From postmortem inventories, we see that these slaveholders maintained an average of 20 to 30 slaves during the entire period, with at least 50 percent of them being of productive age.[31] Acquisitions of slaves, even though restricted to the regional market, and the natural increase in their numbers appear to have allowed the owners to maintain, if not to expand, the functioning of the larger units of production. Likewise, they were able not only to replace the older coffee plantings on a regular basis but to diversify as well, increasing considerably their production of such commodities as manioc flour, in response to the growing demand for primary food products (see Tables II and III).

The persistence of slave labor on local plantations until the eve of the definitive extinction of slavery indicates the importance of slave labor in the commercial production of foodstuffs in this period. It also gives evidence of the possible existence of alternative strategies for survival for

---

not a specific topic of study, is amply illustrated in the work of Celeste Zenha for the same period and region, in which it is made clear, among other things, that the larger landowners controlled almost all the positions in the local judicial structure. "As práticas da justiça no cotidiano da pobreza: Um estudo sobre o amor, a riqueza e o trabalho através de processos penais" (Master's thesis, Universidade Federal Fluminense, 1984).

31. From 15 to 40 years is taken to be the productive age for slaves.

the rest of the population, since, in addition to the fazendeiros, there was a largely mestizo segment of the Capivary free population which only with difficulty could be converted into a suitable work force for commercial agriculture.

This difficulty was especially felt by those producers whose mode of coffee and manioc flour production for the local and regional markets included the use of slave labor, but who were economically dependent on the larger local producers and were without sufficient financial resources to replace their slaves as needed. As a general rule, local farmers who used slave labor did not have enough disposable capital to initiate their own agricultural enterprise. In numerous cases, they depended on financing by fazendeiros of the region, in exchange for political loyalty. Until the 1870s, more than 70 percent of the negotiated mortgage and loan notes in the local registry consisted of advances provided without interest by the planters to small producers attempting to establish themselves.[32] The terms almost always were counted in years, and were frequently deferred. Consequently, we are not dealing here with a simple diversification of investment on the part of fazendeiros with capital at their disposal, since the money invested did not produce any profit. Political loyalties became interwoven in a web of economic dependence among the voting citizens of the municipality.[33] Moreover, as small slaveowning producers for the regional market, local farmers were inhibited by low levels of capital accumulation from fully replenishing their supplies of slaves—something which they had been able to do in the '50s.[34] As a consequence, they were not able to respond to the growing demand for foodstuffs at higher prices, nor were they able to effectively replace their plantings of coffee (see Tables IV and V).

Thus, we have an idea of the dimensions of the internal market of the province of Rio de Janeiro during the second half of the nineteenth century. It was able to both absorb the coffee production of the Baixada (though the latter was at a disadvantage vis-à-vis the Paraíba Valley in export terms) and stimulate some enlargement of productive structure through the growth in demand for primary food products in the period

32. The analysis of credit was made on the basis of all the loan and mortgage documents registered in the local notarial offices, taking also into account the mention of creditors and debtors in *AL*. The complete analysis of the data can be followed in Castro, *Ao sul da história*, 61–70.

33. Cf. articles 90, 91, and 92 of the 1824 constitution cited by Nancy P. Naro et al., *A polícia na Corte e no Distrito Federal* (Rio de Janeiro, 1981), 48–49 and Berenice Cavalcanti Brandão et al., *A polícia e a força policial no Rio de Janeiro* (Rio de Janeiro, 1981).

34. The average number of slaves in the commercial farms, as indicated by the inventories studied, decreases from about nine in the decade of the 1850s to less than six after 1875 (Castro, *Ao sul da história*, 38–45).

TABLE IV: Manioc Farming on *Sítios* in Capivary, 1855–88

Period	Average number of plants per productive unit
1855–64	2,654.6
1865–74	2,920.7
1875–88	955.4

Source: Same as Table II (57 cases).

TABLE V: Percentage of Coffee Trees More Than 16 Years Old on *Sítios* in Capivary, 1855–88

Period	Percentage
1855–64	25.67
1865–74	24.10
1875–88	42.74

Source: Same as Table II (57 cases).

which followed the extinction of the slave traffic. Nevertheless, the low level of capitalization and profitability of local production meant that its expansion did not lead to a situation of land monopoly, nor were producers able to attract free workers by other means. The local fazendeiros were aware of this situation, so that by the mid-'70s they preferred guarantees of liquidity to new investment in the productive or political (loan-based) structure which they controlled. In the decade of the '80s, more than 50 percent of the fazendeiros' wealth was invested in public debt instruments.[35] Between 1872 and 1890, furthermore, the white population of Capivary decreased by 6 percent, reflecting a significant exodus of local planters, who tended to sell off the lands they controlled in small plots. Drastically compromised in their ability to accumulate capital, the small farmers in this area came close to approximating the standards of subsistence agriculture. The social stratification of the município as it was organized until the close of the '80s simply could not subsist without slave labor. At the same time, the black and mestizo populations grew by more than 50 percent during the period, thereby reaffirming the attraction that the possibility of being an independent worker held for former slaves and poor people of the region.[36]

35. Ibid., 66.
36. See Recenseamentos Gerais do Brasil, 1872 and 1890. For a more detailed analysis of the demographic evolution, as well as of the changes in agrarian structure and social stratification of the município after abolition, see Castro, *Ao sul da história*, especially the

Subsistence Agriculture as a Strategy
for Survival in Capivary

According to the general census of 1872, almost one-half (48.0 percent) of the free population of the town was composed of persons without a profession or dedicated to domestic service. These numbers probably refer to women and children. The remaining one-half, which I shall call the active free population for this analysis, was composed 68.1 percent of *lavradores* (farmers). This reinforces the argument that the possibilities opened up by available land around the municipality produced a population of "poor farmers" not always in legal ownership of the land they were exploiting. This meaning of the term *lavrador*, associated with independent agricultural labor, is reinforced in the same census where the slave population of two essentially rural parishes is not found classified by profession as *lavradors* (a term reserved for the free population), but primarily as "servants and day laborers."[37] The concept of the term *lavrador* held by the local census takers made it difficult for them to consider the inclusion in that category of field slaves, who were undoubtedly the predominant group in the local slave population.

Nevertheless, a significant number (1,514, or 21.9 percent of those whom I would designate as an active free population) are also classified as "servants and day laborers." Probably these are a contingent of the population which could not gain its subsistence through independent agricultural work, and thus received a classification suggestively similar to that of the slave population (see Table VI).

In relation to urban occupations, only in the town of Capivary, seat of the município, does one find an elaborated socioprofessional diversification. The other nuclei (Correntezas and Gaviões) register only the presence of clergy (whom they needed in their condition of parish and curacy), notaries (who were responsible for the local registries created in the previous decade), pharmacists, teachers, and merchants, all in numerical inferiority to the municipal seat. In all cases, the parish of Nossa Senhora da Lapa de Capivary contained more than half of the persons dedicated to these occupations. The same disproportionate ratio can be found among seamstresses, carpenters, masons, and cobblers. This small network represents virtually the entire socioprofessional diversification to

last two chapters, "O monopólio da terra: O direito e o fato" and "O reverso do projeto: A caipirização pós-escravidão."

37. According to the 1872 census, the slave population of Capivary was distributed among occupations as follows: workers in leathers and skins, 1 (Gaviões); workers in footwear, 5 (Correntezas), 1 (Gaviões); farmers, 285 (Gaviões); servants and day laborers, 1,397 (Capivary), 396 (Correntezas); domestic service, 385 (Capivary), 197 (Correntezas), 56 (Gaviões); no occupation, 739 (Capivary), 171 (Correntezas), 311 (Gaviões); total, 3,944.

TABLE VI: Free Population of Capivary by Profession, 1872

Occupation	Number	Percent of total free population	Percent of active free population
No profession	2,080	15.53	—
Domestic service	4,419	32.99	—
Lavradores "Farmers"	4,701	} 51.48	68.1
Servants and day laborers	1,514		21.9
Urban and artisanal occupations	681		19.8
Total	13,395		

Source: Recenseamento Geral do Brasil, 1872 (Instituto Brasileiro de Geographia e Estatística).
a. "Active free population" is defined in the text.

which the division between agricultural work and artisans in the municipality gave rise, as reflected in the census under study.

In the criminal records found in the Segundo Ofício de Notas of the município for the period beginning in 1840 and ending in 1890, are 932 witnesses from the free population resident in Capivary.[38] I have used this sample of the free population in the period under analysis as a source for a slightly more in-depth study of the means of support employed by residents of the community. These testimonies are classified according to occupation, sex, and place of birth in Table VII.

The small proportion of persons not classified in terms of occupation (10.3 percent) stands out, on first observation, as does the presence of a majority of men in the total assortment of recorded witnesses, which facilitates a more detailed analysis of the possible types of jobs held by the active local population. In addition, we can identify the noticeable presence, among the residents of the municipality recorded in the documents, of persons born in other towns or regions. The latter detail gives evidence of the extreme spatial mobility of the free population in that area during the period under analysis (50.2 percent), as well as of the municipality's character as an economic and demographic frontier.

In considering the group of those involved in nonagricultural occupations, detailed presentation cannot go much beyond the information offered in the professional census of 1872. Public employees can be categorized more concretely as postal workers, legal staff, and jailers, among others. In addition to priests, the church employed sacristans. To the specialized occupations listed in the 1872 census can be added such occu-

38. A detailed analysis of the criminal records found in the Cartório do 2° Ofício de Notas de Silva Jardim for the period studied was compiled by Zenha in the work cited above. She graciously provided a list of names and identifying data.

TABLE VII: Witnesses Listed in the Criminal Records of Capivary (1840–90) According to Profession, Sex, and Place of Birth

Place of birth	Nonagricultural occupations			No information			Landowners registered in the *Almanack L.*			Landowners not registered in the *Almanack L.,* and other agricultural occupations			Total
	Men	Women	Total	Men	Women	Total	Men	Women	Total	Men	Women	Total	
Capivary	99	06	105	39	16	55	48	—	48	235	21	256	464
Other	125	02	127	31	10	41	69	3	72	219	09	228	468
Total	224	08	232	70	26	96	117	3	120	454	30	494	932

Source: Procesess Penais do 2° Ofício de Notas de Silva Jardim (1840–90).

pations as "saddle maker," "blacksmith," "baker," "coachman," "cabinet maker," as well as "horsebreaker," which, in limited numbers, made up occupations necessary for the life of the community. There appears to be a significant number of commercial houses which did not advertise in the *Almanak Laemmert*, which indicates that they were involved strictly with the local market. At the same time, it is interesting to note that of the 33 persons classified as clerks (i.e., commercial employees), 29 were between the ages of 10 and 30. Likewise, in addition to ordinary tailors and seamstresses, we find 2 master tailors (*officiais de afaiate*), both under the age of 30. Starting in the second half of the '70s, railroad construction in the município created new employment opportunities for mechanics, foremen, and manual workers—the latter (only 2) both under the age of 20. Unskilled employment and youth appear to have had some kind of connection. Of the 28 agricultural day laborers, 20 (71.42 percent) were unmarried and were less than 30 years old. Thus, it is plausible that this very same population of young people, often still linked to the productive units of their parents—who complemented the familial income with occasional salaried work in business establishments and commercial farms—could have made up the greater part of the category "servants and day laborers" in the 1872 census (see Tables VII and VIII).

Out of a total of 484 testimonies of individuals dedicated to agricultural activities who are absent in the *Almanak Laemmert*, we find 61 persons listed as black or mulattos (*pardos*). Twenty-four of them were identified as *lavradores*, 5 of them free Africans; 28, including 1 free African, were "living from farm work"; 4 were called former slaves and "field workers"; 2 were "day laborers," and 3 "brushwood workers" (*trabalhadores de mata*). Taking color as an indicator of social position, these data allow us to perceive, on the basis of 52 of the 61 cases, the access gained by freed people and their descendants to independent agricultural production, even if on land belonging to someone else (as specified in two cases). This group does not necessarily represent all blacks or mulattos found in the sample: often no classification based on color was given in the documents.

In order to analyze the conditions of production and consumption of the agricultural poor in Capivary, we will consider, from the group of postmortem inventories, those referring to individuals who did not appear in the lists found in *Laemmert* and whose production methods did not suggest any large-scale commercialization of agricultural products (mills moved by water or steam).[39] The type of agricultural production reflected

39. Out of all the proceedings and inventories found in the Cartório do 2° Ofício de Notas de Silva Jardim (230 cases), I omitted from the analysis 23 referring to unmarried women,

TABLE VIII: Witnesses Whose Testimonies Appear in the Criminal
Records (1840–90), by "Urban" or Artisanal Professions

Profession	No.	Profession	No.
Public employment		Coachman	1
Public employees	12	Cabinetmakers	2
Postal employee	1	Fishermen	2
Orphan court employee	1	Barber	1
Solicitor	1		
Jailers	4	Total	48
Clerk	1	Liberal professions	
Notary public	1	Pharmacists	6
City Hall porter	1	Professors	6
Judicial officers	10	Lawyer	1
Police corps	9	Doctor	1
Total	41	Artists	4
Church		Total	18
Vicars	2	Commerce	
Sacristan	1	Businessmen (in *Almanack L.*)	14
Total	3	Businessmen (not in *Almanack L.*)	56
Skilled jobs		Clerks	33
Tailors	8	Total	103
Masons	3	Railroad	
Cobblers	2	Foremen	3
Saddlemaker	1	Mechanics	3
Carpenters	19	Workers	2
Blacksmiths	7	Administrator	1
Baker	1	Total	9
Horsebreaker	1		

Source: Same as Table VII.

in the 79 inventories appeared as one of the principal elements of homo-
geneity, while the range of crops produced in these units did not differ
greatly from those establishments classified as slaveholding and commercial: coffee, manioc, fruit orchards, and a selection of small periodic harvest crops, principally corn and beans. Coffee was planted by 70 of the
79 inventoried, who, however, never exceeded the small number of 2,000
coffee plants per agricultural unit, nor did they present any tendency
toward increasing or decreasing that level of production, which could
easily be tended by one person. At the same time, the descriptions of the
farms themselves rarely gave the age of the coffee plantings, in contrast
to the group of inventories whose title holders appeared also in the lists

minors, and individuals with unidentifiable urban occupations; 21 referring to individuals
who were not represented in *AL* but had plantings that used 5 to 9 slaves and processing
equipment that appeared to indicate commercial enterprises; and 8 referring to proprietors
of business houses. These 52 cases are used qualitatively when appropriate in the analysis.

of producers in *Laemmert*. There was also no mention of any types of processing equipment in these establishments.

Manioc, although not a permanent crop, could remain in the ground for two years after maturation without being harvested, thus allowing for later storage, literally in the earth itself. It was regularly harvested according to the producers' needs. One can find in any of the inventories analyzed approximately 400 plants (equivalent to ten bags of flour) "stored in the soil" per agricultural establishment, over and above any harvested manioc or sacks of prepared flour. According to data compiled by Schmidt,[40] a harvest such as this might be completed by one person in just 12 days, which indicates what this reserve could represent in commercial terms.

Yet, 53.1 percent of these farm units were not equipped for simple production of so-called dry flour or commercial flour, which, refined or crude, was sold widely in regional markets.[41] Found uniformly throughout the registry for the entire period was the mention of one or two burros used for transport of foodstuffs and of small animals for domestic consumption (pigs and chickens), or installations for the raising of such animals (chicken coops and hog houses).

The analysis of documents of deceased persons enables us also to perceive something about the living conditions of the group under study, as well as about the role of commercial relations in their social reproduction. For example, Dona Maria Joaquina de Oliveira, deceased in 1877, lived with her husband and two small children in a thatched-roof house with a living room and two bedrooms. Annexed to the house was a small building, also covered with a thatched roof. Furniture was limited to a "well-worn sofa," a table also "well used," "an old bench," two benches "already very worn," and an "old bathtub," valued at 25 milréis.[42] In the cases studied, the homes never had wooden floors, the ground being covered instead with straw or, more rarely, with tile. The only items of furniture entered on the lists were those objects which could have some monetary worth. Furniture or wooden objects were systematically valued, revealing possessions of extremely limited nature, such as the example of the home of Dona Maria Joaquina mentioned above. Notable in the lists by their almost total absence are pots and pans, dishware, cups, tableware, and other domestic utensils. From a comparison with inventories of more well-off farmers, which systematically mention iron pots and pans, metal tableware, and dishware in general (almost always with compara-

40. Carlos Borges Schmidt, *O pão da terra* (São Paulo, 1959).
41. Castro, *Ao sul da história*, 85–87.
42. Forum de Silva Jardim, Cartório do 2° Ofício de Notas, Processo no. 1,776, maço 82, 1877.

tively high appraisals), it can be deduced that the household objects of this group were, in the majority of cases, domestically produced, almost always of clay, and had no commercial value worth mention in the reports of inventoried goods.

The individuals featured in these documents would acquire sparse but regular amounts of some products sold in the local general stores. Mention of these products was often accompanied by numerous current accounts annexed to the debt entries of their inventories. During 1864–66, João Rodrigues de Figueiredo[43] acquired with some regularity from the store of the firm Braz Paulo Muniz e Cia. pieces of cloth, soap, bacon, salt, tobacco, and small amounts of wine. He asked the firm directly for money at least two times each year, for a total amount of 85$260. During that time he further acquired a hoe, a scythe, three pairs of socks, a pair of trousers, a shirt, and a straw hat. Payments were made with coffee sacks full of coconut or manioc flour, for a total of 147$010. In 1869, the balance in favor of the merchant totaled 188$965, 16.18 percent of the total value of the inventoried goods (1:167$500). This type of indebtedness rarely totaled more than 20 percent of the total value of an inventory and would be paid annually, partly in kind. Moreover, the small merchant appears to have been a true "financier" of this type of production. Many times his role resembled that which one expects to see played by larger landowners or important neighbors.

Stores were found scattered in almost all areas of the município, on the side of roads, within the fields of plantations, and in villages. They almost always carried on business in small houses "covered with tile" and rarely having wooden floors, with "business goods" valued at between 100 and 300 milréis. They sold practically everything needed in a rural world that was in fact profoundly specialized in production of a few basic products. Listing of the small and diverse stock of goods of those businesses, which oscillated between 700 and 2,500 milréis in value in the cases studied, almost always began with the dry goods on hand, which were one of the things most in demand. Pieces of cotton, calico, sailcloth, among others, summed up, as a rule, almost one-half of the total value of their listed merchandise. More rarely, the large stores sold ready-to-wear clothing, such as coats, shirts, and cloth hats. From the analysis of the store goods inventoried, one can see the common practice of making clothing domestically from cloth easily found at any small roadside store. Such stores also provided the necessary tools for seamstress work, such as trim, lace, silk ribbons, hooks and clamps, needles, thread, and pins. In addition, they offered the entire gamut of useful objects, principally those destined for

43. Ibid., Processo no. 1,939, maço 54, 1869.

production and transport of agricultural products, such as hoes, scythes, hatchets, and cutting tools. They did not lack stationery articles, nor articles of adornment, such as earrings, small pieces of gold, pens, pencils, or paper. For foodstuffs, the establishments carried dried beef, salt, olive oil, jars of oil, wines and cachaça, cans of sweets, or fish acquired from local fishermen. The list is practically infinite and impossible to reproduce in all its unimaginable details. In general terms, these stocks could be classified as "articles of clothing and farm equipment," "groceries and cupboard supplies," and "hardware," in addition to coffee and manioc flour, which were almost always taken in as payment from the farmers of the area. Representing the second most valuable category of goods in stock, coffee and manioc flour tied up almost one-third of the capital in the lists.

The mere listing of goods bought and sold by the general stores goes far in clarifying the commercial functions of these stores in the rural areas. At the same time as they sought to cover almost all the local consumer necessities, the minimal level of monetarization prevailing in that rural society meant that their cash reserves came essentially from their commercialization of the commodities that they received in exchange for their merchandise—and whose production they in large part financed.

The numerous current accounts found in the small inventories of the general stores attest to their significant intermediary role between local subsistence agriculture and regional markets. In these accounts there is not one case in which payment was listed in the form of money given by the debtors; on the contrary, cash was furnished by merchants to their clients with greater frequency than any of the consumer goods habitually purchased (such as salt, sugar, cloth, etc.). At the same time, these businesses did not perform the same functions as the wholesalers of the regional commercial centers with whom the fazendeiros and more well-off farmers maintained regular commercial relations. Their accounts receivable mentioned amounts of coffee and manioc flour that only for the group of merchants as a whole represented appreciable quantities, and which more than likely they commercialized in the regional centers exactly as the large-scale farmers did with their own products. Moreover, the accounts reveal an impressive level of specialization in this type of "subsistence" agricultural production, in that local residents made payment in coffee and manioc flour even for beans and corn. Although the merchants also dealt with the wealthier farmers of the region (who without abandoning the use of credit were also able to pay in currency), the importance of the commercialization of this subsistence-type small agricultural production is clearly revealed in the accounts receivable of the business proprietors, which were never entirely paid off and in effect guaranteed them a steady supply of agricultural produce to be sold in the larger commercial centers.

Only 11 inventories referring to proprietors of general stores were found and analyzed in detail for this initial study. This represents a small but significant sample by virtue of its uniformity in respect to the items considered up to now. Moreover, the current accounts appearing in these inventories represent almost one-half of the small landholding farmers under study. On the other hand, if the stores, their stocks, and functions appear to be uniform in nature, the same cannot be said about their proprietors. (Nor does the group of owners of general stores whom I was able to identify through the inventories and complementary sources correspond to the retail merchant, as that social type is normally understood.) Of the 11 store owners whose cases were analyzed, 5 appear in the lists published by the *Almanak Laemmert*. While these showed in their business larger stocks and more capital than the others, their "sales" did not appear qualitatively different from the group as a whole. They managed, however, to accumulate larger stores of goods to be commercialized in the regional marketplaces. Aiming at the wholesale merchants more than the local consumer, they made themselves known in the *Almanak*. Yet of the total number of merchants whose names appear in the criminal testimonies, only 20 percent (14 names) are listed in the *Almanak*. It is thus clear that the network of general stores in the municipality was considerably greater than could be perceived by reading that one source.

The retailers in a strict sense, i.e., the individuals supporting themselves exclusively by income from their business, as a rule had few or no slaves. In addition, they had in the total of their entries of supplies, installations, and debts collectible more than 40 percent of their liquid assets. In general, though, they owned small tracts of land, and they never gave up cultivation of subsistence crops. Eventually, the breadth of and profits from their business transactions might allow them to diversify their investments, buying land and slaves, and thereby become wealthy farmers in the regional context. Francisco Xavier Espínola, proprietor of a general store for several years in the parish of Correntezas—a business large enough to justify an entry for him in the *Almanak Laemmert* as a general store proprietor ever since 1850—at his death in 1883 left 27 slaves and one of the largest agricultural properties recorded in the documentation. According to all indications, he formed this from the profits of his business, in which he continued to work until the time of his death.[44]

There are also cases, however, of planters who diversified their investments by opening their own businesses. In these cases, the agricultural properties represented more than 75 percent of the inventoried wealth. Two of the inventories are typical examples of this possibility, which illus-

44. Ibid., Processo no. 1,929, maço 89, 1883.

trates the fundamental role in the concentration of capital and financing of local agricultural production played by a particular social type, the fazendeiro-merchant.[45] Moreover, these examples give evidence of the absence of strict barriers between farming and commerce in the region. From the small retailer with a business located on someone else's land to the large fazendeiro-merchant, the shop always served a double commercial function: to answer the consumption needs of local farmers, especially those who did not have access to the region's wholesale markets, and to provide an outlet for the surplus of the município's subsistence farmers in those larger markets, just as was done directly by the more well-off farmers in regard to their own production.

This analysis still has not taken into account, however, the basic factor which has generally defined the frontiers between rich and poor, socially and economically, in nineteenth-century agrarian Brazil—the ownership of land. Neither has it taken into consideration perhaps the major lacuna extant in the studies and analyses of the so-called poor free people in slaveowning Brazil—their access to and relations with slave property.

Francisco Pinto Pereira, deceased in 1869,[46] left the following goods to be divided among six sons: "a slave by the name of Felício, 15 years old, field work, valued at 1:300$000; one bed frame without value, a leather basket worth 1$000, and a wooden-framed house covered with straw, on land owned by Sr. João Gomez da Cunha," value illegible. There is no doubt concerning the "poverty" of Francisco Pinto Pereira, which appears to have been shared with Felício, his only slave and the most valuable of his belongings. There are many Franciscos and many Felícios among the 79 inventories of poor farmers. Until 1875, only 23 percent of the cases studied did not register ownership of slaves. This index increases to about 40 percent after the second half of the 70s, consonant with the process of regional and social concentration of ownership of slaves throughout the course of the extinction of slavery. It is assumed, of course, that slave labor was the basis for "wealth" in Brazilian society of the last century. Equivalent to capital, the surplus labor extracted from the slaves comprised the basic foundation of all the process of valorization of agricultural production destined for export or for regional markets. What was the significance, then, of the utilization of that source of labor by farmers whom we could consider to be both empirically and conceptually outside this economic circuit?

In the first place, one cannot forget that the number of slave workers associated with the effort to participate in the regional commodities

45. Ibid., Processos nos. 1,860 and 2,055, maços 85 and 96, 1881/1887.
46. Ibid., Processo no. 1,393, maço 64, 1869.

market constituted a basic parameter for our classification of the empirical data gathered from inventory lists. This approach proved highly effective in analyzing the commercial and slaveholding production of Capivary. It is not a question, however, of denying the role of slave ownership in the socioeconomic ranking of the propertied groups in the Rio agricultural areas during the period under study, and its influence on their real possibilities for investment expansion and accumulation. It is just that, before the labor crisis brought about by extinction of the slave trade began to produce its full effects, slave ownership was diffused well beyond the frontiers of commercial agriculture, export oriented or not. Several other recent studies have pointed in the same direction.[47]

Moreover, one cannot forget the very low levels of productivity which characterized the utilization of slave labor by the farmers analyzed up to this point. Until 1875, the 32 small farms (situações) which counted on the use of such labor possessed, on the average, three slaves per unit, of which, as a rule, only one was between the ages of 15 and 40. The presence of one female slave with minor-aged children was very frequent, as was that of aged slaves, very often infirm. After the mid-1870s, the average number of slaves per productive unit was less than two, many of them children or aged.

The opposite tendency seemed to operate with regard to ownership of land by the group of farmers studied. Francisco Pinto was the owner of one slave and of a situação on land belonging to João Gomes da Cunha. In much the same way, almost 60 percent of the cases analyzed up to 1875 refer to farmers on land not belonging to them, or, more rarely, terras devolutas (technically vacant government lands). However, this extremely high ratio begins to decline noticeably (to 33.9 percent) after that date.

The legal concentration of land ownership did not eliminate the pressure for unsettled land in the interior of the properties, which constantly attracted new poor farmers. In Capivary, in particular, where commercial agricultural expansion was not at the same pace as in the higher lands, this pressure became even more apparent, though at the same time the tensions between landowners and squatters were less explosive. The socioeconomic significance of legally owned property in the region during the period studied is thus couched in profound ambiguities. On one hand, the desire for a legal monopoly of land with a view to extending the scope of commercial farming operations was, as a rule, outside the range of possibilities for poor farmers. Yet, they did not have major difficulties estab-

47. See, among others, Francisco Vidal Luna and Iraci del Nero da Costa, "Posse de escravos em São Paulo no início do século XIX" and Stuart B. Schwartz, "Padrões de propriedade de escravos nas Américas: Nova evidência para o Brasil," in Revista de Estudos Econômicos, 1:13 (1983).

lishing themselves in areas not being used by the more well-off farmers. Most of the time, these areas were inside the large landed estates, within which the expansion of coffee cultivation was taking place very slowly. The progress of such small-scale farming in the municipality tended, in truth, to limit the socioeconomic power derived from large landed property. The possession of farm plots and improvements on lands either owned by someone else or *devolutas* was legally recognized by the local judicial system, not only for purposes of inheritance, but also for registering commercial transactions in the notarial records. The squatter was transformed into a typical figure of the rural area under consideration, without being necessarily integrated into the exact type of subsistence economy that I have described. At the same time, not infrequently the poor farmer was actually a landowner, even though his lands were in the majority of cases of very low value. In a still slaveholding agrarian structure, where commercial agriculture was expanding only slowly, land ownership turns out to be an unsuitable parameter for separating wealth from poverty, or for defining in absolute terms the levels of social hierarchy.

What can be concluded from the above is that the so-called "poor free people," an imprecise intermediate stratum of slaveowning Brazilian society, are difficult to define as "dispossessed" from a structural perspective. If they existed, and clearly they did, it becomes necessary to determine just what is meant by the term "poverty" in that society. Wholly different from the figure of the "slaveowning latifundiarist exporter," they would comprise, as a category, almost all of Brazilian society outside the so-called "dynamic centers" identified by Celso Furtado. My own analysis is modest and localized, but it refers to a município where the free population was extremely significant during the entire nineteenth century. It appears that, at least in Capivary, an entire category of poor farmers became owners of small extensions of land or even of some slaves, and sought to protect their own survival space against the agricultural expansion proceeding under the aegis of commercial capital. Poor but not "dispossessed" even when they owned no land or slaves, they managed to gain their subsistence as a result of their labors. Hence, they were fundamentally different from the slave, who, first and foremost, worked someone else's farm. They solved the problem of land scarcity by simply moving to another area; and the abundance of unoccupied land explains their significant presence in the município under study.

Conclusion

Precisely because of its local and monographic nature, the analysis of Capivary permits us to question a series of ideas concerning the poor free

person in the era of slave labor, all of which have been established without
very much concern for a consistent empirical foundation.

The increasingly backwoods nature (*caipirização*) and decapitalization
of Capivary agriculture in the postslavery period illustrate quite clearly
the difficulty of converting the freeborn poor and the former slaves into a
source of labor for commercial agriculture. We can further discern something about their alternatives for survival. Thus, these "vagrants" comprised a group of small producers dedicated to subsistence agriculture,
who, until the middle of the last century, could even count on one or
two slaves. The surplus of their production, exchanged for goods in kind
at the local general stores, could thereby reach the commodities markets
(urban or not), complementing the production capacity of a slaveowning
commercial agriculture dedicated to internal consumption and noticeably
undercapitalized as compared to agroexport production. Their contribu-
tion to internal provisioning illustrates magnificently how little sense it
makes to attempt to classify them according to their "functional" or "dys-
functional" role, and their integration or exclusion in relation to a logically
organized slaveholding system. Not only the "indolence" of the free population, but also the general stores that made it possible, were the target of
anger of those who saw them as a potential work force.[48]

The case of Capivary permits one to question to what extent the models of land monopolization and *coronelista* dominance as they existed under the republic can be applied to the forms of local bossism during the
period of slavery. Until quite late, *agregados* and occupiers of government lands were barely differentiated in terms of any type of normative
obligation from legal landowners. This was the case in such legal proceedings as deeds of purchase, sale or mortgaging of improvements, or the
drawing up of inventories of property of the deceased. But, apart from
its extremely low level of capitalization, would Capivary have been an
atypical or exceptional case in the agrarian world of south central Brazil?
In many aspects it does not seem to have been, for other studies have
been pointing in the same direction. In Campos de Goitacases, also in the
province of Rio de Janeiro, Sheila Faria makes clear that large-scale sugar
production was maintained overwhelmingly by slavery, even to the point
of acquiring slaves from the provinces of the Northeast, while at the same
time family labor was widespread among poor producers and squatters.
More than this, immediately after abolition and throughout the decade of
the '90s there occurred a crisis without precedent in the region, which
reduced to practically nothing the sugar shipments from Campos to Rio

48. See questionnaire responses, Coleção de Documentos, Congresso Agrícola de 1878.

de Janeiro—a crisis that observers of the period said was directly due to labor shortage.[49]

Research by Roberto Martins affirms the persistence of slavery in Minas Gerais and the purchase of slaves in noncoffee-producing areas of the province during all of the nineteenth century.[50] I disagree with his final conclusion when he attempts to describe a "slave-owning economy of Minas oriented toward internal consumption." I believe that the highly aggregated nature of his analysis, covering the entire province, precluded access to local sources, especially notary archives which would have given evidence of a greater division of labor and of the accumulation of capital in the large slaveowning farms of the province. From my point of view, that accumulation is what made possible the new importation of slaves.[51] The research is, however, extremely well substantiated in its treatment of empirical evidence, not leaving the smallest amount of doubt about its fundamental finding that slavery and the net importation of slaves were maintained in the noncoffee-growing regions of the province throughout the nineteenth century. Moreover, I cannot fail to agree with the author that the persistence of slavery in the province and the existence of a numerous free peasantry are different sides of the same coin.

Minas Gerais, the major slaveholding province in Brazil at the end of the nineteenth century (approximately 300,000 slaves in 1872) had, at the same time, a population of 1,700,000 free persons, more than half of whom were blacks and mestizos.[52] The abundance of free lands or lands appropriated de jure but not de facto in the province guaranteed them the necessary resources for their existence. According to Martins, a large part of the province remained completely unsettled and was comprised of lands which were either abandoned or only nominally appropriated. In 1845, it was estimated that 45 percent of the area of the province was effectively occupied.[53]

49. Sheila S. de Castro Faria, "Terra e trabalho em Campos de Goitacazes (1850–1920)" (Master's thesis, Universidade Federal Fluminense, 1986).

50. Roberto B. Martins, "A economia escravista de Minas Gerais no século XIX" (unpublished discussion text, CEDEPLAR, Belo Horizonte, Nov. 1980).

51. For a discussion of the concept of the slaveholding economy of Minas Gerais in the nineteenth century as oriented toward "self-sufficiency," see Amilcar Martins Filho and Roberto B. Martins, "Slavery in a Nonexport Economy: Nineteenth-Century Minas Gerais Revisited," HAHR, 63:3 (Aug. 1983), 537–568; Robert W. Slenes, "Comments on 'Slavery in a Nonexport Economy' (I)," ibid., 569–581; Warren Dean, "Comments . . . (II)," ibid., 582–584; Stanley L. Engerman and Eugene D. Genovese, "Comments . . . (III)," ibid., 585–590; Almicar Martins Filho and Roberto B. Martins, "Slavery in a Nonexport Economy: A Reply," HAHR, 64:1 (Feb. 1984), 135–146; and Slenes, "Os múltiplos de porcos e diamantes: A economia escravista de Minas Gerais no século XIX," Cadernos IFCH–UNICAMP, 17 (June 1985).

52. Recenseamento . . . 1872, IBGE.

53. Martins, "A economia," 54.

The English involved in mining in Minas Gerais during the nineteenth century felt very close to the problem. One of them, James Wells, observed that the free Brazilian, on being contracted for work, was an excellent worker but "the difficulty lies in inducing [him] to accept, for [he] would not work for a wage if it were not for being compelled by a desire for some small thing for himself or his family. On the contrary, he swings in his hammock, smokes his cigarette, and plays on his guitar or sleeps, saying that he is very busy and maybe he will come, God willing, next week or the week after."[54]

I do not intend to trace an idyllic picture of the life of these small producers, for in all senses of the word their existence was precarious, and, moreover, they could easily be expelled from their plots of land. The ineffectiveness of land monopolization in day-to-day terms never inhibited the expansion of commercial agricultural interests. In public lands, or in the interior of the private properties themselves, the extensive growth of large-scale slaveholding production forcefully imposed itself on the shacks and any cleared land it might find in its path. But it is important to note that only at the very moment when, forced off the land, the rural poor took to the highways or forests, did they become truly "dispossessed." And they easily reproduced their former situation. Moreover, the structural precariousness of their access to land did not compromise the relative stability of their existence, for outside of the more dynamic areas of agroexportation, the economic frontier was expanding at a very slow pace.

Based on all these cases, one can state that the ease of access to alternative survival strategies, made possible by the abundance of land, determined the persistence of slavery in the Southeast, and not the other way around. I am not minimizing the impact of cultural and racial prejudice on the thinking of the period, and on the creation of societies for the promotion of immigration. But the practical option of subsidized immigration on the Paulista western frontier was based primarily on the concrete difficulties of obtaining a regular influx of a disciplined, national free work force in an area which had remained, until recently, for the most part forested and sparsely populated but had suddenly accelerated its demand for labor.

In the Legislative Assembly of São Paulo, arguments concerning the "laziness," "indolence," and "undisciplined nature" of the free national population are the same, whether used by the proponents of immigration or by those who favored utilization of free native Brazilians by means of legal incentives and/or coercion.[55] Many times, the division of opinion between the two options reflected regional differences within the province

54. Ibid., 42.
55. Azevedo, *Onda negra*, chap. 2.

itself over the most effective substitute for slave labor. In areas where the demand for slave labor had stabilized, the use of free Brazilians in spite of all difficulties, was a more feasible solution than resorting to immigrant labor, in view of the competition for immigrants with western São Paulo. On the pioneer frontier, however, to utilize the free nationals as the basis of a work force would mean to "colonize" them. Some isolated voices became proponents of using for that very purpose the funds appropriated for subsidization of immigration, but such an ill-thought-out solution would have meant tying up voluminous amounts of capital to attain uncertain and less desirable results. Finally, subsidized immigration permitted the joining of "the useful to the agreeable," since it peopled the province with Europeans at the same time that it solved the problem of an insufficient work force. Indeed, notwithstanding prejudice and fantasies of "whitening," it was the difficulty of obtaining a spontaneous flow of regular, disciplined, and cheap labor for the coffee frontier that made the immigrant solution viable. The continuation of subsidization until the 1920s clearly demonstrates the difficulty of obtaining a self-sustaining supply of labor for the region, to allow it to keep up its rate of accumulation. But Capivary (where commercial farming rapidly declined) and the Paulista West are exceptions from the standpoint of the substitution of slave labor. The rule, based on available knowledge of the agricultural reality of Minas, Rio, and São Paulo during the First Republic, was the continuation of commercial agriculture through the use of Brazilian labor. This, in turn, became the basis upon which the system of *coronelismo* was established in those states.

Because of an abundance of unoccupied or only nominally appropriated land especially in the south central region, the difficulties in subduing, even in part, a work force of free or freed people were so great that agrarian elites preferred using slave labor until the eve of the definitive abolition of slavery. From this fact a question arises, as yet unanswered, and seldom even formulated by the historical literature: in what ways were the mechanisms of rural social control redefined, so as to maintain the viability of commercial agriculture and the class dominance of the rural producers who controlled it? I do not have an answer to this question. Nevertheless, I shall repeat an expression of Fernando Novais, which appears especially apt: "To pose a problem is, perhaps, a fruitful way to conclude."[56]

---

56. Fernando A. Novais, *Portugal e Brasil na crise do antigo sistema colonial (1777–1808)* (São Paulo, 1979), 303.

Black and White Workers: São Paulo, Brazil, 1888–1928

GEORGE REID ANDREWS

O NE hundred years after abolition, Brazil remains a country of marked racial inequality.[1] Brazilians themselves often attribute this to the legacy of slavery, arguing that the experience of bondage so crippled Afro-Brazilians as a social group that they proved unable, in the century after emancipation, to compete effectively against whites for jobs, education, housing, and other social goods.[2] Such an argument has the virtue of linking contemporary

*Research for this article was supported by grants from the Social Science Research Council and the Fulbright-Hays Program. The author thanks members of the Pittsburgh Center for Social History's working group on labor history for their comments on the initial version of this essay.

1. "Aspectos da situação sócio-econômica de brancos e negros no Brasil" (unpublished internal report, Instituto Brasileiro de Geografia e Estatística, Departamento de Estudos e Indicadores Sociais, 1981); Lúcia Elena Garcia de Oliveira et al., *O lugar do negro na força do trabalho* (Rio de Janeiro, 1985); Pierre-Michel Fontaine, ed., *Race, Class, and Power in Brazil* (Los Angeles, 1986); Carlos Hasenbalg, *Discriminação e desigualdades raciais no Brasil* (Rio de Janeiro, 1979).

2. This argument is most powerfully and eloquently developed in the work of sociologist Florestan Fernandes, which will be discussed later in this article. See his *A integração do negro na sociedade de classes*, 2 vols. (São Paulo, 1965; citations in this essay are from the third printing, 1978—an abridged English translation of the book is *The Negro in Brazilian Society* [New York, 1969]); *O negro no mundo dos brancos* (São Paulo, 1972); his coedited volume, with Roger Bastide, *Brancos e negros em São Paulo*, 2d ed. (São Paulo, 1959); and the essay "25 anos depois: O negro na era atual," in *Circuito fechado*, Florestan Fernandes, ed. (São Paulo, 1976), 64–93 (English translation in Maxine L. Margolis and William E. Carter, eds., *Brazil: Anthropological Perspectives* [New York, 1979] 96–113). For additional English translations of Fernandes's work, and that of his collaborator Roger Bastide, see "The Weight of the Past," in *Color and Race*, John Hope Franklin, ed. (Boston, 1968), 282–301; "Immigration and Race Relations in São Paulo," in *Race and Class in Latin America*, Magnus Mörner, ed. (New York, 1970), 122–142; "Beyond Poverty: The Negro and the Mulatto in Brazil," in *Slavery and Race Relations in Latin America*, Robert Brent Toplin, ed. (Westport, 1974), 277–297; "The Development of Race Relations in Brazil," in *Industrialization and Race Relations: A Symposium*, Guy Hunter, ed. (London, 1965), 9–29. See also the work of Fernandes's students Fernando Henrique Cardoso, *Capitalismo e escravidão no Brasil meridional: O negro na sociedade escravocrata do Rio Grande do Sul* (São Paulo, 1962); Octávio Ianni, *As metamorfoses do escravo: Apogeu e crise da escravatura no Brasil meriodional* (São Paulo, 1962), *Raças e classes sociais no Brasil* (Rio de Janeiro, 1972), and

problems to their historical roots. But, in so doing, it focuses our attention on a past which is assumed to weigh like a dead hand on the present, and draws us away from careful examination of conditions and circumstances which came into play after emancipation. Slavery was a traumatic experience for every society which experienced it; but when it came to an end, it was replaced by new social, political, and economic arrangements that transformed racial hierarchy while simultaneously preserving it. Any effort to explore the roots of contemporary racial problems in Brazil, or any other postslavery society, must pay as much attention to these new conditions as to those previously in effect.

This essay examines conditions in the state of São Paulo, where rapidly expanding coffee cultivation had by 1888 concentrated the third largest slave population in Brazil (after neighboring Rio de Janeiro and Minas Gerais). It will focus specifically on labor market competition between blacks and whites[3] in the years after emancipation, seeking to explain the outcomes of that competition in the interactions between, on the one hand, state policies and, on the other, institutions and organized groups in civil society. Several core questions will be addressed. What were the rules of the competition? Was the labor market a genuinely "free" one, or was it defined and structured in certain ways by the state, employers, workers acting through unions, or some combination of factors? If the latter, what were the consequences of a given labor market structure for the workers competing in that market, and for employers bidding for their services? In other words, how did the rules of the competition affect the outcome? And finally, what did black and white workers bring to the competition in terms of their skills, abilities, experience, and attitudes? And what sorts of bargains—among themselves, and with their employers and the state—were they willing to strike?

Escravidão e racismo (São Paulo, 1978); and their jointly authored book, *Cor e mobilidade social em Florianópolis* (São Paulo, 1960).

3. This article will use an essentially dichotomous, black/white conception of race relations, in which *pretos* (people of more or less pure African ancestry) and *pardos* (people of mixed racial ancestry; mulattos) will be treated as a single "black" racial category. This contradicts traditional Brazilian categorization, which recognizes *pardos* as an intermediate category between blacks and whites. My decision to adopt a different approach is based on recent research which demonstrates that, in relation to a number of social and economic indicators, the black and mulatto racial groups resemble each other so closely that they essentially form a single racial group clearly demarcated from whites. The results of this research, much of it carried out by the Instituto Brasileiro de Geografia e Estatística (Brazil's national statistical service), have led IBGE to now publish Brazilian racial data in dichotomous form, grouping *pretos* and *pardos* into a single *negro* category. See the first two items cited in n. 1; the work by economist Nelson Valle do Silva, particularly his essay in Fontaine's *Race, Class, and Power* and his "Black-White Income Differentials: Brazil, 1960" (Ph.D. diss., University of Michigan, 1978); and Sam C. Adamo, "The Broken Promise: Race, Health, and Justice in Rio de Janeiro, 1890–1940" (Ph.D. diss., University of New Mexico, 1983).

Structuring the Labor Market: The Planter State

São Paulo's labor market exhibited none of the rigid, state-imposed racial controls used, for example, in segregationist South Africa or the U.S. South during this same period. Nevertheless, it was powerfully affected by direct state intervention intended to produce results fraught with racial implications: the inundation of the local labor market with a flood of European immigrants.

Paulista coffee planters had been debating the desirability of European immigrant labor since the 1850s, when several planters, responding to the recent abolition of the African slave trade, first experimented with European *colonos* (contract plantation laborers). In 1871 and 1872, the provincial assembly set aside funds to underwrite costs incurred by planters wishing to bring immigrants from Europe to work on their plantations, and in 1884 it moved to create a private but state-funded Society for the Promotion of Immigration. Responsible for informing European workers of employment opportunities available in São Paulo, paying their passage, overseeing their arrival in Brazil, and dispatching them to the coffee groves, the society carried out these functions until 1895, when they were taken over by the State Department of Agriculture (the new federal constitution of 1891 having transformed São Paulo from a province into a state.)[4] European immigration to São Paulo did increase in response to these incentives, but not initially to levels sufficient to replace the slave labor force. Indeed, from the immigrants' point of view, this was precisely the problem: until the slave labor force *was* replaced, and free European workers no longer had to compete against coerced Africans and Afro-Brazilians, the immigrants were not inclined to come to Brazil, especially when they had the more attractive options of going to the United States or Argentina. To paraphrase Finley Peter Dunne, their fear was that employers who made slaves of black folks would make slaves of white folks too. And such fears were amply supported by widely publicized consular reports from European officials in São Paulo, who described working conditions for immigrants on São Paulo plantations as little better than slavery.[5] Thus it was not until 1887, when massive flights of

4. On the early experiments with immigrant labor in São Paulo, see Emília Viotti da Costa, *Da senzala à colônia*, 2d ed. (São Paulo, 1982), 49–90; Warren Dean, *Rio Claro: A Brazilian Plantation System, 1820–1920* (Stanford, 1976), 88–123; and Verena Stolcke and Michael M. Hall, "The Introduction of Free Labour on the São Paulo Coffee Plantations," *Journal of Peasant Studies*, 10: 2–3 (Jan./Apr. 1983), 170–200. On the programs to subsidize European immigrants, see Thomas Holloway, *Immigrants on the Land: Coffee and Society in São Paulo, 1886–1934* (Chapel Hill, 1980), 35–39.

5. Hall, "The Origins of Mass Immigration in Brazil, 1871–1914," (Ph.D. diss., Columbia University, 1969), 90; Pierre Denis, *Brazil* (London, 1911), 185–186.

slaves from the plantations foreshadowed the imminent demise of slavery, that annual European immigration into the province first broke the 10,000 mark. When it did, it jumped promptly to 32,000, more than the previous five years combined. Formal abolition in 1888 almost tripled that number, to 92,000—coincidentally, just slightly less than the number of slaves freed in the province that year by emancipation. Between 1890 and 1914, another 1.5 million Europeans would cross the Atlantic to São Paulo, the majority with their passages paid by the state government.[6]

From the planters' point of view, any benefits which these programs brought to the immigrants were purely incidental. Ever since the first discussions of subsidized immigration, the goal had been clear: to flood the labor market with workers, thus keeping the cost of labor low. The sponsor of the 1870 proposal to subsidize European immigration argued the desirability of creating a market situation in which "workers must search for landowners rather than landowners search for workers." Another supporter of the proposal noted the importance of "bringing in foreign workers, so that the cost of labor can go down. . . ." By the time the 1884 law was being debated, a growing number of fazendeiros understood that "it is impossible to have low salaries, without violence, if there are few workers and many people who wish to employ them." And by 1888, it was said that "it is evident that we need laborers . . . in order to increase the competition among them and in that way salaries will be lowered by means of the law of supply and demand." Supply and demand would now replace the violence and coercion of slavery as a means of organizing production, argued Antônio Prado, one of the province's most prominent planters. "Does the honorable opposition intend that the government should present to the legislature coercive means to force the *libertos* [freed slaves] back to work? What might those means be? Might it not be that freedom is the most effective guarantee that the economic law of supply and demand will conveniently regulate conditions of labor?" And if the law of supply and demand did not work entirely to the planters' advantage, then a little market intervention, in the form of transportation subsidies to the immigrants, was perfectly permissible. After all, as Antônio Prado's

6. An Italian immigrant whose parents brought him to São Paulo in 1890, when he was one year old, recalls that they came specifically in response to abolition, "which opened possibilities for workers from other countries" which had not existed under slavery. "O velho Scaramuzza lembra as origens do Bexiga," *Folha de S. Paulo* (São Paulo), May 14, 1985, p. 19. During this same period (1890–1914), 681,000 immigrants left the state (and, presumably, Brazil), according to official statistics; for the 1888–1928 period overall, 2,078,000 immigrants entered São Paulo, and 949,000 left. Holloway, *Immigrants on the Land*, 34, 179. Lúcio Kowarick, "The Subjugation of Labour: The Constitution of Capitalism in Brazil" (unpublished ms., 1985), 92, notes the coincidence between the 92,000 immigrants entering the state in 1888 and the estimated 107,000 slaves freed.

brother Martinho cogently observed, "immigrants with money are of no use to us."[7]

São Paulo's labor market in the years immediately following abolition was one shaped by an unusual (in the context of the economic liberalism dominant in the turn-of-the-century Atlantic world) degree of state direction and intervention. This was intervention seemingly devoid of any racial content, but in fact, by choosing to invest funds in European workers and refusing to make comparable investments in Brazilians, the province's planters, and the state apparatus which they controlled, had made their ethnic and racial preferences in workers crystal clear.[8] In so doing, they were motivated in equal part by the international currents of scientific racism and Social Darwinism running strong at that time, and by their own autocthonous *ideologia da vadiagem*, a firm and unshakable belief in the innate laziness and irresponsibility of the black and racially mixed Brazilian masses. Visiting French naturalist Louis Couty nicely captured the essence of the *ideologia* in his famous declaration that "o Brasil não tem povo": "Brazil does not have people, or rather, the people that it was given by race mixture and by the freeing of the slaves do not play an active and useful role" in the country's growth and development. The most rapid and efficient way to overcome this situation, argued the São Paulo planters was, as one of them put it, "a transfusion of better blood," or, in Antônio Prado's formulation, "immigration on a grand scale, on the grandest scale possible."[9]

As emancipation drew closer, São Paulo's leading abolitionist newspaper, *A Redempção*, denounced the planters' apparent desire to "open

7. For these various quotations, see Paula Beiguelman, *A formação do povo no compleixo cafeeiro: Aspectos políticos* (São Paulo, 1977), 65; Célia Maria Marinho de Azevedo, "O negro livre no imaginário das elites (racismo, imigrantismo, e abolicionismo em São Paulo)" (*dissertação de mestrado*, Universidade Estadual de Campinas, 1985), 241; Stolcke and Hall, "The Introduction of Free Labour," 182; Fernandes, *Integração do negro*, I, 37; and Hall, "Origins of Mass Immigration," 102.

8. An 1885 proposal to extend the same privileges to Brazilian migrants as those enjoyed by Europeans—paid maritime passages and lodging at state expense at the immigrant hostel in São Paulo city—was rejected by the provincial assembly. Proposals by abolitionist leaders that state funds should be expended on education and training to help the *libertos* compete in the labor market never even made it to the floor for debate. Azevedo, "O negro livre," 281–284.

9. On the influence of scientific racism in Brazil at this time, see Thomas Skidmore, *Black into White: Race and Nationality in Brazilian Thought* (New York, 1974), 52–63. The concept and label of an *ideologia da vadiagem* is used by Laura de Mello e Souza in her *Desclassificados do ouro: A pobreza mineira no século XVIII* (Rio de Janeiro, 1982), 64–72, 215–222; Kowarick's "Subjugation of Labour," passim, discusses the evolution of the ideology during the nineteenth and early twentieth centuries. For the quotations, see Louis Couty, *O Brasil em 1884: Esboços sociológicos* (Rio de Janeiro, 1984); Azevedo, "O negro livre," 250; Fernandes, *Integração do negro*, I, 36–37.

the doors to the immigrants" and deny the *libertos* "the work that they [the planters] infamously extorted from the slaves." By 1888, it indeed appeared that this was to be the meaning and result of abolition. The Europeans were being transported to São Paulo to compete with the *libertos*, and it was assumed at the outset that this would be a contest which the latter would lose. On the day after abolition, São Paulo's *Diário Popular* reflected that the event was "a great good, not because of how it will benefit the black race, which, because of its backwardness, will continue to suffer almost as much as before. . . ." Rather, the beneficiaries will be those "appropriately educated and prepared to deal with the challenges posed by the new order of things. *The right man in the right place*, as the Americans say," and that man clearly was not going to be black.[10]

Even more ominous was an article written a year after emancipation, entitled "The Segregation of the *Liberto*," which announced the virtual conclusion of the labor market competition and the definitive victory of the immigrants. Ignoring the substance of the earlier legislative debates, the article argued that no such competition had been intended or anticipated. "Nobody was thinking about a contest between the old laborers and the new. There was room for everyone." But the *libertos'* flight from the plantations, and their refusal to continue in their old positions, left the planters no choice but to turn to the immigrants. "The Brazilian worker abandoned the position he had conquered, he made the immigrant replace him, he forced the landowner to opt for the latter." And now, "the gap left by the former laborer has been filled forever. . . . The *liberto* is segregated, rendered useless, lost to the productive life."[11]

One is startled by the rapidity with which the contest had run its course—it had been only a year since abolition, and the vast majority of those Europeans who would enter São Paulo had not yet set foot on Brazilian shores—and by the rigid finality of its conclusion: not just defeat and displacement for the *libertos*, but segregation and exile, forever, from "the productive life." One is struck as well by the placement of blame for this tragic situation: it lies squarely on the shoulders of the former slaves themselves.

These articles, and others like them, should be read not as empirical descriptions of what was happening in São Paulo at the time, but rather as expressions of what the state's elites hoped and indeed expected would come to pass: the displacement of black labor by white. White labor had

10. Azevedo, "O negro livre," 383, 385; "O que ganhamos," *Diário Popular* (São Paulo), May 14, 1888, p. 1.
11. "Questões e problemas: A segregação do liberto," *A Província de São Paulo* (São Paulo), May 22, 1889.

been granted a privileged position over black, and was expected to take full advantage of it. But precisely how far would those privileges extend in practice? Would white workers in Brazil exploit their preferred position to create a racially exclusionary union movement and a racially exclusionary labor market, as their peers in the United States and South Africa were doing at the same time?

Structuring the Labor Market: Organized Labor

Between 1900 and 1920 São Paulo's immigrants forged a labor movement led by, and comprised largely of, Europeans. Precise statistics on membership are not available, but a study of 106 labor leaders from this period discovered that fewer than one-third of them were native born; of that third, most were concentrated in Rio de Janeiro rather than São Paulo.[12] The immigrants' domination of the labor movement, their insecurity in the face of the government's immigration policies and the resulting oversupply of labor, and the marginalization of black and mulatto workers in São Paulo might easily have led to outcomes like those in the United States and South Africa, where white workers demanded, and received, institutionalized barriers against black competition.[13]

Such was not the case in São Paulo, however. In searching for strategies with which to improve their position and confront their employers and the state, São Paulo's workers seem never to have even considered the possibility of the racial exclusion and segregation being pursued elsewhere. If anything, their approach was exactly the opposite. Acutely aware of the tactical opportunities which an ethnically and racially divided working class offered to employers and the state, and inspired by the egalitarian

12. Sheldon Leslie Maram, *Anarquistas, imigrantes, e o movimento operário brasileiro, 1890–1920* (Rio de Janeiro, 1979), 19–22. On the Brazilian labor movement generally, and São Paulo in particular, see Maram; Boris Fausto, *Trabalho urbano e conflito social, 1890–1920* (São Paulo, 1977); Beiguelman, *Os companheiros de São Paulo* (São Paulo, 1977); Paulo Sérgio Pinheiro and Hall, *A classe operária no Brasil, 1889–1930*, 2 vols. (São Paulo, 1979), I; and Edgar Carone, *Movimento operário no Brasil, 1877–1944* (São Paulo, 1979).

13. Not all labor organizations in either the United States or South Africa made such demands. Several industrial unions, such as the International Ladies Garment Workers Union and the United Mine Workers, took an early stand against racial discrimination and played an important role in pressuring the Congress of Industrial Organizations to extend such policies to all its member unions. But before the creation of the CIO in 1936, the American Federation of Labor took little effective action to combat racial exclusion in its affiliates, and such exclusion tended to be the norm. On the racial policies of organized labor in the United States and South Africa during this period, see Stanley Greenberg, *Race and State in Capitalist Development: Comparative Perspectives* (New Haven, 1980), 273–356; William J. Wilson, *The Declining Significance of Race: Blacks and Changing American Institutions*, 2d ed. (Chicago, 1980), 42–87; and William H. Harris, *The Harder We Run: Black Workers since the Civil War* (New York, 1982).

doctrines of socialism, anarchism, and anarcho-syndicalism, labor organizers repeatedly invoked the goal of eliminating such divisions.

O Amigo do Povo spoke for the labor press as a whole when it denounced what it described as the government policy of "dividing in order
to rule" by "pitting the foreign worker against the national worker. . . ."
Organizers recognized that, by dividing the labor force into immigrant
workers and Brazilians, and granting preference to the former, employers
had produced a state of "latent warfare in the very heart of the working
class" which could be fanned into flame at any time. A "heterogeneous
population . . . separated by hatreds" was peculiarly vulnerable to such a
strategy, and those hatreds were further exacerbated by the discontent and
resentment of Brazilians locked out of the labor market. Urging its readers
to renounce "false prejudices and false pride of race," the Italian-language
paper Avanti! concluded that ethnic and national cleavages within the
working class formed the single most important obstacle to the success of
São Paulo's labor movement.[14]

Such a conclusion was the product of bitter experience. The tactic
of exploiting racial divisions within the labor force was first used in São
Paulo just three years after abolition, in the 1891 dockworker strike in
Santos. The Docas de Santos Company brought in unemployed libertos
who had fled to Santos during 1887 and 1888 and then remained, and used
them as strikebreakers to defeat the predominantly immigrant strikers.
The same weapon was employed again in 1908, this time using the black
laborers who worked in the company's gravel quarries, fazendas, and road-
building crews. After the 1908 strike, the paper of the dockworkers' union
devoted several articles to the company's campaign to promote "discord
and racial struggle among the workers of Santos," and a recent study
of these strikes concludes that the company was indeed "successful in
presenting the conflict between strikers and strikebreakers as the result of
'color prejudice' among immigrant workers."[15]

Efforts to promote ethnic and racial antagonism within the labor force
were particularly evident during the 1917–20 period, years of unusually
active labor agitation in São Paulo. The successful general strike of 1917,
an unprecedented event in Brazilian labor relations, provoked a wave of
repression by employers and the state during the years that followed, and

14. Initial quotation from "Os acontecimentos do Rio e do Ceará," O Amigo do Povo
(São Paulo), Jan. 17, 1904, p. 1. The rest, from O Amigo do Povo, Dec. 6, 1903; Il Pungulo,
May 1, 1909; and Avanti! (São Paulo), July 25 and Nov. 28, 1914, are taken from Hall,
"Immigration and the Early São Paulo Working Class," Jahrbuch für Geschichte von Staat,
Wirtschaft, und Gesellschaft Lateinamerikas, 12 (1975), 397–399.
15. Maria Lúcia Caira Gitahy, "Os trabalhadores do porto de Santos, 1889–1910" (tese
de mestrado, Universidade Estadual de Campinas, 1983), 67–68, 79, 109–110, 290–291, 302.

repeated attacks by public officials and the establishment press against subversive, traitorous foreign radicals. Newspapers which had rejoiced at the immigrants' arrival several years earlier now turned on them as importers of the alien, anti-Brazilian doctrines of anarchism and socialism, and employers who had welcomed the immigrants into their factories and plantations now denounced them as disloyal ingrates and proclaimed the simple virtues of the loyal, hardworking Brazilians.[16]

Seeking to overcome these xenophobic appeals and forge a genuinely unified labor movement, São Paulo's unions promoted the principle of ethnic, national, and racial equality among all workers, and devoted particular attention to organizing and mobilizing the Brazilian population. A 1903 article attacked the practice of conducting meetings and public speeches in Italian, and urged that organizers do more of their proselytizing in Portuguese. The first issue of the *Jornal Operário* announced that it had come into existence to fill the need for a Portuguese-language workers' paper to speak directly to Brazilian workers.[17]

As they spoke to their immigrant and Brazilian readers, the labor papers hammered home the message of equality: "We're not in the time of slavery any more—every individual, white or black, ugly or handsome, Brazilian or foreign, according to the laws of this country is a citizen, and as such can take part in the affairs of the state and demand accounts from his oppressors." A more pessimistic approach was that black and white workers were equal not in their rights, but in their common degradation, since all workers, regardless of race, remained enslaved and oppressed by capitalism. "Wages are the modern form of slavery"; "slavery died in name but not in fact." This implicit equalizing of blacks and whites occasionally became explicit, as in an article denouncing the twentieth anniversary of abolition as "lies, hypocrisy, Jesuitisms, we say. . . . Between the *black slaves* who worked in their masters' fields, and the white slaves who labor in the factory . . . between the blacks from the Congo employed on the fazendas prior to 1888 and the white workers from the most civilized countries of Europe who work *today* to enrich a gang of parasites, there is, and there cannot be, any difference whatsoever."[18]

16. On the antiforeigner campaigns of the late 1910s, see Maram, *Anarquistas, imigrantes*, 60–89 and Fausto, *Trabalho urbano*, 233–243.

17. "Pela propaganda," *O Amigo do Povo*, Feb. 14, 1903; "Jornal operário," *Jornal Operário* (São Paulo), Sept. 17, 1905.

18. "1 de maio," *O Grito do Povo* (São Paulo), May 1, 1900; "13 de maio," *A Lucta Proletária* (São Paulo), May 16, 1908; "O salariato é a forma moderna da escravidão," *O Amigo do Povo*, Aug. 14, 1903; "Entre operários," *O Amigo do Povo*, June 21, 1902. *Terra Livre* (São Paulo), May 16, 1916, noted the similarities between immigration and the slave trade, and the importance of the state in promoting the former. "It used to be that private enterprise, the slave trader, took charge of going to hunt or buy the blacks. . . . Today the

The labor movement made explicit appeals to an Afro-Brazilian con-
stituency. A 1908 article denounced as an outrage the practice among
Catholic churches in Campinas of dividing white and black women into
separate organizations and sisterhoods. A 1911 article on São Paulo's peasant population made clear that it was discussing Afro-Brazilians (it described their singing sambas and *cantigas de desafio*, the Brazilian answer-
back song, in black dialect), and pointedly contrasted their innocent rural
virtue with the corruption and viciousness of the urban bourgeoisie. The
article went so far as to hold up this peasant idyll as a model for the future
anarchist society: "the delicate sentiments of those good people are like
the affectionate embrace that will someday unite free men on a free earth."
And a 1919 article in the newspaper of the construction workers' union,
written during the heat of the antiforeigner campaign in São Paulo, noted
that the government's denunciations of immigrant agitators might make
it look as though Brazilians were not involved in the labor movement.
Nothing could be farther from the truth, the author argued. Despite the
fact that "we are descendants from a slave race, that our fathers died in
the stocks or under the lash, while our mothers—as a foreigner put it—
still have the marks of the master's whip on their buttocks," Brazilians are
as active in the struggle as any European.[19]

These efforts to promote interracial solidarity notwithstanding, one
must agree with Sheldon Maram's judgment that the early labor movement
was not very successful in achieving its goal of creating a racially and ethnically unified working class. The immigrant response to the labor movement was far from overwhelming, and the Brazilian response weaker still.
One reason for that weak response is hinted at in the laconic "as a foreigner
put it" in the quotation immediately above. Despite their appeals for racial
equality and working-class solidarity, many immigrant labor leaders could
not break completely free of feelings of ethnic and racial superiority over
their Brazilian colleagues. A 1903 article in *O Amigo do Povo* expressed
despair at the idea of ever organizing the Brazilian *povo*, which lies vege-
tating in ignorance, sunk in poverty and lethargy. To make the revolution,
the paper argued, will require "wills and characters that are stronger,
physically and morally, than those possessed by the Brazilians, who are
the product of a debilitated nation. . . ." Articles in the labor press some-

entrepreneur who runs this business is the state. It doesn't buy the slave, but it pays his
passage. And the slave is called a colono." Quoted in Silvia I. L. Magnani, *O movimento
anarquista em São Paulo* (São Paulo, 1982), 154.

19. Maram, *Anarquistas, imigrantes*, 67; "O preto Simeão," *O Combate* (São Paulo),
May 13, 1915; "O velho anarquista Rodrigues," *Folha de S. Paulo* (São Paulo), Oct. 27, 1984,
p. 46; "Azafama clerical," *A Lucta Proletária*, Mar. 7, 1908; "O sol da liberdade," *Aurora
Social* (Santos), special anniversary issue, no date (internal evidence suggests Jan. 1911); "Os
brasileiros e a questão social," *O Grito Operário* (São Paulo), Dec. 28, 1919.

times took on explicitly racial overtones. A 1917 article criticizing recent repression of strikes argued that police had completely overstepped the bounds of Brazilian law and behaved like savages. Contrasting Brazil with the kingdom of Senegambia, "a vast region of blacks on the black continent," the paper argued that "this republic is not a Liberia, it's not a republic of blacks, of barely clad savages and primitive laws." No, Brazil is a cultured country, with the sole exception of its police. "The police are not, and never have been, Brazilian; the police are from Senegambia, they follow Senegambian laws, and their officers are Senegambians." A satirical play published in an anarchist monthly in 1905 presented a symbolic social scale running from nobleman to dog. A black butler ranks just above the dog and below a beggar, who expresses his humiliation at being removed from the mansion "by a well-fed black." This effort was at least satirical; not so a 1918 article on the origin of black people, which recounted various racist folktales about how God had happened to give black people broad noses, kinky hair, and light-colored palms. The editor of the paper, which served the workers of the Sorocabana Railway Company (many of whom were black), described these legends "as most clever and well done."[20]

It was probably inevitable that the racial attitudes and tensions which characterized the society at large would emerge in the labor unions. But adding to the generalized racism of the time was the fact that the exclusion of black workers from industrial employment created a classic "reserve" labor force—an army of unemployed who could be called up at any time to break strikes, undermine efforts to unionize, and keep wages low. So limited were opportunities for black workers elsewhere in the economy that sufficient numbers could always be found to respond to employers' appeals for *furagreves*. One black paper noted that strikebreaking had been the means by which black men had finally penetrated the ranks of conductors and drivers for the São Paulo Light, Power, and Tramway Company, which before the strike of 1917 had restricted black men to laying track.[21] Many labor leaders understood how difficult it would be for unemployed workers to refuse opportunities like these, but this did not stop them from voicing irritation with black workers who did so, and particularly with those who signed on as thugs and hoodlums hired by employers to break up strikes and demonstrations. "[W]hat hurts and embitters is to see the sons of yesterday's slaves today replacing the old *capitães do mato* [hunters of runaway slaves] in the disgraceful mission of filling the ranks

20. Maram, *Anarquistas, imigrantes*, 89; "Pobre povo brasileiro," *O Amigo do Povo*, Dec. 27, 1903; "No reino da Senegambia," *A Plebe* (São Paulo), Sept. 15, 1917; "A escala," *Aurora* (São Paulo), Apr. 1, 1905; "Os negros," *A Sorocabana* (São Paulo), Sept. 1, 1918.

21. *Getulino* (Campinas), Dec. 9, 1923. For a reply which argues that Afro-Brazilians should make common cause with white workers rather than undermine them, see the short essay by Moacyr Marques, *Getulino*, Mar. 30, 1924.

of those who beat up workers who are in search of their economic liberty and the improvement of their class by the only means at their disposal— the strike." [22]

It is important to note that the strikebreakers of this period were by no means exclusively black. A 1905 article argued that a disproportionate number of strikebreakers were "yokels" from Sicily and Venice—though, significantly, the piece was entitled "Slaves and Savages from Europe," implicitly equating strikebreaking with blackness. A 1904 article on the desperate condition of Portuguese immigrants in São Paulo noted that their situation was so bad that many of them, "in order that their families not die of hunger," had been driven to the ultimate betrayal of their fellow workers: enlisting in the police force. [23] Despite their preferred position, European workers proved no less vulnerable to the pressures of the labor market than their Afro-Brazilian peers—which explains, in part, the collapse of this first phase of the Brazilian labor movement during the early 1920s.

The anarchists and socialists had sought to bridge the gap between Brazilian and European workers, and had failed. Or rather, the degree to which they succeeded was not sufficient to produce a labor movement which could prevail against the forces of the Republican state. Nor did it make any progress in introducing racial equality into the workplace. In the absence of such intervention, and as shaped by the immigration policies of the planter state, what were the outcomes of the labor market competition between São Paulo's black and white workers?

The Struggle for Jobs: Outcomes

In analyzing the results of black/white labor market competition, it is helpful to divide the discussion into rural and urban spheres. In the countryside, white workers, who were almost exclusively immigrants, quickly became concentrated in the most prosperous regions of the state, and in the most desirable jobs in those regions. Black and caboclo [24] workers either retreated to more depressed parts of the state or held the

22. "O 13 de maio," *A Plebe*, May 15, 1920.
23. "Escravos e selvagens da Europa," *Jornal Operário*, Oct. 15, 1905; "O emigrante," *A Pátria* (São Paulo), Jan. 3, 1904.
24. *Caboclo* is defined as "a civilized Brazilian Indian of pure blood" or "a Brazilian half-breed (of white and Indian)." *Novo Michaelis dicionário ilustrado*, 2 vols. (São Paulo, 1961), II, 200; see also Holloway, *Immigrants on the Land*, 106. In practice, in São Paulo, caboclo seems to have meant a dark-skinned ruralite of indeterminate race, usually engaged in subsistence agriculture or day labor on the plantations, and forming part of the rural *caipira* (peasant) culture. On *caipira* culture in the nineteenth century, see Maria Sylvia de Carvalho Franco, *Homens livres na ordem escravocrata* (São Paulo, 1969); on the twentieth century, see Antônio Cándido Mello e Souza, *Os parceiros do Rio Bonito*, 2d ed. (São Paulo, 1979).

least desirable jobs on the more profitable plantations. Planters in the badly eroded Paraíba Valley, for example, in the northeast section of the state, were unable to provide competitive salaries and working conditions. For these planters, as well as for those in the neighboring coffee-growing areas of Rio de Janeiro and Minas Gerais, as a contemporary observer put it, "white labor was a luxury which they could not maintain." As a result, by 1905 only 4 percent of the labor force in the Paraíba region was European.[25]

In the booming central-western region of the state, by contrast, the agricultural labor force was two-thirds European by the same date. Within that labor force, a clear system of racial preference prevailed. Warren Dean finds that "immigrants were generally preferred for *colono* contracts, undoubtedly the best positions on the plantation." Thomas Holloway agrees that "when the Paulistas decided to go to Europe for their workers, the Brazilian peasantry, including many ex-slaves and the native mixed-blood backwoodsmen, was relegated to a marginal position in the regional economy. . . . By the early twentieth century the die was cast, and work in the coffee fields of the west was universally identified with immigrants." When black and racially mixed Brazilians were hired at all, it was to perform "the seasonal, precarious jobs that were not sufficiently well paid to be attractive to the immigrants. They became *camaradas*, general laborers, who were paid by the month. When there was a local excess of immigrants, the freedmen might be further demoted to day laborer." Observing this situation, political scientist Paula Beiguelman describes it as a two-tier, racially segmented labor market, with an upper level of "foreign wage-earners, who worked toward the eventual accumulation of cash savings; and a second, Brazilian, for the painful and difficult tasks rejected by the first."[26]

In the cities immigrants enjoyed the same preference in hiring that they experienced in the countryside. The 1893 census of São Paulo city showed that 72 percent of employees in commerce, 79 percent of factory workers, 81 percent of transport workers, and 86 percent of artisans were foreign born. A 1902 source estimated the industrial labor force in the capital as more than 90 percent immigrant; in 1913 the *Correio Paulistano* estimated that 80 percent of the capital's construction workers were Italian; and a 1912 survey of the labor force in 33 textile factories in the

25. Denis, *Brazil*, 314, 316; Holloway, *Immigrants on the Land*, 63; Beiguelman, *Formação do povo*, 72–73, 108–109. For a detailed discussion of the labor situation in the Paraíba region, see Stanley J. Stein, *Vassouras: A Brazilian Coffee County, 1850–1900*, 2d ed. (Princeton, 1985), 259–274.
26. Dean, *Rio Claro*, 172; Holloway, *Immigrants on the Land*, 63; Beiguelman, *Formação do povo*, 108.

TABLE I: Ratio of Percentage of Immigrants in Labor Force to
Percentage of Immigrants in Population, São Paulo City

	1893	1920
Commerce	1.4	1.9
Artisanry	1.7	—
Manufacturing	1.6	1.5
Transport	1.6	1.9
Domestic service	1.2	1.1

Sources: *Relatório . . . de 1894; Recenseamento do Brasil, 1920.*

state found that 80 percent were foreign born, the great majority of them
Italian.[27]

The 1920 census, while providing no information on race, suggests at
first glance that native Brazilian workers had recovered some lost ground.
They now accounted for 49 percent of the capital's 96,000 factory workers,
38 percent of transport workers, and 38 percent of employees in commerce. When one factors into these figures, however, the fact that the
capital's foreign-born population had fallen from 50 percent of the city's
inhabitants to 35 percent, one still finds a situation of clear labor-market
preference in all categories save domestic service (where the preference
is weak), and actually strengthened preference (in relation to 1893) in the
areas of transport and commerce (see Table I). Scattered evidence further
suggests that many of the Brazilians employed in urban occupations in
1920 were themselves the second-generation offspring of immigrants who
had arrived in the 1890s and early 1900s; by 1920, therefore, descendants
of native-born Brazilian families were probably worse off in the labor market competition than they were in 1893.[28]

27. *Relatório apresentado ao . . . secretário dos negócios do interior do Estado de São
Paulo pelo director da Repartição de Estatística e Archivo . . . em 31 de julho de 1894* (Rio
de Janeiro, 1894), 82–83; Beiguelman, *Formação do povo*, 117–121; "Condições do trabalho
na indústria textil do Estado de São Paulo," *Boletim do Departamento Estadual do Trabalho*,
1: 1–2 (1912), 35–80.
28. Figures from *Recenseamento do Brasil, 1920*, vol. IV, 1st part, tomo I, 170–173.
On Brazilian-born offspring of immigrant parents, see Hall, "Immigration," 394–395 and
Fernandes, *Integração do negro*, I, 139. Inspectors from the State Department of Labor
reported visiting a textile factory in 1912 which employed 20 adults, 151 foreign-born minors,
and 112 Brazilian minors. Of this last group, 106 were children of Italian parents. "Condições
de trabalho na indústria textil," 60. While carrying out research in the personnel files of
the Jafet textile factory in São Paulo, I found numerous Italian-surnamed Brazilian-born
minors and young adults working in the factory in the 1910s and '20s, many of them related
to older Italian-born employees. Unfortunately, I failed to count these second-generation
Italian-Brazilians as a separate category of employee, and thus cannot offer firm figures on
this score.

Brazilian sociologist Florestan Fernandes argues that this was indeed the case, and that the disadvantages which affected Brazilian participants in the labor market were particularly pronounced for Afro-Brazilians. By 1920, he argues, their position in the urban economy was even worse than it had been 20 or 30 years earlier, despite the phenomenal growth in industry, construction, and commerce that had taken place in the meantime. Blacks were almost completely barred from factory work, and black artisans had virtually disappeared from the city. Poor and working-class black people found their job opportunities restricted to domestic service and what today would be termed the "informal sector." Two Afro-Brazilians who lived through that period recall the conditions under which they worked.

> There were almost as many blacks as Italians in those days, in São Paulo, [but] they lived in a state of total disintegration. . . . The immigrants were in the factories and in commerce. The only work left for the blacks was to clean houses and offices, cart wood, and other chores. We were all underemployed. You always used to see blacks pushing carts through the city and lining up in Quintino Bocaiuva Street, with their buckets and brushes, waiting for the call to clean a house here, scrub a floor there.
> The blacks had to hustle, as they say today. They had to create various sources of work, as porters, gardeners, domestic servants, sweeping the sidewalks, washing cars. . . . All those jobs that didn't exist before, the blacks created—shoeshine boys, newspaper venders, day laborers, all those jobs they created for their subsistence, because the fazendeiros wouldn't hire blacks. . . .[29]

Some black men were able to find regular work laying track for the railroads or for the São Paulo Light, Power, and Tramway Company, which was building the city's tramway and electric systems at the time. And the exclusion of black workers from factory employment was not absolute, since there was occasional mention of factory workers in the social columns of the black press, as well as in employment records.[30] Such opportunities

---

29. "Os jornais dos netos de escravos," *Jornal da Tarde* (São Paulo), June 12, 1975; "Frente negra brasileira, 1930–1937" (collaborative *trabalho de pesquisa*, Pontifícia Universidade Católica-São Paulo, 1985), anexo 2.

30. On São Paulo Light, see "Frente negra brasileira," anexo 2. For factory workers in the black press, see, for example, *A Rua* (São Paulo), Feb. 24, 1916, p. 3, which mentions "certain young women from the Trapani factory" and "certain young women from the silk factory"; or the obituary of Deodato de Moraes, employed at "the hat factory in Villa Prudente. . . . Workers from various factories attended his funeral," *O Alfinete*, Sept. 22, 1918, p. 2. My own 20-percent sample of workers hired at the Jafet textile plant between 1905 and 1930 showed that, of those Brazilian-born workers of known race, 10.9 percent were Afro-Brazilian. However, the first Afro-Brazilian worker does not appear on the company's rolls

were clearly limited, however, and the great majority of black people found themselves forced into domestic service or the irregular, poorly paying jobs described above.

Why did this happen? Why was the state's Afro-Brazilian population so consistently marginalized and pushed aside in the labor market competition? Certainly that contest had been structured by state policy in such a way as to make it exceptionally rigorous; but did this mean that black people inevitably had to lose?

Explaining the Outcomes: The Fernandes Thesis

According to Florestan Fernandes's pathbreaking book, *A integração do negro na sociedade de classes* (1965), there was no way that blacks could have fared better than they did. Based on research undertaken during the 1940s and '50s as part of a UNESCO-sponsored project on race relations in Brazil, Fernandes's writings, and those of his students, have become the most widely accepted and influential explanation of why black people were not integrated into Paulista society (and into Brazilian society more generally) on terms of equality with white people.[31] Fernandes focused on the heritage of slavery, which he saw operating in two ways.

First, it left a strong inheritance of racism which made whites unwilling to accept blacks as equal and to grant them equality of treatment and opportunity after emancipation. Even if such opportunities had been offered, however, Fernandes argues that the great majority of black people would have been unable to take advantage of them because of the second aspect of the slave heritage: the ways in which slavery had crippled its victims intellectually, morally, socially, and economically. Slaves learned no marketable skills under slavery; quite the contrary, slavery had taught them to avoid work wherever and whenever possible. Slavery had not built up the black family; rather, it had undermined and destroyed it. And slavery had done nothing to instill a sense of community and self-worth into slaves; for reasons of security, it had sought to root out and destroy whatever instruments of solidarity and mutual support the slaves may have brought with them from Africa or tried to construct in the New World.

---

until 1922—though some may be concealed among the workers of unknown race recorded during the 1910s—and over 90 percent of the black workers hired by the firm during this period were taken on only after 1925.

31. For titles of work by Fernandes and his students, see n. 2. On the UNESCO project and the significance of its findings in correcting earlier views of Brazil, associated with Gilberto Freyre, as a "racial paradise," see Pierre-Michel Fontaine, "Research in the Political Economy of Afro-Latin America," *Latin American Research Review*, 15: 2 (1980), 122–126. For an insightful discussion of Freyre's and Fernandes's ideas, and the historical circumstances which gave rise to them, see Viotti da Costa, "The Myth of Racial Democracy: A Legacy of the Empire," in her *The Brazilian Empire: Myths and Histories* (Chicago, 1985), 234–246.

Therefore, when the Europeans arrived in São Paulo and began to compete with black people in the rural and urban labor markets, there simply was no competition, reasoned Fernandes. Black people were "automatically" pushed aside by Europeans who were more highly skilled, more imbued with a capitalist work ethic, and more effectively supported by family and community structures of solidarity. The "isolation" and marginalization of São Paulo's black population was "a 'natural product' of their inability to feel, think, and act socially as free men." São Paulo did not reject the Afro-Brazilians, he argues; rather, by their failure to assume the new, "modern" roles of citizen, employee, wage earner, etc., the Afro-Brazilians in effect rejected the modernizing, capitalist society of twentieth-century São Paulo.

Fernandes's book was a courageous, and at times brilliant, effort to unmask the reality of Brazilian race relations, and to give the lie to the notion of Brazil as a land of racial equality and "racial democracy." Nevertheless, a close examination of his arguments concerning the first decades after abolition, and the process of labor market exclusion which took place at that time, suggests some problems. Fernandes bases much of his explanation for the marginalization of the black population on a set of characteristics attributed to each racial group: dynamic competitiveness and a relatively high level of professional skills on the part of the immigrants; anomie, apathy, and ignorance on the part of the Afro-Brazilians. Are these assertions supported by the evidence available?

The first problem with the Fernandes thesis is that, as early as 1872, the majority of São Paulo's black and mulatto population was not slave, but free.[32] Well before the abolition of slavery, and increasingly so in the years leading up to 1888, most of the province's Afro-Brazilians had escaped the devastating effects of slavery, and were at liberty to construct lives and careers of their own choosing. Far from floundering helplessly in the labor market, as Fernandes's argument would lead us to expect, many of these free blacks and mulattos succeeded in establishing themselves as artisans and merchants, in São Paulo as throughout Brazil. It was only when the immigrants came, he notes, that these black craftsmen and entrepreneurs started to disappear from the urban scene.[33]

32. Brazil's first national census in 1872 assigned São Paulo a total population of 837,354: 433,432 whites, 39,465 caboclos, 208,215 free blacks and mulattos, and 156,612 slave blacks and mulattos. Samuel Harman Lowrie, "O elemento negro na população de São Paulo," *Revista do Arquivo Municipal de São Paulo*, 4: 48 (1938), 12.

33. Fernandes, *Integração do negro*, I, 64–66; Roberto J. Haddock Lobo and Irene Aloisi, *O negro na vida social brasileira* (São Paulo, 1941), 29. On free black urban workers and artisans in Brazil more generally, see Herbert Klein, "Nineteenth-Century Brazil," in *Neither Slave Nor Free*, David W. Cohen and Jack P. Greene, eds. (Baltimore, 1972), 325–330.

They simply didn't have the skills to face the Europeans, he argues
—in either skilled labor, commerce, or factory work. But the evidence is
far from convincing. Fernandes's own informants recall that the "quality
of the blacks' work was no worse than the whites'." And while Fernandes
asserts that the Europeans were better educated and had more extensive
experience with urban industrial work than did the Brazilians, either black
or white, a number of historians take issue with him. Michael Hall argues
that "most of those who came to the capital [São Paulo] appear, by all accounts, to have had no prior industrial or urban experience. While some
artisans and other urban workers undoubtedly went to São Paulo, such
immigration was not encouraged and it seems fairly clear that the overwhelming majority of the labor force was composed of men and women
from the rural areas of Southern Europe." Looking specifically at Italian
immigration, which accounted for almost half of the immigrants arriving
in São Paulo, and studying it at its point of origin rather than its desti-
nation, Rudolph Bell found that between 1880 and 1910 "persons with
skills useful in an urban or industrial setting tended to move to northern Europe, particularly Germany and Belgium," lured by higher salaries
and low transportation costs; "they clearly failed to take advantage of any
opportunities in North and South America."[34]

Since most factory workers in turn-of-the-century São Paulo learned
their skills on the job, the question of previously acquired industrial skills
may not even be relevant. This was particularly the case with minors, who
comprised almost one-third of the workers (3,152 out of 10,204) in the
33 textile factories surveyed by the State Department of Labor in 1912.
Brazilians, Africans, and Europeans all seem to have been equally capable
of mastering the basic operations of factory work. Nineteenth-century
slaveowners had experimented successfully with slave labor in a variety
of industries; after abolition, Brazilians, among them sizable numbers of
Afro-Brazilians, would form the majority of industrial laborers in Rio de
Janeiro and other states which could not afford São Paulo's program of
subsidized immigration.[35]

34. Fernandes, Integração do negro, I, 74; Hall, "Immigration," 395; Rudolph M. Bell,
Fate and Honor, Family and Village: Demographic and Cultural Change in Rural Italy since
1800 (Chicago, 1979). Further supporting these findings is Virginia Yans-McLaughlin's book
on Family and Community: Italian Immigrants in Buffalo, 1880–1930 (Ithaca, 1971), which
finds that the overwhelming majority of immigrants were agricultural workers. "Those few
immigrants who had engaged in manufacturing did not compose an industrial proletariat"
(p. 27). See also Beiguelman, Formação do povo, 122.
35. "Condições do trabalho na indústria têxtil," 38–39. For discussions of the use of
slave labor in industry, see Beiguelman, Formação do povo, 122; Viotti da Costa, Da senzala
à colônia, 21; Douglas Cole Libby, Trabalho escravo e capital estrangeiro no Brasil: O
caso do Morro Velho (Belo Horizonte, 1984); and Jorge Siqueira, "Contribuição ao estudo
da transição do escravismo colonial para o capitalismo urbano-industrial no Rio de Janeiro:

We may concur then with Lúcio Kowarick's judgment that "the use of foreigners in São Paulo's industry was not due to better qualifications on the part of immigrants; indeed, they very rarely brought any previous industrial experience with them from their countries of origin."[36] This was even more so in the countryside, on the coffee plantations. I could find no instance of any planter ever arguing that former slaves lacked the necessary skills to carry out plantation labor. Such an argument would have been patently absurd, given that Afro-Brazilians and Africans had formed virtually the entire labor force in the coffee economy ever since the export boom began, in the early 1800s. Working with plantation records from the first decade of the century, Warren Dean concludes that there was no significant difference in productivity between Brazilian and immigrant plantation workers. Thus, the preferred position granted the latter "was partly founded upon discrimination against the national [Brazilian] workers, especially the blacks. Had they been paid equally on the basis of productivity without making distinctions of whiteness, the Italians might not have come at all."[37]

The reasons for the displacement of black labor, therefore, are not to be found in different levels of skill. Rather, the state's planters and industrialists argued, it was a question of attitude. And it is on precisely this point that Fernandes is most emphatic. Black people did not succeed in São Paulo's labor market because of their failure to don the mental armor of disciplined, motivated competitors in the marketplace. Their attitudes were "precapitalist," even "anticapitalist," he argues. They actually preferred poorly paid, irregular employment to the grinding discipline of the factory and the plantation. Lacking the "courage" and either the "material or moral" preparation to compete with the immigrants, the Afro-Brazilians retreated into "a self-condemnation to ostracism, dependence, and destruction" which "can be seen as a *silent protest* or as a suicidal effect of a complex of *social disillusionment*."[38]

A Companhia Luz Stearica (1854/1898)" (*dissertação de mestrado*, Universidade Federal Fluminense, 1984). A recent study of workers at textile, dock, urban transport, and electric power firms in Rio de Janeiro during this period found the overwhelming majority of their employees to be Brazilian; the percentage of Afro-Brazilians in each firm's work force varied between 30 and 40 percent. Adamo, "The Broken Promise," 55. English traveler Lilian Elwyn Elliott Joyce reports visiting a textile mill in the heavily Afro-Brazilian northeastern state of Pernambuco employing 3,500 workers, almost all of them locally born. "The manager of the mills, an Englishman, spoke highly of the Brazilian operatives; the company has never taken any measures to import other labour than that of the district." Elliott Joyce, *Brazil: Today and Tomorrow*, 2d ed. (New York, 1922), 231–232.

36. Kowarick, "Subjugation of Labour," 114; see also Hasenbalg, *Discriminação*, 165–166.

37. Dean, *Rio Claro*, 173–174.

38. Fernandes, *Integração do negro*, I, 17, 20, 51–58, emphasis in original.

These unfortunate attitudes were, in turn, part of a greater problem, that of the anomic social milieu which the black population created for itself. Disorganized family structure, alcoholism, crime, and obsession with sex all combined to lock the black community into a state of anomie and social pathology which, when added to the low skill levels and aversion to work which were their inheritance from slavery, eliminated whatever hope the Afro-Brazilians might have had of competing successfully for jobs and opportunities in São Paulo's expanding economy.[39]

Certainly São Paulo's turn-of-the-century planter and urban elites would have recognized their black population in Fernandes's writings, since the anomic, irresponsible, shiftless black people pictured there are perfectly in keeping with the elites' vision of the Afro-Brazilians. Recent research on Afro-Brazilian criminality and family structure during this period, however, has suggested that Fernandes overstates both the degree of social pathology and "disorganization" within the black community, and the effect which that "disorganization" had on black people's participation in the labor force.[40] Perhaps even more importantly, the Fernandes thesis fails to acknowledge the degree to which similar conditions prevailed among the immigrant population.

The black newspapers of the period offer clear evidence of the community's concern over the social problems facing it. Articles appeared regularly urging readers to adopt "modern" morality: to abandon alcohol, gambling, and other vices; to maintain public decorum; to refrain from adultery and loose living; and to educate their children in a respectable trade or profession. "At every step we see black men living from vice, a large number of women lewd and unkempt, vagabond children roaming

39. Ibid., I, chap. 2, 98–245.
40. On the black family, see Robert Slenes, "Escravidão e família; Padrões de casamento e estabilidade numa comunidade escrava (Campinas, século XIX)" (unpublished ms., no date); Moema de Poli Teixeira Pacheco, "'Aguentando a barra': A questão da família negra" (unpublished ms., 1982). Fernandes recognizes the existence of family solidarity among the black population and the importance of the family as a means of support for members experiencing economic difficulties. But since such a large proportion of family members was likely to be unemployed at any given time, he argues, such family solidarity actually became an obstacle to the advancement of its members. While immigrant families "used domestic solidarity to defeat economic adversity and 'to move upward,' among the blacks exactly the opposite occurred: domestic solidarity absorbed the best fruits of labor and of daily sacrifice, lowering the standard of living, savings, etc., and enforcing equality from below." If this was indeed the case, clearly it was a function of differential economic opportunities rather than family "pathology," which seems to have worked similarly in the two communities. Nevertheless, Fernandes concludes that this "domestic solidarity" among the Afro-Brazilians was "an anachronistic manifestation of tribal solidarity" and that "even the Italian 'disorganized family,' for example, possessed decided advantages over the 'black family.'" Fernandes, Integração do negro, I, 162–163, 198, 216. On black criminality in São Paulo during this period, see Boris Fausto, Crime e cotidiano: A criminalidade em São Paulo, 1880–1924 (São Paulo, 1984), 13–14, 51–57, 119, 167–172.

the streets. . . ." Clearly the community was suffering from at least some of the anomie which Fernandes attributes to it.[41]

That anomie does not seem to have been the exclusive property of the black population, however. It is striking to find, when one turns to the labor or neighborhood newspapers aimed at the immigrants, perfect mirror images of those articles, bemoaning the same kind of "moral decay" that was affecting the blacks.[42] In fact, one of the earliest such papers, the Spanish-language *El Grito del Pueblo*, while noting clear disparities in employment patterns between Afro-Brazilians and immigrants, found no appreciable differences in their respective levels of "anomie." The paper noted that Brazilian workers are always ready to turn out for the labor movement's parades or rallies, where they "applaud the orators, and cheer deliriously for Social Revolution. The next day, however, some go off to serve as fodder for the factories, others to the kitchen, others to clean the gardens and palaces of the bosses," and nothing changes. Why is this? Because "the Brazilian worker was only recently plucked from slavery, or he is the son or grandson of slaves. Because of this, his sense of civic responsibility is scarce, and he retains the meekness and brutishness instilled in him by the horrible torments of slavery." But the immigrants are no better. "[O]wing to their sufferings in Europe, they are content with little salary, and settle into tenement slums and huts, housed like beasts, eating black bread and bananas. They live worse than pigs." The paper concluded that "these unhappy people differ little from the ex-slaves of Brazil. If the latter were prostituted by the lash of slavery, the former were overcome by the misery of their wages."[43]

The immigrant and labor press tended to concur in viewing modern industrial life, rather than slavery, as the cause of the social ills which afflicted the entire working class, white as well as black. "Modern industry, calling women to the factory, ruins the life of the family and the home. Children run in the streets, unprotected, uneducated save by an environment corrupted by poverty, and the father takes refuge in looking the other way." As for the father, "factory labor turns him into a brute

41. "Grave erro!," *O Bandeirante* (São Paulo), Sept. 1918.

42. Clearly such articles reveal as much about the moralizing, middle-class outlook of the editors of these papers as they do about the black and immigrant workers being described. What is important to note is that observers of the black and immigrant communities who held such values found as much to criticize among the immigrants as among the blacks. On the editorship and readership of the black and labor presses, see, respectively, Bastide, "A imprensa negra do Estado de São Paulo," in his *Estudos afro-brasileiros* (São Paulo, 1973); Miriam Nicolau Ferrara, "A imprensa negra paulista (1915–1963)" (*dissertação de mestrado*, University of São Paulo, 1981); and Maria Nazareth Ferreira, *A imprensa operária no Brasil, 1880–1920* (Petrópolis, 1978).

43. "Sin creencias," *El Grito del Pueblo*, Aug. 20, 1899.

. . . lured into pointless gossip, to the bars, to alcohol, to gambling, to cursing." Another labor paper replied to charges that workers only use their holidays to get drunk, gamble, dissipate themselves, and commit crimes. There may be some truth to this, the paper confessed, but if so it is the fault of the factory system, which brutalizes its victims, and forces children to work before they are old enough to get a decent education.[44]

The black and labor presses displayed striking agreement in their judgment of the moral challenges which their respective communities faced. Alcohol, which was no respecter of race or ethnicity, was clearly the worst. Closely tied to alcohol abuse were the dance halls and annual carnival celebrations in which "men, women and children, all in the senseless insanity of a disgusting libertinism, reveal a state of moral degeneracy that almost provokes nausea." The black press worried, too, about the excesses of these popular celebrations, but saw the excesses as just as likely to come from white celebrants as from black. The black paper O Alfinete warned its readers against a number of particularly notorious dance halls, where "most of the dancers are white women, and our black women also take part, to our shame, and our race's moral corruption."[45]

While illegitimate births and the absence of male providers was clearly a concern in the black community, it was perceived as a problem among the immigrants as well. One paper ran a story urging its readers to stop giving charity to unmarried women who bear child after child. Interestingly, the specific case it cites is not a black woman but a young white one, "her face as white as a lily. . . ." The labor and black newspapers both recognized that domestic service posed one of the gravest risks to a young woman's honor (and, if she became pregnant, her future livelihood), and both published articles urging parents to send their daughters into any other occupation. Prostitution also received the attention of the labor press, which analyzed it not as the result of social anomie or exaggerated sexuality, but rather in purely economic terms. "It is in order to earn her living that a woman, today, becomes a prostitute. As evidence for this observation, simply note that the immense majority of residents of brothels had a humble origin and, before their fall, suffered the most

44. "O Alcoolismo," *Jornal Operário*, Oct. 29, 1905; "O dia dos operários," *O Grito do Povo*, May 1, 1900.

45. Articles on alcoholism appeared regularly in the black press; in the labor and immigrant press, see "O alcoolismo," *Jornal Operário*, Oct. 29, 1905; "Abaixo o alcool!," *O Carpinteiro* (São Paulo), June 1, 1905; "O alcoolismo," *O Proletário* (São Paulo), Oct. 1, 1911; "Contra l'alcoolismo," *Palestra Social* (São Paulo), Jan. 12, 1901; and others. On dancing and parties, see "Depois do baile," *O Grito Operário*, Feb. 4, 1920; "O carnaval," *O Internacional* (São Paulo), Feb. 6, 1921; "Carnaval," *O Internacional*, Jan. 17, 1922; "Carnaval," *O Grito Operário*, Feb. 18, 1920. On notorious dance halls, see "Carta aberta," *O Alfinete*, Oct. 12, 1918.

atrocious poverty. It is the enormous working class that keeps the whore-houses supplied."[46]

There is certainly evidence to indicate that, in the decades immediately following abolition, São Paulo's black community did suffer from the crime, poverty, and "social disorganization" described by Fernandes, though perhaps not to the degree which he suggests. But crime, poverty, and anomie were by no means confined to black people. To the degree that the Fernandes thesis conforms to the previously mentioned *ideologia da vadiagem*—and at times it is difficult to detect much difference between the two—it would apply to poor whites and immigrants as well as to blacks. In fact, it would apply to virtually every inhabitant of São Paulo, argued one of the labor newspapers, in response to elite assertions that if there were any people suffering from poverty in the state, it was because they were *vadios* (bums) who didn't want to work. If that is so, responded the anarchist paper *A Plebe*, then 90 percent of the state must be *vadios*, because 90 percent of the state is poor.[47]

In the absence of evidence documenting that the immigrants possessed clear-cut advantages in work skills and social integratedness over black people, the Fernandes thesis in its present form is impossible to sustain. One large chunk of it, however, is salvageable: its emphasis on the expectations, attitudes, and demands which the immigrants and Afro-Brazilians brought with them to the labor market.

Bargaining: Libertos, *Immigrants, and Employers*

As free wage labor replaced slave labor in the countryside and in the city, an unprecedented process of bargaining and negotiation took place between São Paulo's workers and employers. As Antônio Prado had predicted, supply and demand were replacing violence and coercion as the means of allocating labor, and the planters were by no means certain that they liked the change. What will happen, asked the *Província de S. Paulo*, "when the *libertos*, with this education [of freedom] behind them, organize to impose salary conditions, hours of work, protection for their children?" Such fears were by no means unfounded: the former slaves were not slow to perceive the possibilities opened by this new system, and had already begun to exploit them even before abolition. German visitor Maurice Lomberg, who traveled through the province in 1887, observed that

---

46. "A aleijada," *O Dois de Fevereiro* (São Paulo), Aug. 1905. On the perils of domestic service, "Uma menor violentada," *O Proletário*, July 15, 1911; "Cuidae de vossas filhas," *Getulino*, Apr. 13, 1924; "Reparando," *O Alfinete*, Sept. 28, 1921. On prostitution, "O fenómeno da prostituição," *A Plebe*, Jan. 19, 1935.

47. "O pobre é um vadio," *A Plebe*, June 9, 1917.

the passivity and sullen obedience which had characterized their behavior as slaves were starting to disappear. "They raised their heads and began to speak aggressively to their masters; they imposed the conditions under which they wanted to continue to work, and at the smallest offense they threatened to leave."[48]

What were the demands that former slaves presented to their erstwhile employers? In comparison with the United States, where postemancipation bargaining is richly documented in plantation records, the archives of government agencies, and testimony by former slaves themselves, the historical record of such bargaining in Brazil is sparse and patchy. Nevertheless, those features of the negotiations that emerge in contemporary accounts offer clear similarities to the tug-of-war which took place in other slave societies following abolition.[49]

While undeniably important, wages appear to have been almost a secondary consideration, and one pushed aside by the more pressing issue of working conditions. The *libertos'* overriding concern was to place as much distance as possible between themselves and their former status as slaves, and to ensure that their new conditions of employment bore as little resemblance as possible to servitude. For most freedmen and women, this meant not accepting employment on plantations where they had been slaves. As one *liberta* declared in explaining why she was leaving the plantation where she had been born and raised, "I'm a slave and if I stay here, I'll remain a slave." "The idea of remaining in the house where he was a slave is repugnant to the *liberto*," one contemporary observer noted, with the result that the mass flights from the plantations which had provoked abolition continued even after emancipation.[50]

Still, *libertos* trained in agricultural work and seeking employment in an overwhelmingly agrarian society had few alternative opportunities open to them. While some migrated to the cities, most remained in the countryside and sought plantation work, though under conditions which they insisted be quite different from those which had characterized slavery. Foremen and overseers were to carry whips no longer, and the locks were to be removed from the barracks in which the slaves had lived. Most

48. "Tiram as consequéncias," *A Província de S. Paulo*, Nov. 15, 1889; Maurício Lomberg, *O Brasil* (Rio de Janeiro, 1896), 342. My sincere thanks to Thomas Holloway for providing me with the latter citation and several subsequent ones.

49. For careful analyses of such bargaining in the United States and Cuba, see Leon F. Litwack, *Been in the Storm So Long: The Aftermath of Slavery* (New York, 1979); Eric Foner, *Nothing But Freedom: Emancipation and Its Legacy* (Baton Rouge, 1983); and Rebecca J. Scott, *Slave Emancipation in Cuba: The Transition to Free Labor, 1860–1899* (Princeton, 1985), 201–278.

50. Stein, *Vassouras*, 257; Francisco de Paula Lázaro Gonçalves, *Relatório apresentado à Associação Promotora de Immigração em Minas* (Juiz de Fora, 1898), 10–12.

former slaves preferred to leave the barracks entirely and live in individual huts or shacks located far from the main house and free of direct supervision by the employer. On plantations where these demands were met, the *libertos* were willing to accept employment. After all, as Lomberg had noted, these were the conditions under which they *wanted* to continue to work.[51]

The *libertos'* demands on these scores contrasted sharply with the initial willingness of the European immigrants, particularly the Italians, to work under conditions harsh in the extreme and, according to some observers, not far removed from those of slavery.[52] Such willingness was a function partly of the motives which had brought the immigrants to Brazil, and partly of the structure of the immigration program. One historian of Italian emigration notes that, at the turn of the century, "all of Italy's rural folk desired the fruits of economic progress. [But in regions] where aspirations for material betterment were expressed in broad associative behavior [such as cooperatives, political mobilization, etc.] there was little emigration. Where economic aspirations were integrated only with the welfare of the individual's nuclear family, emigration rates were high." Migrants were much more likely than nonmigrants to pursue goals of individual and family-based upward mobility at whatever cost, particularly since migration itself was often viewed as a short-term expedient to earn

51. Lomberg, *O Brasil*, 342–344; Pierre Denis, *Brazil*, 317–320. Denis reports on conditions in the neighboring state of Minas Gerais, where an absence of European immigration had forced planters to make what he considers to be excessive concessions to the *libertos*.

[T]he negroes lived scattered over the estate, far from the master's eyes, and assemble when they please at the fazenda, where the master waits for them, often in vain, to commence the day's work. . . . [T]he negro is indolent; work inspires him with a profound horror; he will allow himself to be driven to it only by hunger or by thirst; when all other resources fail him, only then he presents himself at the morning roll-call and offers his services. . . . One must have visited a few of the Minas plantations before one can realize precisely what advantage the São Paulo planters have derived from the free immigration of European laborers (318–320).

It is interesting to read a Brazilian anthropologist's account of his research during the late 1970s on an isolated rural black community in São Paulo, many of whose inhabitants refuse to this day to submit to plantation labor. One of the village's elders denounces modern plantation work as "the return of slavery. You won't believe it, but a long time ago the old people in the village used to tell us about how slavery used to be obligatory. But not today. The people are being enslaved again, but not everybody—just those who give themselves over to it," i.e., those who accept wage employment on local fazendas. Renato Queiroz, *Caipiras negros no vale do Ribeira* (São Paulo, 1983), 81. On the relaxed rhythm of agricultural work in the village, see 58–62.

52. Holloway reports a 1912 incident in which a black servant on a Campinas plantation, after being given an order which she considered beneath her station, retorted, "what do you take me for, an Italian?" Holloway, *Immigrants on the Land*, 105. On working and living conditions for immigrants on São Paulo fazendas, see Hall, "Origins of Mass Immigration," 121–140 and Holloway, 70–110.

money and return home with capital. As *Avanti!* observed in 1914, "the immense majority of the Italian immigrants here seek only to earn a living as best they can and put aside a nest egg which will allow them to return home or to venture into commerce and industry here in order to secure a higher social position." And since most of the immigrants "brought into the country little of capital or of personal accomplishment," the only way to build such a nest egg was through brute physical labor, paid at whatever wage was available.[53]

As previously mentioned, the immigration program played a central role in ensuring that immigrants would arrive in Brazil with "little of capital or of personal accomplishment." Emigrants with job skills and, more importantly, personal savings sufficient to pay their transatlantic fares were more likely to migrate to northwestern Europe, the United States, or Argentina. São Paulo's subsidies attracted the poorest of Europe's emigrants, who bargained with their new employers from a correspondingly weak position (as Martinho Prado had foreseen when he expressed his uninterest in "immigrants with money").[54]

Further adding to their vulnerability was a second aspect of the immigration program: its emphasis on families. Besides bringing in the poorest of Europe's emigrants, it brought them over in family units, seeking at all times, as a contemporary observer noted, "to reduce to a minimum the proportion of single men among those introduced at the public expense." Eighty percent of the people who passed through the immigrant hostel in São Paulo city came as families, averaging roughly five people per unit. Immigrants who sought work, therefore, had to worry not just about their own livelihood and their survival but about their spouses and children as well. When added to the immigrants' poverty, this produced a labor force which, during the early years of immigration, offered little resistance to employer demands.[55]

Besides weakening the immigrants' bargaining position, the priority placed on family units had a second, and perhaps even more important,

53. John D. McDonald, "Italy's Rural Social Structure and Emigration," *Occidente*, 12:5 (1956), 454; Hall, "Immigration," 399–401; Robert F. Foerster, *The Italian Emigration of Our Times* (Cambridge, MA, 1919), 316. See also Yans-McLaughlin, *Family and Community*, 34–36.

54. In response to persistent reports of the maltreatment and exploitation of its nationals on São Paulo plantations, the Italian government in 1902 forbade its citizens to accept subsidized passages to Brazil, a prohibition which remained in effect until the end of the subsidy program in 1927. Italians able to pay their own way remained free to emigrate. Holloway, *Immigrants on the Land*, 42–43. On "the melancholy condition" in which the immigrants arrived in São Paulo, "all covered with rags, disheartenment writ upon their brows," see Foerster, *Italian Emigration*, 316.

55. Denis, *Brazil*, 196, 216; Beiguelman, *Formação do povo*, 79; Holloway, *Immigrants on the Land*, 55.

motive, argues Verena Stolcke: providing cheap (often free) and abundant child and female labor for the plantations.[56] Plantation labor under slavery had been a family affair, involving women and children as well as adult males. Slave women worked in the fields, sorted coffee, performed household chores, cultivated subsistence plots, and cared for their children, who in turn helped in progressively heavier tasks as they got older. Following emancipation, the most intractable of the *libertos'* labor demands, and the most significant, as viewed both by the planters and by the former slaves themselves, was that women and children would no longer be used in field labor. Many families went further and withdrew their women and children from wage labor altogether, leaving the fazendeiros and their wives to complain bitterly about having to do their own washing and prepare their own meals. "If the *liberto* does little, the *liberta* does absolutely nothing. They laze in the doorway of their houses, yawning and napping, killing time in one long, unconscious *dulce far niente.*"[57]

As the planters structured the subsidized immigration program, they sought to ensure that their new workers would supply the female and child labor that the old workers were no longer willing to sell. To their great good fortune, this proved to be the case. Italian families in particular proved willing to put all their members to work, in a continuation of practices rooted in the old country. In the four Italian villages studied by Rudolph Bell, women had comprised between one-third and one-half of the agricultural labor force in 1881; even in families which did not permit women to accept paid employment, "an expected part of a wife's year-round labors would include joining the family in crop harvesting." This use of female labor continued in São Paulo, actively encouraged by the planters, as did the intensive use of child labor, which was widespread in Italy despite government efforts to curb it. As a result, noted a contemporary student of the Italian experience in São Paulo, "every child past toddling earns more than its current cost."[58]

The immigrants' willingness to send all members of the family to work

56. Stolcke, "The Exploitation of Family Morality: Labor Systems and Family Structure on São Paulo Coffee Plantations, 1850–1979," in *Kinship Ideology and Practice in Latin America*, Raymond T. Smith, ed. (Chapel Hill, 1985), 266–274.

57. Quotation from *A Província de São Paulo*, Feb. 6, 1889. On *libertos'* antipathy toward female and child labor, see Gonçalves, *Relatório*, 11 and Stein, *Vassouras*, 262. This desire of black families to protect women and children from the rigors of field labor would seem to undercut Fernandes's observations concerning the lack of family feeling among Afro-Brazilians.

58. On labor practices in Italy, see Bell, *Fate and Honor*, 118–137; Yans-McLaughlin, *Family and Community*, 183–184; and Foerster, *Italian Emigration*, 85, 319. On the importance of family labor on the São Paulo plantations, see Stolcke, "Exploitation of Family Morality" and Zuleika M. Forcioni Alvin, "Emigração, família e luta: Os italianos em São Paulo, 1870–1920" (*dissertação de mestrado*, Universidade de São Paulo, 1983), 97–157.

not only won them a preferred position on the plantations, but also enabled many of them to accumulate the cash savings which eluded the Afro-Brazilians. Indeed, given the low wages on the plantations, only with multiple members of the family working was it possible to even make ends meet. "Only under the most ideal conditions," the Italian consul reported in 1901, "can a single colono make enough to live on." Family labor became not simply a means of upward mobility, but the key to survival on the plantations.[59]

Much the same was true in the factories of the capital, where workers' employability was determined less by their skill level than by their willingness "to submit to the discipline of production regulated by whistles which subdivided working days often longer than 12, 13, or 14 hours, in which women and children took part. . . ." As on the plantations, the immigrants' decision to subject themselves and their children to such conditions gave them a distinct competitive advantage over the Afro-Brazilians. The initial stages of industrialization in São Paulo would therefore be based on immigrant labor rather than black, and on labor carried out by every member of the immigrant family. The importance of this fact, and its implications for the industrial development of São Paulo, were intuitively recognized by British traveler Lilian Elwyn Elliott Joyce, who exclaimed that "to see this [São Paulo's industrial growth] and to watch the crowds of pretty chattering Italian girls pouring out of Braz and Mooca factories at noon or evening is to obtain a revelation of the newer South America."[60]

This "newer South America" offered no place for the Afro-Brazilians. They had bargained too hard, and demanded too much. Some of the more enlightened employers could understand the motives behind those demands, and how the experience of slavery had produced a deep determination among all Brazilians, and particularly black ones, to avoid conditions of employment at all reminiscent of the slave regime. But even these sympathetic observers joined in the general rejoicing over the coming of the immigrants, "which contributed greatly to rescue our fazendeiros from their dependence on the *libertos*, and from the just demands presented by the latter, after so many years of barbarous oppression."[61] Those demands

59. Holloway, *Immigrants on the Land*, 141–142; see also Alvin, "Emigração" and Stolcke, "Exploitation of Family Morality." For similar observations on the importance of family labor in coffee production in Colombia, see Charles Bergquist, *Labor in Latin America: Comparative Essays on Chile, Argentina, Venezuela, and Colombia* (Stanford, 1986), 320–329.

60. Kowarick, "Subjugation of Labour," 114; Elliot, *Brazil*, 268. Labor organizers despaired of ever mobilizing these "pretty chattering Italian girls" because of the iron control which their fathers, husbands, and brothers exercised over them, and the refusal of these latter "to give up, even for a little while, the miserable sum" which their wives, daughters, and sisters brought home. *Avanti!*, Dec. 16, 1907, quoted in Hall, "Immigration," 402. Yans-

formed part of a bargain that São Paulo's employers did not care to accept and, because of their ability to import and hire European workers, did not have to accept.

By keeping the labor market oversupplied with white workers, São Paulo's government ensured that the goal first articulated by state legislators in the 1870s would be realized: that workers would have to seek out employers rather than vice versa. Of course, employers at the time did not see it that way. Bitter complaints about the short supply and instability (i.e., its tendency to flit from job to job in search of better wages) of immigrant labor persisted throughout this period, from planters and industrialists alike, who argued that it was the chronic shortage of adult workers that forced them to resort to child labor. But as several historians and contemporary observers of the period note, child labor was widespread in São Paulo's plantations and factories not because of the shortage of adult labor, but rather because of its abundance. Adult wages were so low that, in order to survive, families had no recourse but to send their children to work—which of course drove wages even lower. And by giving preference to immigrants who came with their families, the state had acted to ensure a more than adequate supply of child, as well as adult, labor.[62]

So lavish was the oversupply of labor in São Paulo that it helped produce an unexpected and unintended outcome: the growth of industry in the state. This was hardly the goal which the planters had had in mind when they first designed the subsidy program, but the combination of coffee export earnings (which provided investment capital and the beginnings of a local market) and abundant labor turned São Paulo by the 1920s into the most important industrial center in Brazil, surpassing Rio de Janeiro.[63] And despite the demand for labor generated by this growth, according to the U.S. consul in São Paulo in 1922, as a result of immigration "it is doubtful that there exists anywhere an industrial sector that offers better

---

McLaughlin similarly notes the enormous pressure placed on Italian children in Buffalo to contribute wage income to the family economy. "Because of this transference of family discipline into the factory, [employers] had few problems obtaining the highest possible output from children" (*Family and Community*, 192).

61. João Pedro da Veiga Filho, *Estudo econômico e financeiro sobre o Estado de São Paulo* (São Paulo, 1896), 69.

62. On wage trends during this period, and the high incidence of child labor in response to those trends, see Hall, "Origins of Mass Immigration," 143–144; Maram, *Anarquistas, imigrantes*, 119–124; and Pinheiro and Hall, *Classe operária*, II, 135–138.

63. The impact of an abundant labor supply on São Paulo's industrialization is discussed in Wilson Cano, *Raizes da concentração industrial em São Paulo*, 2d ed. (São Paulo, 1977), 126–128. Cano notes that industrial wages in São Paulo lagged significantly behind those of Rio de Janeiro and Rio Grande do Sul, giving Paulista industry a competitive edge over the rest of the country (p. 248, n. 24).

working conditions from the point of view of the employer. Workers in the various industries and workshops are abundant, hardworking, and they earn low salaries. The Portuguese workers in particular will do anything to preserve their jobs. . . ." The consul described the Italians and Spaniards as more "independent" in spirit, but executives at the Canadian-owned São Paulo Light, Power, and Tramway Company found Italian workers just as tractable as the Portuguese: speaking of their motormen and conductors, they noted that "a large majority of these men are Italians who would do anything rather than lose their daily pay. . . ."[64]

Restructuring the Labor Market: The Immigrants Lose their Preference

The desperation of these relatively privileged members of São Paulo's labor force is perhaps the most convincing proof of the efficacy of the state's labor policies. The planter state had sought policies which would keep labor cheap and insecure, and it found them. Such victories are never permanent, however. In the short run or in the long, they produce resistance and response. In the case of the immigrants, that resistance and response took various forms. One was the simple act of returning to their countries of origin, or pursuing more promising opportunities in Argentina or the United States. Another reaction was to shop about from plantation to plantation, or from factory to factory, in search of marginally better wages or working conditions, much as the *libertos* had done after abolition. A third was to pursue individual goals of upward mobility, pooling the combined earnings of family members to buy a small farm in the countryside or open a small business in the city. And a final response was collective: joining an urban labor movement which enlisted growing numbers of adherents in the cities, and taking part in strike actions in both the cities and the countryside during the early decades of the century.[65]

These efforts by the immigrants to further improve their labor market position led to a gradual cooling of the Paulista elites' initial rejoicing over immigration. By 1900, articles in the planters' *Revista Agrícola* complained about the immigrants' "inconstancy" and "ingratitude" in terms

---

64. Pinheiro and Hall, *Classe operária*, II, 126; "Increased Salary of Motormen and Conductors" (no date, but internal evidence suggests early 1920s), Arquivo do Eletropaulo (São Paulo), pasta 29.005, 1906–1924.

65. On these various strategies of resistance, see Holloway, *Immigrants on the Land*; Alvin, "Emigração"; Stolcke and Hall, "The Introduction of Free Labour"; and Fausto, *Trabalho urbano*. Historians have tended to underestimate the importance of strikes in the countryside because of their lack of success. For evidence that they occurred not infrequently, and were taken quite seriously by planters, see Stolcke and Hall, 185–186; Dean, *Rio Claro*, 179–180; and Holloway, *Immigrants on the Land*, 104–108.

much the same as those applied to the *libertos* in the 1890s: "nothing ties them to the soil; . . . they readily change their employers after each harvest. No more nomadic people could be imagined; they change incessantly from fazenda to fazenda." Particularly galling was the purchase by immigrant workers of their own small farms and homesteads. *O Combate* noted in 1919 that "certain fazendeiros have come to detest land sale agents today in the same way that those of yesteryear detested the abolitionists." Just as the abolitionists had lured slaves away from the plantations by inciting them to flight, so by the late 1910s real estate agents were luring workers away by offering to sell them their own homesteads.[66]

As employers' enthusiasm for the immigrants waned, so too did the state's, at least in that arm of the state responsible for labor policy. A series of articles published in the bulletin of the State Department of Labor during the 1910s traced the dangers of the labor gluts which periodically swept the state. While such gluts undoubtedly redounded to employers' short-term advantage, they also promoted criminality, *vagabundagem*, hunger, and generalized social tension. As wages fell in the countryside, the official publication argued, the result was an inflow of poverty-stricken immigrants into the capital, where they live "as parasites, as beggars, as invalids, feeding themselves on charity, by hustling, and by crime. . . ." During the hiatus of European immigration caused by World War I, department staffers even began to rethink some of the negative consequences of "the privilege conferred on foreign immigration to supply workers for agriculture," the result of which had been to marginalize São Paulo's black and caboclo workers in the land of their birth. Articles published in the bulletin during the war years urged employers to reconsider the many virtues and abilities which Brazilian workers brought with them to the workplace—foremost among which, they noted, was the Brazilian worker's well-known disinclination to join unions or strike.[67]

66. *Revista Agrícola* (1899), 50, 350–352, 382–386; (1901), 166–167, 311; (1902), 75–84; (1904), 218–221. Again, my thanks to Thomas Holloway for acquainting me with this material and making it available to me. The observation from *O Combate* is quoted in Alba Maria Figueiredo Morandini, "O trabalhador migrante nacional em São Paulo, 1920–1923" (*tese de mestrado*, Pontifícia Universidade Católica-São Paulo, 1978), 78.

67. In the *Boletim do Departamento Estadual do Trabalho* (São Paulo), see: "O Departamento Estadual do Trabalho em 1914," 3: 12 (1915), 471–472; "A legislação do trabalho sob o ponto de vista immigratorio," 6: 23 (1917), 270; "O trabalhador nacional," 5: 20 (1916), p. 352; "Localização dos trabalhadores nacionais," 7: 27 (1918), 301–340; and others. These articles acknowledge quite openly the labor market preference granted to the immigrants over Brazilians.

Abandoned to their fate, with no assistance from the government, [the *libertos* and caboclos] were easy and defenseless prey to the illnesses which conquered them, wasting their bodies, reducing their capacity for work, and destroying their race. While this was happening, we opened our pocketbook to the European immigrants,

São Paulo's elites still had considerable financial and ideological capital invested in the notion of the superiority of immigrant labor, and after the war ended Governor Washington Luís announced the state's intention to continue its policy of maintaining "the cheapness of labor, and particularly agricultural labor, by the introduction on a large scale of honest, hard-working immigrants." But as the 1920s continued, and more immigrants either bought their way out of the wage labor market or continued to engage in hard bargaining with employers, the aura surrounding foreign-born workers darkened and faded away. A poll of Paulista fazendeiros in 1925 found a majority of them now willing to employ Brazilian labor, and two years later the program of subsidized European immigration was finally terminated.[68]

The impact on labor relations in the state was immediate. In 1928, for the first time since records had been kept, Brazilian migrants into São Paulo outnumbered European immigrants. The following year, one of the black newspapers in São Paulo city reported on the turnaround in labor conditions in the countryside.

> [T]he men of color of our hinterland, those whose labor consists of the cultivation of the soil and the business of agriculture, are in excellent conditions as workers, enjoying the same advantages and benefits as the other men of the soil. Black workers are as highly valued as the Italians, who are São Paulo's agricultural workers par excellence. Which is to say that the black of the hinterland, the colono or day laborer of color, has succeeded, more rapidly than

---

who have no love for this land and their eyes fixed on their distant Fatherland, where many of them return after having saved some money. We gave them everything: land, housing, food, tools, medical assistance, and guaranteed work ("O saneamento da população agrária do Brasil," 6: 23 [1917], 245–246).

Kowarick nicely captures the "rehabilitation" of the Brazilian worker during the war years.

His lack of ambition came to be seen as the parsimoniousness of one who is content with little, is not after easy gain, and above all, does not make demands; lack of constancy was translated into versatility and aptitude for new kinds of work, while lack of discipline was metamorphosed into stoutheartedness and dignity. The former wanderer was ready to go wherever he was needed. His love of adventure and scrapping changed into fearlessness and courage to perform risky tasks, while his wariness became a sound characteristic with which to reject spurious ideas, so much in vogue at the time. . . . His indolence came not from sloth or a vagabond nature, but from lack of opportunity to work, while his vices were now seen as a result of the misery in which he had been bogged down for centuries and from which he must now be removed ("Subjugation of Labour," 119).

68. Morandini, "O trabalhador migrante," 76; Joseph Love, *São Paulo in the Brazilian Federation, 1889–1937* (Stanford, 1980), 11, 75.

the blacks of the city, in establishing himself vis-à-vis his peers, obliging them to recognize his value and worth.[69]

Though the dominance of European workers would last longer in the cities, by the 1930s and '40s Afro-Brazilians were entering factory employment in ever larger numbers as well, coming to form part of São Paulo's industrial proletariat. As a white worker who lived through this period recalls, their entry into the urban workplace was due to the same factor as their earlier exclusion: state policy governing the labor market. If immigration had not been reduced and "there hadn't been a shortage of manpower, the blacks would never have managed to get into the factories. Everything would have stayed the way it was. If the immigrants had continued to come the bosses would have given them the preference, leaving the Brazilian worker behind."[70]

Conclusions

Throughout this essay I have sought to stress how evolving interactions among employers, workers (both black and white), and the state explain the marginalization of Afro-Brazilian workers in São Paulo's postabolition economy and society. Clearly, the legacy of slavery helped shape this process, by producing both employers unaccustomed and unwilling to bargain with their former slaves, and a former slave population with very specific demands concerning the conditions under which they would work as free men and women. But that legacy applied throughout most of Brazil, yet "in no other place in the country [besides São Paulo] were white immigrants so clearly the 'winners' and blacks the 'losers' [in the process] of economic development and prosperity."[71]

The explanation for São Paulo's uniqueness is to be found in state policy which undercut workers' bargaining position by flooding the labor market with European immigrants. In addition to keeping wages low and weakening a labor movement committed to racial equality and interracial solidarity, this policy enabled employers to turn their backs on those workers who sought to drive the hardest and most demanding bargains.

69. "Pequenas considerações," *O Clarim d'Alvorada* (São Paulo), Jan. 6, 1929.

70. Fernandes, *Integração do negro*, I, 157. Afro-Brazilian entry into the industrial labor force was further assisted by state action at the national level in the form of the Lei de Nacionalização do Trabalho, enacted by the Vargas regime in 1931, which required at least two-thirds of the labor force in industrial and commercial establishments to be native-born Brazilians. Agriculture was explicitly exempted from this requirement. *Diário Oficial dos Estados Unidos do Brasil*, Aug. 25, 1931, pp. 13,552–13,558.

71. Hasenbalg, *Discriminação*, 254.

Those workers were initially the former slave *libertos;* but by the first decades of the 1900s, the immigrants and their children had become increasingly aggressive and effective in the pursuit of their individual and collective interests. Turning the preferences which they had been granted by the state government to tangible advantage, they started to make demands that both the Paulista elites and the small, native-born middle class found increasingly objectionable. The result was the redefinition of state policy in the mid-1920s to end the official preference given to Europeans, and the subsequent gradual restoration of Afro-Brazilians to a competitive, if subordinate, position in the market for manual labor.[72]

This 40-year hiatus from the labor market was extremely damaging to the Afro-Brazilians, as emerges both in testimony from the period and in the marked disparities between São Paulo's black and white populations documented in the censuses of 1940 and 1950.[73] By depriving Afro-Brazilians of work experience and income, and reinforcing racist assumptions concerning the unemployability of black people, it would make that much more difficult their struggle in subsequent years to play a full and equal role in the life of their society. Florestan Fernandes has argued that understanding the nature of race relations in his country is essential to understanding and shaping "the very destiny of democracy in Brazil."[74] As a democratic government celebrates the centennial of the abolition of slavery, it would do well to consider how its predecessors worked to bar blacks access to jobs, livelihood, and the pursuit of happiness, both during the years of slavery and after, and what it might do, even at this late date, to right those historical wrongs and remove the obstacles to black advancement created by earlier state policy.

72. On rising anti-immigrant feeling among the middle class, see Steven Topik, "Middle-Class Brazilian Nationalism, 1889–1930: From Radicalism to Reaction," *Social Science Quarterly*, 59:1 (1978), 93–103 and Boris Fausto, *A Revolução de 1930: Historiografia e história*, 8th ed. (São Paulo, 1982), 36–37. On the entry of Afro-Brazilians into the industrial proletariat, see Fernandes, *Integração do negro*, II, 160–324 and Maria Isaura Pereira de Queiroz, "Coletividades negras. Ascensão socio-económica dos negros no Brasil e em São Paulo," in her *Cultura, sociedade rural, sociedade urbana no Brasil* (São Paulo, 1978), 231–262.

73. For discussions of the inequalities documented in those censuses, see Fernandes, *Integração do negro*, II, 120–160 and Hasenbalg, *Discriminação*, 163–193.

74. Fernandes, *Integração do negro*, I, 10.

"Mud-Hut Jerusalem": Canudos Revisited

ROBERT M. LEVINE

THE rise and fall of the holy city of Belo Monte, at Canudos in the northeastern Brazilian backlands (1893–97), traumatized the new republic and shattered its facade of harmonious national progress. The settlement was founded on the site of an abandoned ranch in the remote Bahian sertão as a holy refuge by Antônio Conselheiro, a charismatic lay preacher and rebuilder of churches and cemeteries. It grew virtually overnight to number more than five thousand clay-roofed huts scattered below a ring of hills and low mountains. By 1896, its swollen population made it the largest urban nucleus in the state after Salvador, the capital, seven hundred kilometers distant. In late 1897, Canudos was crushed after a year-long war waged by the Brazilian government to destroy the settlement and its fearsome leader.[1]

Popular movements are often seen as collective expressions demanding social change, or as collective struggles to resist change which has already taken place. In some ways both modes of analysis are useful in Canudos's case. I propose, however, that understanding of the events at Canudos is best accomplished by situating Canudos within the cultural context of the rural population.[2] Such an approach emphasizes the composition of the lower-class actors at Canudos and the role of its leader, seen less as

1. I would like to thank my colleagues Linda Lewin, Warren Dean, Joseph L. Love, Steven Topik, Teresita Martínez-Vergne, Gerald M. Greenfield, Todd Diacon, and José Carlos Sebe Bom Meihy for their suggestions, and the staff of the Centro de Estudos Euclydes da Cunha (Yara Bandeira de Ataide, Renato Ferraz) and José Calasans for their help during my stay in Salvador.
2. This approach is described by James C. Scott in his article "Resistance without Protest and without Organization: Peasant Opposition to the Islamic *Zakat* and the Christian Tithe," *Comparative Studies in Society and History,* 29:1 (July 1987), 417–420, and by Patricia R. Pessar, "Unmasking the Politics of Religion: The Case of Brazilian Millenarianism," *Journal of Latin American Lore,* 7:2 (Winter 1981), 255–278. See also Pessar, "When Prophecy Prevails: A Study of Millenarianism in Brazil" (Ph.D. diss., University of Chicago, 1976) and "Revolution, Salvation, Extermination: The Future of Millenarianism in Brazil," in *Predicting Sociocultural Change,* Susan Abbott and John van Willigen, eds. (Athens, GA, 1980), 95–114.

a crazed fanatic than as an orthodox lay Catholic with intense feelings of social justice and opposition to slavery.

The Canudos "rebellion" left an indelible legacy on the republic. Taken to be a symbol of the clash between urban "progress" and rural "backwardness" in the early republican years, Canudos has been recalled frequently over the decades, often in a romanticized vein. The seminal narrative treatment is Os sertões, published in 1902 by Euclides da Cunha.[3] Called the hallmark of Brazil's intellectual coming of age, it has become a sacred text—leaving its interpretation of Canudos, in turn, virtually untouchable. Da Cunha intermixes a passionate description of the events, colored by his anguish over what he saw as an urban southerner and a war correspondent, with his deep ambivalence over the nature of the fanatical backlands peasantry, the national-racial question, and the peasants' tenacious struggle to preserve their lives.[4]

Da Cunha proclaimed to his countrymen that Canudos was "our Vendée."[5] Sensitive to the suffering he saw during the final military assaults on Canudos and to the brutality exhibited on both sides of the conflict, da Cunha's account reflected his dualist view of Brazilian society as irrevocably divided between the archaic primitivism of the backlands and the progressive culture of the coastal cities. Ambivalence tormented him: he profoundly respected the tenacity of the rural peasantry, but considered them racially degenerate. His deep-seated positivism led him to believe that the republic was threatened by Conselheiro's stubborn resistance to modernity, of which one aspect was nostalgia for the monarchy. Dismayed by both military factionalism and monarchist plots after the birth of the republic, internecine jockeying among the states, and a severe economic depression in the early 1890s, da Cunha and others of like mind came to see Canudos as a challenge to the new civilian government in the federal capital and a threat even to the nation itself.

The chroniclers describing and interpreting Canudos have claimed evi-

---

3. Samuel Putnam, translator's introduction to Rebellion in the Backlands (Os Sertões) (hereafter RB) (Chicago, 1944), iii. In 1984, Canudos was the focus of a novel by the prominent Peruvian novelist, Mario Vargas Llosa, translated into English as The War of the End of the World, Helen R. Lane, trans. (New York, 1984). A similar novel appeared in France in 1953, by Lucien Marchal. It was translated as The Sage of Canudos by Charles Duff (New York, 1954).

4. See Agrippino Grieco, Evolução da prosa brasileira (Rio de Janeiro, 1933), 281–286; Stefan Zweig, Brazil: Land of the Future (New York, 1941), 159–160; Bezerra de Freitas, História da literatura brasileira (Pôrto Alegre, 1939), 251–252; Eduardo Portella, Literatura e realidade nacional, 2d ed. (Rio de Janeiro, 1971), 36–37; Nicolau Sevcenko, Literatura como missão: Tensões sociais e criação cultural na Primeira República (São Paulo, 1983), esp. chap. 4.

5. Indeed, Putnam tells us that da Cunha thought of using "our Vendée" instead of Os sertões as his title. See RB, 162, n. 179.

dence of primitive and even psychotic factors underlying the settlement of this place of refuge. They have painted Conselheiro larger than life, much in the way the rumors of his saintliness reached backlands peasants, and in the same way that his reputation as an antisocial threat to the republic reached members of the region's dominant elite. Canudos entered the Brazilian consciousness as a fearful symbol of primitive impulses of racially mixed peasants manipulated by a false messiah. But what can be pieced together from the historical record of Conselheiro's life and career from the point that he emerged as a peripatetic holy man to his death and the destruction of his holy city brings to light not a reckless, malevolent antisocial movement of religious deviants but a story of a hopeful and innocent settlement of rural migrants, neither apocalyptic nor evil. Canudos was, no more and no less, borrowing E. P. Thompson's phrase, "the institutional expression of social relationships." To examine those relationships is the goal of this revisitation of Conselheiro's tragic "mud-hut Jerusalem."

Several new emphases emerge from a reappraisal of the historical record.[6] In 20 years of wandering through the northeastern backlands until mid-1893 and in most cases until the destruction of Canudos itself, Antônio Conselheiro exercised the role of a dedicated lay missionary who counseled against civic and religious disobedience. His followers were not aberrant primitives mesmerized by religious fanaticism, as chroniclers described, but a heterogeneous community whose members included emancipated slaves (crioulos), Indian-Caucasian mamelucos, rural peasants, men and women from small towns and other urban settlements, and even some linked by family ties to leading elite networks on the coast. The settlement was populous, especially for the backlands, but probably nearer to 15,000 or 20,000 residents than the oft-cited total of 25,000 and even 30,000. Peasants comprised the majority. In the main they were caboclos, northeasterners of mixed African, Amerindian, and European racial origin, although the residents of Canudos represented a much broader socioethnic spectrum than conventionally believed.[7] To outsiders, they all were jagunços, as cowboys of the backlands were traditionally

6. Sources consulted include the records of the Brazilian army stored at the 6th Military Region headquarters in Salvador, the archives of the Bahian State Police, records of the Curia of the Catholic church in Salvador, Antônio Conselheiro's own homilies and sermons, manuscripts in the Arquivo Público in Salvador, and material collected at the Núcleo do Sertão of the Centro de Estudos Brasileiros.

7. The term caboclo has varied meanings in Brazil. In the most general sense, a caboclo is the Brazilian approximation of the Spanish American mestizo, commonly a lower-class peasant. Some maintain that the caboclo is essentially a northern type; others contend that the caboclo is a phenomenon of the South. See James B. Watson, "Way Station of Modernization: The Brazilian Caboclo," Watson et al., eds., Brazil: Papers Presented in the Institute for Brazilian Studies, Vanderbilt University (Nashville, 1953), 9.

called to distinguish them from agricultural peasants of the coast. After the events of Canudos, the term *jagunço* took on a pejorative connotation, that of *cangaceiro* or outlaw—one among many ways in which Canudos burrowed into the national psyche.

The decision to neutralize and finally demolish Canudos resulted from a convergence of factors all linked to state, regional, and national over-reaction in the wake of the instability of the new republic. Rural bosses, the *coronéis*, naturally felt threatened by Conselheiro's growing spell over sertão residents. Moreover, though openly tolerated and even wel-comed by many backlands parish priests, some of whom were also local merchants, Conselheiro threatened the church hierarchy at the bishop-ric level. The main reason was that ultramontanist pressures from Rome, initiated in the late nineteenth century, demanded that bishops reassert control over parishes which for decades—and not only in the case of Conselheiro in the rural Northeast—had acted independently and with zeal. The deeply felt religious expression of faith which outsiders labeled "mystical" and "fanatical" represented a continuation of a spiritual revival among both laity and rural clergy which had begun in the 1860s.

A fact which is not generally known is that many Canudos residents escaped as the fighting intensified. Some males who survived were not executed, and more than a hundred women and children were brought to Salvador and ultimately reunited with family members or cared for under the aegis of a committee of civic leaders. Nevertheless, Canudos repre-sented a trauma that raised far-reaching questions about Brazil's national identity and racial composition. Underlying the bravado of the era's opti-mism lay the reality that representative forms of government rested on a national population 85 percent illiterate and mostly living in misery.[8] In these circumstances, the attempt of Canudos's believers to live together outside the arm of the menacing institutional world of republican Brazil generated real fears about the ability of the republic to survive, yet it actu-ally represented only one of many "disturbances" and uprisings of masses of the population throughout Brazilian history.[9] Perhaps the most impor-tant lesson that Canudos offers is that it confirmed the elites' attitudes of rigid biologic determinism, of latent fear of the rural underclass, and re-veals the fragility of the First Republic and the brutal lengths to which its officials were willing to go to crush discord.

8. The 1872 census counted 84.2 percent of the total population as illiterate; the 1890 census found 85.2 percent illiterate. In rural areas, the percentages certainly were higher. See Armin K. Ludwig, *Brazil: A Handbook of Historical Statistics* (Greenwich, 1985), Table V–8.

9. See Putnam, translator's introduction, *RB*, xiv.

Antônio Conselheiro

Antônio Vicente Mendes Maciel was born in 1828 in the *sertanejo* vila of Santo Antônio de Quixeramobim, in Ceará. His father, Vicente, was initially a successful businessman who owned several "good houses" on Quixeramobim's square. The boy was coffee-colored (*moreno*) in pigmentation, perhaps with Calabaça Indian ancestry, and described as pallid, since he spent most of his time indoors, working for his father. He was short of stature, rawboned, with black eyes and an aquiline nose, and small hands and feet. As a boy he was enrolled in a school taught by Professor Manuel Antônio Ferreira Nobre and was taught Portuguese, French, and Latin. Some of his schoolmates later took their places in the regional elite —including Major Eufrásio Nogueira, police chief in Quixeramobim, and João Brígido dos Santos, a newspaperman, lawyer, and polemicist.[10] The Mendes Maciel clan was a "good family," in the language of the day, part of the "conservative classes," although not particularly wealthy. Members of the clan who lived in the backlands between Quixeramobim and Tamboril had been engaged in a blood feud since 1833 with the more powerful and affluent Araújos, and Antônio's grandfather had been one of several Maciéis arrested for their part in the feud and lynched while in police custody. Antônio Mendes Maciel himself is not known to have participated in any of the hostilities.

His mother, Maria Joaquina de Nascimento, died when he was six, and his father, described in a memoir by João Brígido (written before Antônio became notorious) as a "semivisionary and iconoclast," died when his eldest son was 26. Vicente had been an alcoholic, aggressive to the point of violence, even against his wife when she was alive. His death in 1855 followed a gradual decline in the family's economic fortunes worsened by overspeculation.[11] Now responsible for three unmarried sisters, Antônio inherited little; most of the assets in his father's estate went to pay debts. He took over his father's business and filed papers to back the remaining loans with a mortgage. He was married in 1857, to a cousin from Quixeramobim, Brasilina Laurentina de Lima, known for her ill temper and pugnacity. Still in debt, Antônio liquidated the business and became a

10. Abelardo Fernando Montenegro, *Antônio Conselheiro* (Fortaleza, 1954), 11; José Calasans, "Canudos não euclidiano," in *Canudos: Subsídios para a sua reavaliação histórica*, José Augusto Vaz Sampaio Neto et al., eds. (Rio de Janeiro, 1986), 13. Da Cunha's morbid fascination with Conselheiro's mysticism produced a distorted portrait which for the most part has been accepted uncritically.

11. See João Brígido, *Ceará (Homems e fatos)* (Rio de Janeiro, 1969), 43. The article was published in June 1893, before the Masseté incident reached the public. Calasans notes that it devoted more attention to Vicente Mendes Maciel than to his son, Antônio.

tutor in Portuguese, arithmetic, and geometry at a nearby fazenda. In 1859, he worked as a shop clerk, then opened a dry goods store in Tamboril and another in Campo Grande. Both failed.

Antônio tried to earn money as a *requerente* (a kind of nonlicensed lawyer), taking simple cases in the *foro* (tribunal) in Ipu. There, his wife ran away with a sergeant in the Ceará militia, João de Melo; some years later, she abandoned him, becoming a beggar in the streets of Sobral, crazed, before dying. Maciel's financial fortunes and presumably his emotional state continued to decline, although he struggled to reassert his former position within the system, not outside of it, becoming even at one point a traveling salesman. We know nothing further about this period in his life.[12] Antônio emerged in the early 1870s wandering in the backlands of southern Ceará and continued to roam through the arid regions of Bahia, Pernambuco, and Sergipe, "cadaverous," having taken the role of a penitential pilgrim. Walking from town to town, he asked to be permitted to rebuild dilapidated walls of churches and cemeteries fallen into disrepair. In time he also designed and constructed small reservoirs, chapels, and even small churches, aided by local parishioners who worked without wages and by disciples who followed him. His first recorded employment was to rebuild the Rainha dos Anjos chapel in Itapicurú (Bahia) in 1874.[13]

Antônio embraced an austere Catholicism, characterized by a brooding spirituality and message of pious responsibility. His unshakable faith has never been questioned; to those who encountered him he projected a "sense of foreboding . . . pervasive and unappeasable." Indeed, he was a spellbinding orator: when he gave sermons, a survivor of Canudos said later, "his listeners felt as if they were flying up to the clouds."[14] Although later analysts criticized his emphasis on frugality and penitential redemption as "primitive" or rural "folk" Catholicism, no evidence suggests that he advocated heresy or even digressed significantly from the Catholic precepts common to the region. Some of his prophecies were enigmatic, but he mostly spoke of things which touched the lives and concerns of hinterlanders—debts, morality, the government, and individual destiny. Consistent with lay Northeast traditions antedating Conselheiro's career, handfuls of *beatos* (disciples) wandered with him across the dusty sertão

12. José Carlos de Ataliba Nogueira, *Antônio Conselheiro e Canudos: Revisão histórica*, 2d ed. (São Paulo, 1978), 4–5. De Melo was a *furriel*, an intermediate rank between *cabo* and *sargento*.

13. Unless indicated otherwise, all place names pertain to Bahia.

14. The last-quoted words are by Dona Evangelina, taken prisoner during the fourth military expedition. (Manoel Funchal Garcia, *Do litoral ao sertão* [Rio de Janeiro, 1965], 172.) The preceding description was written ironically, about John Calvin, but it fits Conselheiro perfectly. See John Gross, review of William J. Bouwsma's *John Calvin: A Sixteenth-Century Portrait* (Oxford, 1987), in *The New York Times*, Dec. 8, 1987, p. 29.

trails. Some of the women had formerly been prostitutes.[15] Observers noted his pilgrim's clothing, his air of grim austerity, and his unconcern with worldly goods. He slept only a few hours each night, usually on the floor without a blanket. It was said that he was especially kind to victims of political wrongdoing and police arbitrariness.[16] As time passed, his reputation grew, and he amplified his role as "councilor," permitting men, women, and children to join him as pilgrims to a promised land of his description. Most of those who left their miserable huts were peasants with little to lose, although the fact they migrated to new locales is still noteworthy, since few rural peasants ever permanently left their place of birth except in dire necessity. Evidence shows that not all of his followers were poor or dark skinned: some were "white" women from "good families," some of whom brought money, jewelry, or other valuable items with them.[17]

The evolution of the names by which Conselheiro was known is interesting in itself. As a boy he was called Antônio Vicente; as a young adult, Maciel. At the outset of his lay ministry he was known as Irmão (Brother) Antônio, then, variously, Antônio dos Mares, Santo Antônio dos Mares, Santo Antônio Aparecido, and finally Antônio Conselheiro. By the mid-1870s, he was known as Conselheiro, which signified that he was considered not merely a *beato* but a wise counselor, a nineteenth-century title which a few religious men in the backlands attained. *Beatos* begged for alms for the poor, while *conselheiros* preached and offered advice. Both were common in the region, so understaffed by secular or regular clergy.

Maciel followed in the footsteps of others. The practice of rebuilding churches, chapels, and cemeteries was a clearly enunciated church policy initiated in the region in the 1860s to improve ecclesiastical property and to reach out to the lower classes. José Maria de Ibiapina, born in Ceará, had traveled as an itinerant missionary through the backlands between 1862 and 1883 founding *casas de caridade*, institutions serving as orphanages for abandoned girls, shelters for runaways, and schools for

15. Putnam claims that the *beatas* who followed Conselheiro were women of a dissolute life who were expiating their sins by penance (*RB*, 132, n. 130) but offers no evidence beyond da Cunha's own reference to the fact that *some* of the women at Belo Monte were "old maids," the backlands term for loose women (p. 156).

16. Ataliba Nogueira, *Antônio Conselheiro*, 6. See also Hélio Silva and Maria Cecília Ribas Carneiro, *O poder civil* (Rio de Janeiro, 1975), 58–60.

17. Only one or two members of the entire adult male population of Canudos are described as "white" in the documentation. See, for example, *Relatório da commissão especial nomeada para recolher as creanças sertanejas, feitas prisioneiras em Canudos* (Salvador, 1898) (or a briefer version, *Rel. do comitê patriótico constituido na Cidade do Salvador*, published in *Comércio* [São Paulo, 1897]). The racial breakdown of Conselheiro's flock is discussed in greater detail below.

the daughters of merchants and landowners. A direct influence on Conselheiro, he emphasized lay Catholic roles in a region sparsely served by clergy.[18] Other *conselheiros* included Conselheiro Guedes, in Pernambuco, who dressed in a Carmelite habit and was the father of ten children, who walked with him, and Conselheiro Francisco, a "jovial *cabra*" (mulatto) who helped build a church in Cumbe near Canudos, and who went to Canudos every two weeks to say mass. An even better-known example is Padre Cícero Romão Batista, who had exercised a perfectly conventional chaplaincy between 1872 and 1889 in the Cariri Valley in Ceará but deviated from orthodoxy after he participated in an alleged miracle whereby the Host being administered to a *beata* in Joaseiro turned into the blood of Christ. Ralph della Cava notes that priests other than Padre Cícero publicized and exploited the event, organizing pilgrimages to the site from all over the Northeast. By the time Antônio Conselheiro established his holy city at Canudos some hundreds of pilgrims had settled in Ceará's Cariri Valley, at Joaseiro—residents of another holy city which lasted more than 50 years despite Cícero's suspension from priestly orders in 1892.[19]

Unlike Padre Cícero, who did not object to others publicizing his miracle and who skillfully enlisted political allies as well as a personal following, Maciel behaved modestly. He often chided penitents who genuflected before him, remarking, "I am a Maciel by name and a Conselheiro [only] in my heart." He did permit the curious to follow him around; and he did not dissuade them from addressing him as "my father." He often began speaking with a few sentences in Latin, which had the effect of mystifying his listeners and establishing his authority. Sometimes he stared for long minutes, as if he were in a trance. Witnesses later said that he was "saintly," and "prophetlike."[20] Sometimes, too, he was joined in his pilgrimage by individual missionaries sent by the church from Europe. He led prayer meetings (*orações*) and gave sermons, never inside churches but outdoors, in public squares. He exhorted his listeners against Masonry, Protestantism, and secularism, and from time to time he declaimed against slavery.

The first published reference to Conselheiro appeared in a weekly newspaper, *O Rabudo*, in Estância, Sergipe in 1874. The article, filling

18. See Celso Mariz, *Ibiapina, um apóstolo do Nordeste* (João Pessoa, 1942); José de Figueiredo Filho, "Casa de Caridade de Crato," *A Província* (Crato), 3 (1955), 14–25; Ralph della Cava, "Brazilian Messianism and National Institutions: A Reappraisal of Canudos and Joaseiro," *HAHR*, 48:3 (Aug. 1968), 404–405.

19. Della Cava, "Brazilian Messianism," 409–415.

20. Testimony of Bacharel Genes Fontes, a judge, in a letter to *A República* (Rio de Janeiro), 1897, cited in Calasans, "Notícias de Antônio Conselheiro" (unpublished ms.), 4–5, in Centro de Estudos Brasileiros, Núcleo do Sertão, courtesy of Dr. Calasans. We do not know, however, whether he actually offered prophesy, as the legend asserts.

half of the weekly's four pages, mocked Maciel, and suggested that his penitential dress indicated that he had committed some kind of crime or was fleeing from justice.[21] He was mentioned in the Bahian press two years later, described as an ascetic with "great influence over our . . . ignorant and simple peasants of the lower classes."[22] In the larger towns, opposition began to be voiced from clergy as well, who complained about him to one another and sometimes to the provincial chief of police. A story is told that in the absence of the vicar in Natuba, in the province of Bahia, Conselheiro gathered stones to rebuild the church. But when the former returned, he ordered the work halted because he had not been consulted and Conselheiro had "taken" stones which did not belong to him. Conselheiro left the city, and the church remained unfinished.[23]

Among rural northeasterners, Conselheiro evoked the mystical appeal of Portuguese King Sebastian, lost in 1578 in battle in Africa against the Moors, beloved as a saint whose return to earth in full glory with his armies would herald the Second Coming. Much more than on the coast, Sebastianism was deeply rooted in *sertanejo* folk religion. A major Sebastianist movement occurred at Rodeador in Pernambuco in 1817–20, and in 1837 at Pedra Bonita, also Pernambuco, there had been a terrible episode centered around a Sebastianist cult of about 300 peasants who sacrificed 53 souls, 30 of them children, to free the saint from a large rock where he was believed to have been imprisoned.[24]

The first attempt by officials to interrupt Conselheiro's ministry coincided with the decision by a powerful local *coronel*, the Barão de Jeremoabo, in collusion with the archbishop of Salvador, to deal with his growing influence. Claims that peasants were beginning to call him "Messiah" and reports of ever larger bands of followers led to his arrest in Itapicurú de Cima, a dependency of the baron, in June 1876. Conselheiro was accused of having murdered his mother and wife. For this he was

21. *O Rabudo*, 7 (Nov. 22, 1874). Cited by Calasans, "Canudos não euclidiano," 2–3.

22. Paraphrased from an article in *Diário da Bahia* (Salvador), June 27, 1876.

23. Correspondence between Padre João José Barbosa (vicar of N. S. do Apora), Padre João Alves da Silva Paranhos (vicar of N. S. do Livramento do Barracão), Padre Emílio de Santana Pinto (vicar of Divino Espírito Santo de Abrantes), and correspondence between Monsenhor Luís d'Armour, vicar in Salvador, and the provincial chief of police, Dr. João Bernardo de Magalhães, in the Gabinete Arquiepiscopal (Correspondência das Repartições Públicas, Salvador, XVI, 1874–77).

24. See the *cordel* poet João Melquíades Ferreira da Silva, *A guerra de Canudos*, and J. Sara, *Meu folclore* (1956), cited in *Literatura popular em verso-estudos* (Rio de Janeiro, 1973–), I, 112–115; Maria Isaura Pereira de Queiroz, *O messianismo no Brasil e no mundo*, 2d ed. (São Paulo, 1976), 200–201. On Sebastianism, see René Ribeiro, "Brazilian Messianic Movements," in *Millenial Dreams in Action: Studies in Revolutionary Religious Movements*, Sylvia L. Thrupp, ed. (New York, 1970), 58, 66 and *Grande enciclopédia portuguesa e brasileira*, 40 vols. (1936–60) XXVIII (Lisbon, 1945), 19.

ordered to be extradited to Ceará, the letter of extradition noting that the accused was a bad influence among the "ignorant folk" of Itapicurú, and that he had shown disrespect to the local vicar. Even if he is not found to be a criminal, it concluded, it would be wise "not to permit him to return here," since that would "provoke disagreeable results among the fanatics angered by the arrest of their idol."[25] Taken first to Salvador, he was beaten by the soldiers accompanying him and taunted by bystanders. He was then taken to Fortaleza on the coastal steamboat *Pernambuco* and from there to Quixeramobim.[26] No sooner did he arrive than it was verified that his mother had died when he was a child, and that his wife was still living. The charges were therefore dismissed, although he was beaten once more by the soldiers who had transported him from Bahia to Ceará.[27] He returned to the sertão region of Bahia and Sergipe and again took up his old work of rebuilding ruined churches and adobe cemetery walls.[28]

Conselheiro's fame spread faster after his arrest and release. Other factors contributed as well. From February 1877 to May 1880, the devastation of what became known as the Great Drought sent hundreds of thousands of refugees from five Northeastern provinces fleeing across the sertão in the direction of the coast or to the Amazon. Sixty-four thousand died from epidemic disease in Fortaleza in 1878–79.[29] The desperate situation sharpened tensions—and made many people more receptive to drastic solutions in the fight to survive. In the midst of this volatile atmosphere, the monarchy entered its last decade; slavery virtually disappeared in the Northeast as slave owners sold their chattel to the more

25. Extradition letter, L. B. Magalhães, Secretaria de Polícia da Província da Bahia, 2a seçao, no. 2182, June 5, 1876 to sr. chefe de polícia de Ceará. See Garcia, *Do litoral ao sertão*, 184.

26. See *Diário da Bahia*, June 27 and July 7, 1876; *Jornal da Bahia*, July 6 and 7, 1876; *Diário de Notícias* (Salvador), July 6 and 7, 1876. A summary of these descriptions appeared in the *Folhinha Laemmert* in Rio de Janeiro later in that year, the first notice of Antônio Maciel in the imperial capital.

27. See Fortunée Levy, "Crentes e bandidos," *Anais do Museu Histórico Nacional*, 8 (1957), 41. Another secondary source (Nertan Macedo, *Memorial de Vilanova* [Rio de Janeiro, 1964], 113) states that Maciel was arrested for nonpayment of debts.

28. This system of labor, akin to the *mutirão*, or communal labor form of constructing houses and community buildings, was very common in the region, although not usually carried out on church property. One of the reasons that cemetery walls had to be rebuilt is that population growth necessitated cemetery expansion. Also, the dead were often interred in the walls themselves, their bones removed to ossuaries after two years if fees were not paid. Thus, by enlarging cemeteries, Conselheiro paid respect to the dead by providing more room for permanent burial.

29. See Roger L. Cunniff, "The Birth of the Drought Industry: Imperial and Provincial Responses to the Great Drought in Northeast Brazil, 1877–1880," *Revista de Ciências Sociais*, 6:1–2 (1975), 65–82; Gerald Michael Greenfield, "Recife y la gran sequía," in *Cultura urbana latinoamericana*, Richard Morse and Jorge Enrique Hardoy, eds. (Buenos Aires, 1985), 203–226.

prosperous South, turning to caboclos and emancipated slaves for labor; the church remained woefully underfinanced and understaffed; and Conselheiro continued his work and his wanderings.

Conselheiro was accepted by all social levels of the rural population. From 1880 through 1892, he was listed as godfather, and personally attended, at 92 baptisms in Itapicurú de Cima alone. In nearly half of these cases, the godmother listed was "Nossa Senhora" (the Virgin Mary). *Compadrio* (the godparent system) was a highly meaningful institution in the rural interior, a kind of ideological and spiritual coparentage, building interpersonal ties as strong as blood relationships in a region where the real need for personal protection made choice of a godfather extremely important.[30]

Remarkably, in spite of the legends that grew up around him, Conselheiro did not emphasize miracles in his sermons, only faith and hard work. He did not usurp sacerdotal functions, nor did he perform healing or provide medicine.[31] Outsiders, including Euclides da Cunha, referred to him as "Bom Jesus Conselheiro," but no evidence survives proving that he ever used that name. He never asserted that he had been sent from God, or that he was a prophet: he remained within the boundaries of formal Roman Catholicism as a lay preacher and *beato*. His works were performed in the name of the church, and at the service of local priests.

In February 1882, Archbishop Dom Luís Antônio dos Santos circulated a letter prohibiting nonordained persons from preaching. Rural priests were now to be caught up in the effort of the church hierarchy to preserve its authority. Yet it is instructive that the church never condemned Conselheiro's religious practices or his theology. He was always orthodox in his Catholicism, and he continued to enjoy good relations with many local clergy. They gave him free access to their churches, and, in many cases, publicly embraced his efforts to repair church property. Priests in several localities ignored the archbishop's order against lay preachers.[32]

The journalist and writer Sílvio Romero, in a tract published after Canudos was already established, made reference to its "army of believers committing depredations of all kinds." Conselheiro had wandered through Lagarto, Romero's birthplace in Sergipe, where he obviously left an im-

---

30. Parochial records of N. S. de Nazaré do Itapicurú de Cima. See Francisco José de Oliveira Vianna, *Instituições políticas brasileiras* (Rio de Janeiro, 1949), 263; Consuelo Pondé de Sena, *Introdução ao estudo de uma comunidade* (Salvador, 1979), 157.

31. Ataliba Nogueira, *Antônio Conselheiro*, 8.

32. This was the case with the vicar of N. S. da Piedade do Lagarto, Sergipe, João Baptista de Carvalho Daltro, in Jan. 1886. See Daltro's letter to Archbishop D. Luís Antônio dos Santos, cited by Calasans, "Canudos não euclidiano," 6–7.

pression. Usually friendly to manifestations of local folk culture, Romero had been repelled by the "dour fanatic" who detested ostentation and who forbade the women in his flock to use hair combs and wool shawls, ordering them to burn possessions representing personal vanity.[33]

Few of the other allegations appearing in print and in rumor about Conselheiro were based either on meetings with him or on observation of his works. An exception was the experience of Durval Vieira de Aguiar, a colonel in the Bahian state police and at one time its commanding officer. Vieira de Aguiar ran into Conselheiro in Cumbe, in or about 1882. Conselheiro was starting work on a new church, having completed a chapel in Mucambo, today Olindina. The colonel described Conselheiro as "short, emaciated, dark skinned, with dark hair and a long beard, dressed in a beltless blue tunic, living alone in an empty house, where he is attended to by *beatas* with food." He watched Conselheiro dispense advice and pronounce homilies and sermons. The local population flocked to hear him, listening raptly and obeying his words unquestioningly. Aguiar noted that the local vicars earned handsomely from the baptisms, marriages, festivals, novenas, and every other kind of service rendered by the church, while Conselheiro "earned nothing."[34]

A second personal encounter was related by Dr. Genes Martins Fontes, a judge in nearby Monte Santo in the early 1890s, loyal to the Barão de Jeremoabo to whom he owed his post. As a student at the Recife Law School in 1881, he had come across Conselheiro during a trip to Sergipe. Like Vieira de Aguiar, he described Conselheiro's long, unkempt hair and his skin-and-bones appearance; he also noted his dirty hands and body lice. Conselheiro, he observed, exuded an expression of indefiniteness, "characteristic of mystics and dreamers." Martins Fontes came away marked by the encounter.[35] Some years later, as a magistrate, Martins Fontes wrote again to a newspaper, changing his story. Conselheiro, he now said, had clearly exhibited an air of leadership, capable of "dominating multitudes."[36] He was not the only member of the elite to embrace the Conselheiro-as-devil theme after initial doubts.

33. See Sílvio Romero, *O vampiro do Vaza-Barris: Intermezzo jornalisto em resposta ao vigário Olympio Campos. Complemento ao opusculo "A verdade sobre o caso de Sergipe"* (Rio de Janeiro, 1895) (the "vampire of Vaza-Barris" was Olympio Campos, not Conselheiro). See also Romero's *Estudos sobre a poesia popular no Brasil*, 2d ed. (Petrópolis, 1977), 41 (first published in 1888). Also, Calasans, "Canudos não euclidiano," 4.

34. Durval Vieira de Aguiar, *Descricões práticas da província da Bahia* (Salvador, 1888), 76. Calasans avers that da Cunha read Aguiar's book and used part of it without consulting his source ("Canudos não euclidiano," 7).

35. Letters to *A República*, cited without dates by Calasans, "Canudos não euclidiano," 11.

36. Letters to *A Notícia* (Aracajú), Jan. 28–29, 1897.

Cícero Dantas Martins, the baron of Jeremoabo, also met Conselheiro personally and recorded his impressions. Not only was the baron the leading fazendeiro in the municipality of Itapicurú, where more than any other place in the sertão Conselheiro stayed for long periods of time, but he had been the leading *coronel* in the region around Canudos since the late empire.[37] A hesitant Republican, he joined the dominant state Republican party (PRF-Ba) when it was founded, and allied himself with other sertão *coronéis* under the nominal leadership of José Gonçalves. When the PRF split apart in 1893 over patronage and internal power, Martins became one of the principal founders of a new opposition party, the Republican Constitutional (PRC), with its power base in the interior.[38] Canudos was established in that same year.

Like many of the other landowners in the region, Jeremoabo initially tolerated Conselheiro but then backed away, especially after the holy city of Belo Monte started to grow. As early as 1887, Itapicurú's police chief, who was one of the baron's clients, had petitioned Salvador to take steps against the "fanatic." After the Republican party schism, Conselheiro and his aides turned to the faction headed by former Conservative party leader Luiz Vianna for protection, banking on its gaining control of the state assembly and the governorship. Unfortunately for Belo Monte, Vianna's enemies seized power in Ilhéus, the Lavras, and the sertão portion of the state. By the time Vianna reclaimed power and was inaugurated governor in 1896, it was too late. The anti-Vianna faction then put pressure directly on the federal government to act, creating new sources of fear by painting Conselheiro's group as seditious monarchists protected by Vianna. Conselheiro's allies cooperated with Vianista *coronéis*-fazendeiros, increasing Jeremoabo's anger. Ultimately, the alliance of sertão *coronéis* in the state with anti-Vianna forces at the national level would force Vianna's hand and doom Canudos.[39]

37. See J. C. Pinto Dantas, Júnior, *O Barão de Geremoabo (Dr. Cícero Dantas Martins), 1838–1938* (Salvador, 1939), 9–22. Dantas Martins preferred to use either his imperial title of nobility (Barão de Jeremoabo) or the title conferred on him by his law degree (*Bacharel* Dantas Martins). If not a nobleman, he would probably have been known as a *coronel.*

38. Eul-Soo Pang, *Bahia in the First Brazilian Republic: Coronelismo and Oligarchies, 1889–1934* (Gainesville, 1979), 56–59. For detailed analysis of the political economy of the rural Northeast in the late nineteenth and early twentieth centuries, see Linda Lewin, *Politics and Parentela in Paraíba: A Case Study of Family-Based Oligarchy in Brazil* (Princeton, 1987).

39. Circumstances in the national government conspired against Conselheiro as well. President Prudente de Morais returned to office after a long illness only days after news of the defeat of the third expedition and the death of its commander, Colonel Moreira César, was received. This led to violent antimonarchist outbreaks and fueled demands for total victory, with no mercy to the vanquished. See June E. Hahner, *Civilian-Military Relations*

It is clear that the conventional view that Conselheiro was opposed because of his anti-Republicanism is misleading. As in other cases, da Cunha's burning desire to paint Conselheiro as a revolutionary fanatic obscures the real source of Conselheiro's dissatisfaction with the new regime, which was something equally opposed by the Catholic hierarchy: compulsory civil marriage.[40] Only in 1893, at Bom Conselho, did Conselheiro openly commit an act of political defiance, the burning of tax edicts in the public square.

Once at a weekly outdoor market in that town he was said to have been present when an old *curuca* (crone) attempted to seat herself to sell a straw mat. When the municipal fee collector demanded that she pay more than the value of her merchandise for the right to sell, she began to cry out and sob, drawing a crowd; in a sermon that evening, Conselheiro referred to the old woman's plight and chastised the republic for attempting to deliver the people back into slavery.[41] According to *Os sertões*, Conselheiro "gathered the people, and, amid seditious cries and noisy demonstrations, had them make a bonfire of the bulletin boards in the public square."[42] In reality, municipal taxes in Bahia were no higher or lower during the early republic than they had been during the empire, but Conselheiro's action, whose only illegal aspect was destruction of public property, probably had more than its desired effect: it gave Conselheiro's enemies a pretext on which to demand retaliation. For the rest, reports of Conselheiro's active opposition to the republic before Canudos itself was established were hearsay and in all probability false except for his frequent denunciations of the republican law recognizing civil marriage.[43]

The Bom Conselho events followed closely the schism in the ruling state Republican party. Conselheiro's tax edict bonfire may have been a show of loyalty for Vianna, temporarily out of power after having lost his

in *Brazil, 1889–1898*, 2d ed. (Columbia, SC, 1971), 170–177. See also Pereira de Queiroz, *O messianismo*, 203–219; Pang, *Bahia in the First Brazilian Republic*, 59–60; Barão de Jeremoabo (Cícero Dantas Martins), "Antônio Conselheiro," *Jornal de Notícias* (Salvador), Mar. 4–5, 1897.

40. The 1891 Marriage Act was also widely misunderstood. Legitimacy being a criterion of social status, many women who otherwise would have been legally married by virtue of their church weddings now risked being juridically considered mothers of illegitimate children. This encouraged wife abandonment in the eyes of many, a serious transgression of backlands puritanical Catholic mores. My thanks to Linda Lewin for underscoring this point.

41. Manoel Benício, *O rei dos jagunços* (Rio de Janeiro, 1899), 163. This book appeared three years before *Os sertões*, and in a way was a model for da Cunha.

42. *RB*, 141–142.

43. The new law's impact was greatest on the propertied classes, since without civil marriage their children would no longer be regarded as able to divide their legal estates as legitimate heirs. Small landholders like those at Canudos were very much affected by it.

assembly majority. Further, when the new majority ordered a contingent of 30 soldiers from the state police to intercept Conselheiro and his few hundred followers on the Monte Santo road, it may have been an attempt by Vianna's opponents to punish "their enemy's backlands ally" by using the same tactic Vianna would gain a reputation for later—to use the state police as his personal *jagunços*. Firing into the group of "beggarly penitents" in the vicinity of Masseté, a "sterile and foresaken tract of land between Tucano and Cumbe in the vicinity of the Ovó range," the soldiers discovered that Conselheiro's band was accompanied by its own *jagunços* carrying weapons. The bodyguards met the police in battle and wiped out their adversaries. Conselheiro marched straight north, following the trails which would take his band to Canudos where they would be more protected from the influence of Jeremoabo and the other regional *coronéis*.[44]

Vianna supporters in the elite continued to defend Conselheiro. When word of the Masseté incident reached Vieira de Aguiar, he wrote to the *Jornal de Notícias* in Salvador avowing that Conselheiro was no dangerous agitator but merely a simple, deeply religious missionary seeking to be of help by building and rebuilding temples and cemeteries.[45] A letter from another citizen, Maximiano José Ribeiro, a commercial employee in Salvador writing to the same newspaper three days later, reported that he had spent some time in conversation with Conselheiro in Bom Jesus (Crisópolis), and that Conselheiro rather than offering personal advice had referred him to the regular church representative in the parish, the vicar of Itapicurú.[46] Continued political infighting and victory for Vianna's party in 1896 meant that for the time being Belo Monte was not threatened, while its reputation as a haven for the faithful grew. However, from 1893 until the inauguration of Vianna as governor in May 1896, most public mention of Conselheiro and his followers was negative. Journalist clients of Gonçalves railed against the "pernicious monarchist cell."[47] The Masseté clash was reported in the federal Chamber of Deputies in Rio de Janeiro, and Bahia's Gonçalvista acting governor, Dr. Rodrigues Lima, demanded that Brazilian chief of state Floriano Peixoto avenge the attack on the police contingent. It is thus evident that Conselheiro's flock was caught up in the generations-old factional struggles among members of the Brazilian

---

44. Pang, *Bahia in the First Brazilian Republic*, 58; della Cava, "Brazilian Messianism," 412–423. See also Antônio F. Moniz de Aragão, *A Bahia e os seus governadores na República* (Salvador, 1923), and Montenegro, *Antônio Conselheiro*, 44 and Dante de Mello, *A verdade sobre os sertões (Analise reivindicatória da campanha de Canudos)* (Rio de Janeiro, 1958), esp. chap. 5.

45. Durval Vieira de Aguiar, letter to *Jornal de Notícias*, June 13, 1893.

46. Maximiano José Ribeiro, letter to *Jornal de Notícias*, June 16, 1893.

47. See Calasans, "O *Diário de Notícias* e a campanha de Canudos," *Universitas* (Salvador), 18 (Sept.–Dec. 1977), 89–96.

oligarchy. Yet what was not reported was that Conselheiro was only one of several points of political unrest in Bahia. Tax-decree bonfires occurred in 1893 not only in Bom Conselho but elsewhere in the state in Itapicurú, Soure, and Amparo.[48] At the same time that Conselheiro was constructing his mountainous retreat, the city of Lençôes had been attacked by *sertanejo* bandits; ruffians were threatening nearby Lavras Diamantinas; the village of Mendes Brito was under siege to a mob; and the town of Jequié reportedly the scene of numerous and violent crimes. What was also not said publicly but was known by anyone familiar with backlands life was that for decades the rural population had hated the police, who were undisciplined, poorly paid, and often permitted to run rampant and terrorize individuals and entire villages.

Conselheiro established his permanent residential colony at Canudos, on the site of an abandoned cattle ranch on the banks of the Vaza-Barris, in a valley surrounded by mountains. Title to the land was held by the Baronesa de São Francisco do Conde, whose main lands were in the Bahian Recôncavo. The highest peak was the *morro* (mount) of Favela, which could be used as a watchpost to spot any arrivals to the settlement. When Conselheiro arrived, there were about five hundred mud-thatched wooden shanties scattered in the vicinity, and the manor house had been left in ruins.[49] He chose Canudos as his locale because of its capacity to support agriculture, not, as was claimed later, for its defensive capabilities. The settlement centered in the valley at the widest point of its seasonal river, which reached some one hundred meters in breadth during the wet season. It enjoyed a very unsavory reputation. In 1876, a delegation of priests, including the vicar of Cumbe, had visited it. One later described the idle population there as made up of people "armed to the teeth . . . whose sole occupation, almost, consisted in drinking brandy and smoking certain strange clay pipes with stems (*canudos*) a yard long."[50] In the last years of the empire, the entire district of Santo Antônio das Queimadas, which included Cumbe, Canudos, and a dozen other hamlets, had contained 3,360 souls, 10 percent of them slaves and almost all of them illiterate. The province of Bahia, so proud of its high culture that it called itself the "Brazilian Italy," spent considerably more on its police force than for all levels of public education combined, and most of these allocations were earmarked for the capital.[51]

48. Montenegro, *Antônio Conselheiro*, 44; della Cava, "Brazilian Messianism," 413, n. 37.

49. One chronicler even claimed that the rude habitations of mud and straw covering the hilly slopes of the Favela *morro* were the source for the word *favela*. See Levy, "Crentes e bandidas," 42.

50. Communication from the vicar of Itu, 1898, Curia papers, Salvador.

51. Manoel Jesuino Ferreira, *A província da Bahia: Apontamentos* (Rio de Janeiro, 1875), 36, 64, 119.

The initial few hundred settlers who followed Conselheiro to Canudos worked to construct mud brick houses and to plant and raise goats and horses. No opposition came from municipal authorities. There were no wanted criminals in Conselheiro's flock, as later charged; the life was pastoral, and centered around seasonal planting and daily religious ministrations. Since the die had been cast in Masseté, da Cunha in hindsight permitted himself to describe the scene in the dramatic language of *Os sertões*:

> This transient settlement of wandering woodsmen . . . was within a short space of time to be transformed and expanded into the mud-walled Troy of the *jagunços*. It was to become a holy site, surrounded as it was by a protective ring of mountains, where the long arm of the accursed government never would reach. Its interesting topography in the eyes of these simple folk made it appear as the first broad step of the stairway to heaven.[52]

Ravaged by the most recent regional droughts, the arid Northeast experienced unprecedented demographic dislocation. Tens of thousands of backlanders migrated to the coastal cities; others wandered in the direction of the *agreste* and zona da mata. Others moved within the sertão itself. Canudos grew precipitously. Towns within a range of two hundred kilometers (Olhos d'Agua, Rosário, Natuba, Tucano, Cumbe) lost up to half of their population or more to Conselheiro's settlement. Some smaller hamlets, more distant, became virtually deserted (Mundo Novo, Entre-Rios in the judicial district [*comarca*] of Alagoinhas). According to one newspaper report, Queimadas, in Bonfim, declined from 4,504 residents in 1892 to three occupied houses in September 1897. Some 5,000 adult males from Itapicurú were reported to have taken up residence in Canudos, as well as 400 from Capim Grosso, "great numbers" from Pombal, 300 from Itabaianinha in Sergipe, and a "large number" from Ituiuba in Bahia. Families came from as far away as Feira de Santana in the Recôncavo, outside the capital, and from the state of Sergipe.[53] Large numbers of livestock came from Jeremoabo, Bom Conselho, and Simão Dias.

For the Catholic church, the turning point came in May 1895, when the new archbishop of Salvador, Dom Jerónymo Thomé da Silva, sent a pastoral delegation to Canudos to bring Conselheiro's flock under church control. From the tone set by the visitors, and from the rigidity of their demands, the mission was predestined to fail. That the church sent the mission at the request of state officials despite the formal separation of church

52. *RB*, 142.
53. *O Estado de São Paulo*, Sept. 14, 1897, cited by Cândida Pereira da Cunha and Ilana Blaj, "A urbanização em Canudos como decorrência da necessidade de defesa," *Anais do VII Simpósio Nacional dos Professores Universitários de História* (São Paulo, 1984), 497.

and state after 1889 was not unusual in the Northeast, where republican-
era secularism never fully took hold behind the scenes as long as religious
and political leaders shared common objectives. Heading the delegation
was an Italian Capuchin missionary, Father João Evangelista de Monte
Marciano, flanked by another Capuchin and the curate of Cumbe. Lacking
sufficient numbers of Brazilian priests, the church had turned to Europe
for Capuchin friars to perform evangelical work in the interior—especially
among Amerindians in mission villages. In the sertão, they encouraged
the establishment of *feiras*, or weekly markets, and helped develop agriculture. However, they tended to approach local customs with rigidity
and some disdain. Da Cunha describes how the delegation to Canudos
crossed the river and, walking past the first outlying huts, approached
the square, which was filled with "near to a thousand men, armed with
blunderbusses, shotguns, knives, etc.," Conselheiro having been advised
in advance of the visit. That the *sertanejos* were armed should not have
shocked the clerics, although they did profess to have been, since, for generations, backlanders had carried knives and manufactured ammunition
from saltpeter and other materials found naturally on the banks of the São
Francisco River.

What frightened the visitors most of all was the sheer number of Conselheiro's entourage, as they made their way uneasily to the curate's house;
it had been closed for more than a year, the curate's visits stopped at
church orders. They passed eight coffins being carried by pallbearers to
the cemetery, without any sacramental rites. Conselheiro himself continued working on repairs to the chapel, until the visitors sought him
out. They called out a salutation of peace, "Praised be Our Lord Jesus
Christ," which called for the response: "May our blessed Lord be praised
forever!" Conselheiro greeted them affably and addressed them with the
same greeting.[54]

The visitors noted that Conselheiro appeared pleased by their visit,
and that he dropped his habitual reserve and stubborn silence, showing
them the progress of his work and serving as their personal guide. The
missionary's lack of tact undermined the cordiality. Approaching the choir
loft, he addressed Conselheiro in the form of a warning. He later reported:

> I seized upon the occasion to inform him that my mission was a
> wholly peaceful one, that I was greatly surprised to find armed men
> here, and that I could not but disapprove of all of these families

---

54. *RB*, 164–165. Putnam notes that da Cunha's account follows closely the report
submitted by Friar Monte Marciano and published in Salvador by the Curia. See *Relatório
apresentado pelo Revd. Frei João Evangelista de Monte Marciano ao arcebispado da Bahia
sobre Antônio Conselheiro e seu séquito no arraial dos Canudos* (Salvador, 1895).

living here in idleness, lewdness, and under conditions so wretched that they led to eight or nine deaths a day. Accordingly, by the order and in the name of His Lordship the Archbishop, I propose to give a holy mission and advise the people to disperse and to return to their homes and daily tasks, both for their own sakes and for the general welfare.[55]

He was shocked to hear, instead, shouts of loyalty to Conselheiro from the people. Conselheiro replied: "It is to protect myself that I keep these armed men with me; for your Reverence must know that the police attacked me and tried to kill me at the place called Masseté, where the dead were piled up on one side and the other. In the days of the monarchy, I let myself be taken, for I recognized the government; but today I will not, because I do not recognize the republic." The visitor reportedly replied to Conselheiro: "Sir, if you are a Catholic, you must remember that the church condemns revolts and, accepting all forms of government, teaches that the constituted authorities rule the peoples in the name of God."[56]

The mission, then, began badly and continued for four days in the same spirit. Conselheiro permitted the visitors to offer mass to more than five thousand in the congregation, including men who retained their arms. He stood beside the altar, and, when something was said of which he disapproved, he shook his head, provoking, in turn, vocal protests from the congregation. Note was taken of the "incredible faults of pronunciation" of the Kyrie eleisons uttered by the faithful. The visitors sanctified 55 marriages of "couples living in concubinage," performed 102 baptisms, and heard more than 400 confessions,[57] but little compromise was ventured on either side. On the seventh day of the mission João Abbade, Conselheiro's chief lieutenant, led a mob to the front of the guests' house, where they shouted vivas to Jesus Christ and let the priests know that "when it came to the matter of eternal salvation, the population of Canudos had no need of their ministrations."[58]

Unhappy with the formal separation of church and state under the 1891 constitution, the ecclesiastical hierarchy was sensitive to the charge that devout Catholics were hidden monarchists, especially in rural areas. The language of the eight-page *Relatório* published by the archdiocese in Salvador under Frei Evangelista's signature, condemning Canudos as a "political-religious sect" and as a source of "resistance and hostility to the constituted government in the country," thus reveals the hierarchy's

---

55. He offers no evidence for this.
56. *RB*, 166–167.
57. De Monte Marciano, *Relatório*, 7.
58. Ibid., 5.

position.[59] The document described living conditions in Canudos in some detail, emphasizing the detrimental effect of overcrowding on the general state of public health, the poor sanitation, and the provocative attitudes of Conselheiro's lieutenants in disrespect to civil and church authority.[60] These points could have been made for any urban settlement in the northeastern backlands, but to the inexperienced visitor Canudos seemed both unique and ominous. Indeed, the choice of Frei Evangelista, a zealous missionary unfamiliar with the psychology of Brazilian folk Catholicism, contributed to the report's aggressive and condemnatory mien. Yet not even did the shocked cleric in his cold hostility claim what others falsely charged later. He admitted, for example, that Conselheiro was not arrogating any sacerdotal functions.[61] And the old vicar of Cumbe, who maintained a house in Canudos, resumed his twice monthly visits to perform baptisms and marriages.[62]

Conselheiro was not visibly affected by the visit in any way. He continued to leave the day-to-day administration of the city to his aides, and concentrated his personal attentions on reconstruction of the ruined Canudos chapel and construction of a new church. In his writings there is nothing suggesting any kind of mania or unbalanced behavior; he always signed himself "Antônio Vicente Mendes Maciel," not "Santo," or "Bom Jesus," or "Conselheiro."[63] In Canudos, he continued to dress in the same faded and dirty tunic, his long hair streaked with white, wearing worn sandals, carrying a wooden staff and calling passers-by "my brethren," ending conversations with the phrase "sanctified be Our Father Jesus Christ." The two handwritten books attributed to him which survive further reveal his religious orientation. The first, written in 1895 in Belo Monte, is a collection of several hundred commentaries on the New Testament, some copied verbatim from the *Missão abbreviada*, of the Goan priest Manuel José Gonçalves Couto, a text filled with apocalyptic and millennial passages.[64] Entitled *Preceitos*, Conselheiro's volume bears a date only three

---

59. Ibid., 7. The report was obviously edited by diocesan officials, if for no other reason than to correct the written language, which reflected the Italian missionary's halting Portuguese.

60. See also Gregôrio de S. Mariano, "Os capuchinhos na Bahia," I Congresso de História da Bahia, *Anais* (1950), 273–283.

61. De Monte Marciano, *Relatório*, 4.

62. Euclides da Cunha, *Canudos e inéditos. Diário de uma expedição* (Rio de Janeiro, 1939), 79.

63. Calasans, "Canudos não euclidiano," 17.

64. The *Missão abbreviada* incorporated language close to five Jansenist precepts condemned by the Vatican, including the doctrine of individual salvation, and an exaggerated sense of personal sin. See *Missão abbreviada para despertar os descuidados, converter os pecadores e sustentar o fruto das missões* (Porto, 1873), esp. 198–199, 399, 468 and Pessar, "Unmasking the Politics of Religion," 261.

days after Frei Evangelista's departure, as if to affirm his continued loyalty to orthodox Catholic doctrine.[65] The second of the two works, dated January 1897, contains many of the same homilies and commentaries but also indicates his refusal to recognize the republic (he refers to the "province" of Bahia), and contains as well negative references to slavery (Princess Isabel in signing the Golden Law was only carrying out instructions from God), Masons, Protestants, civil marriage, and Jews, who "only believe in the laws of Moses."[66] Transcribed in the midst of the march on Canudos by the Brazilian army, this work suggests that Conselheiro possibly attempted to leave a message for his adversaries.[67] Both books were found in his meager house, after his death.

Conselheiro devoted most of his attention to building a new church, of his own design, with wood shipped to the region on the São Francisco River to Joaseiro, a hundred kilometers distant. The wood, which was prepaid, arrived but was not sent from Joaseiro. Conselheiro then sent representatives to Joaseiro to intercede. This was the basis of later rumors that he had personally led a band of *jagunços* to invade the city and sack its warehouses. But the prospect of a large band of men setting out from Canudos for Joaseiro, whether to carry back the wood for the church or to loot the city, encouraged the merchant who had handled the transaction in Joaseiro, Coronel João Evangelista Pereira de Melo, to make a second appeal. Governor Vianna, who since his inauguration had found one pretext or another not to intervene, was now forced to act by political pressure.[68] Toward the end of 1896, a hundred state police soldiers, commanded by a lieutenant, set out to intercept the group from Canudos which had stopped in Uauá for prayers, en route to Joaseiro. Eyewitnesses averred later that there was nothing bellicose about the flock, which car-

65. Both books may have been written by the hand of Leão de Natuba, or Leão da Silva, who served as Conselheiro's scribe and personal secretary. See Calasans, "Canudos não euclidiano," 18, referring to "Apontamentos dos preceitos da Divina Lei de Nosso Senhor Jesus Cristo, para a salvação dos homens" (1895), original copy in Núcleo do Sertão, Centro de Estudos Bahianos, Salvador; see also p. 76. Both books are probably authentic. Had they been forged, they presumably would have contained material deemed more volatile. Each is a standard prayer book, common to its era, although painstakingly copied by hand on parchment paper.

66. Antônio Vicente Mendes Maciel, "Prédicas e discursos de Antônio Conselheiro" (title given later), paragraphs 542, 607–608, 619, 656–667. The handwritten book was obtained by João de Sousa Pondé, a young medical officer and a member of the group sent to exhume Conselheiro's corpse, and given to his friend, Afrânio Peixoto, who gave it in turn to Euclydes da Cunha. His survivors in 1973 presented it to Ataliba Nogueira.

67. Reprinted in Ataliba Nogueira, *Antônio Conselheiro*, 55–181; see also Calasans, "Canudos não euclidiano," 18–19.

68. See Aristedes Milton, "A campanha de Canudos. Memoria lida no Instituto Histórico e Geográfico Brazileiro," *Revista Trimensal do Instituto*, LXIII, part II (1902), 33–35, cited by Ataliba Nogueira, *Antônio Conselheiro*, 16–17.

ried rosaries carved from coconut husks, religious banners, and a large wooden cross.

It was claimed that 3,000 men, most of them armed, made up the procession. Actually there were about 500, and more than 150 of them were killed. The police, who were exhausted from 19 days of marching, fired without warning or provocation. The peasants used tree limbs, old rifles, farm implements, knives, iron bars, and cattle prods (chuços) to defend themselves. Ten soldiers died and 16 were wounded at Uauá; the troops then withdrew to Joaseiro. The Vianna administration was vilified in the assembly, facing accusations that it had not seriously intended to attack the problem of Canudos, only disperse the jagunços. Vianna, having backed into an untenable political position, sought reconciliation with his enemies.[69] The price to him was that he request federal intervention. In an interview published in the Gazeta de Notícias of Rio de Janeiro, he boasted that he had warned the president of the republic that the "fanatical horde" at Canudos "neither recognized nor obeyed" the laws, and had committed "acts of extortion, beggary, and frequently robbed neighboring properties."[70]

"La Mer C'est Elevée avec les Pleurs"

Life in the Bahian sertão moved exceedingly slowly. When calamity struck, as in the aftermath of the cyclical droughts whose effects worsened each time owing to the increased demographic density of the region, few sertanejos moved unless life itself seemed to be threatened. Visitors to the sertão found it stark and unbroken, of strange aspect, mostly sterile, fixed in the melancholy of unrelieved horizons. But as the geographer Yi-Fu Tuan has shown, local populations, especially nontechnical societies, develop their perceptual senses to a high degree of acuity, not only seeing detail and subtle coloration differences where outsiders see only monotone but learning intimately "every bush, every stone, every convolution of the ground."[71]

The harshness of the region dismayed the city-bred bacharéis (graduates), medical students, and young military officers who found themselves in the midst of what da Cunha called land cauterized by drought and burning, sterilized air. The outsiders pitied the local inhabitants, whom they found unkempt, lethargic, and disoriented, and marveled at their

69. Della Cava, "Brazilian Messianism," 414, citing Montenegro, Antônio Conselheiro, 48–49.
70. Interview, Governor Luiz Vianna, in Gazeta de Notícias (Rio de Janeiro), Aug. 7, 1897, p. 1.
71. Yi-Fu Tuan, Topophilia: A Study of Environmental Perceptions, Attitudes, and Values (Englewood Cliffs, 1974), 77–79.

ability to work at hard labor for 10 to 12 hours a day with nothing more to eat than a handful of manioc meal and a palm-sized piece of jerked beef. The *jagunços* averted their gaze when addressed, staring at the ground and uttering monosyllabic replies or simply remaining mute. Yet these same clumsy, "primitive" folk functioned with astonishing skills and energy when left to their own devices in their own environment.[72] More than two thousand houses in Canudos were constructed almost overnight, as well as water cisterns, a schoolhouse, warehouses, armories, and Conselheiro's ambitious new church. Visitors and journalists from Salvador, Recife, Rio de Janeiro, and the rest of Brazil were clearly foreigners in their own territory, displaying colonial impatience mixed with disbelief that such statusless men and women could defy the progressive and modern benefits of civilized life. Unlike many nineteenth-century Europeans, who prided themselves on their enlightenment but were disillusioned with tyrannical governments and smallmindedness in their own countries, and who, in turn, tended to see Europe as the "center of darkness surrounded by a broad rim of light," urban Brazilians felt pride in their material as well as their political accomplishments, and shame at the dark, primitive world of the hinterland.[73] Only Euclides da Cunha among the outsiders attempted to understand the power of the *sertanejo's* relationship to the land, and his view was flawed by biological determinism and a reservoir of distaste which underlay his effusive praise and respect for the primitive's tenacity.

Writers on Canudos not only made frequent reference to the dark pigmentation of most of Conselheiro's followers but pointed out that even many members of the sertão's own upper class were dark hued. In the late nineteenth century, racial determinism, rooted in the axiom that the "strong ethnic element tends to subordinate to its destiny the weaker element with which it comes in contact," led, in the Brazilian case, to the widely accepted view that the "rude fellow-countrymen of the north . . . variable of all shades of color and all the shadings of form and character" represented inevitable casualties of miscegenation.[74] The fact that eyewitnesses to the Canudos conflict shared suspicions and fears about the retrograde if not degenerate nature of the *sertanejo* population under-

72. For a general discussion of the skill of "primitives," see Barry Lopez, *Arctic Dreams: Imagination and Desire in a Northern Landscape* (New York, 1986), 248–249.

73. Basil Willey, *The Eighteenth-Century Background*, 2d ed. (London, 1965), 19–21, cited by Tuan, *Topophilia*, 44.

74. *RB*, 87. See Raymundo Nina Rodrigues, *As raças humanas e a responsibilidade penal no Brasil* (Salvador, 1957, reprint of 1894 ed.); Deolindo Amorim, *Sertão de meu tempo* (Rio de Janeiro, 1978), 6–7. For an overview of attitudes toward race in Brazil, see David H. P. Maybury-Lewis's "Introduction" to the 2d paperback ed. of Gilberto Freyre's *The Masters and the Slaves* (Berkeley, 1986).

mines the likely objectivity of the descriptions of Conselheiro's followers. However, to the extent that a picture can be pieced together from available sources, the residents of Canudos came from much broader origins than heretofore recognized. Canudos housed a population ranging in age from newborns to men and women too old to work or even to walk; it was a fully functioning community. Recounting what he considered the bizarre, although the descriptions on which he relied were generally clinical rather than exotic, da Cunha offers a stunning description of the physical and age variation among Canudos's residents. Under the spell of the place, all of the disparate elements gathered from far and wide "were welded into one uniform and homogeneous community, an unconscious brute mass . . . in the manner of a human polyp." Of the women, he wrote that

> [H]ere, finally, were the respectable mothers of families, all kneeling together in prayer. The wrinkled faces of old women, skinny old viragoes on whose lips prayer should have been a sacrilege; the austere countenances of simple-minded matrons; the naïve physiognomies of credulous maidens—all mingled in a strange confusion; all ages, all types, all shades of racial coloring.[75]

At the end, women outnumbered men two to one. While a good number of men deserted Conselheiro in the last months, slipping away through the sertão trails left open, many of them left their wives and children behind. Contemporaries further claimed that the women in Belo Monte were more faithful than the men. This seems puzzling, given Conselheiro's own misogyny. Although women were welcomed to the settlement, he did not deal with them directly, segregating them from the men in the chapel and even avoiding eye contact when he could. His aversion seems to have been chronic, and it may shed light on the reasons for the failure of his marriage. Yet in Canudos he did permit a small number of women acolytes to serve him personally. The one closest to him was "Aunt Benta." Born in Itapicurú, she made her living in Bom Conselho as a midwife and as a matron of a boarding house for boys from other towns who studied at the primary school set up under Conselheiro's auspices. She was described as a "fat mixed-breed" (*cabo verde*), who also was skillful in business matters. She accumulated real estate, which she sold for a good sum when she left the village to follow Conselheiro to Canudos. There she took care of his austere residence and cooked for him. Her fate is unknown.

A handful of women are known to have been permitted to fight in defense of the city. One, Maria da Guerra de Jesus, had served as a nurse at Cocorobó, and in the last days of the battle in Canudos killed a soldier

75. *RB*, 149, 156.

with a sickle.[76] Women performed heavy manual labor, as did children and the elderly. Some worked in the fields with the livestock and doing agricultural chores; some carried stones from a quarry to the site of the new church, or salt from a quarry in Vargem, nine kilometers away. Asked about the heavy work, a survivor said that, if the load was unbearable, Conselheiro "would touch it," and it would become lightened.[77]

Contemporary writers claimed that sexual promiscuity was common in the sertão, although the presumption conflicts with the existence of the draconian code of honor which often led to vengeance killings and bitter family feuds. In any case, Conselheiro imposed a rigorous standard of public morals based on his unease with (and possibly anger against) women. Adolescent girls accused of flirting were punished, and prostitution, common in every Brazilian urban center, was banned.[78] Conselheiro also attempted to prohibit the use of cane rum, or *cachaça*. Whether he was successful is not known, but merchants were warned not to sell it.

The population of Canudos included not only caboclos but a wide range of groups from all races, admixtures, and social classes.[79] There were Indians of Kariri origin, as well as members of their extended mameluco families, mixed with others. Some of the Kariri festivals, including one in mid-August in which participants imbibed liquor brewed from *jurema* berries, smoked tobacco and drank *cachaça* (all supposedly banned by Conselheiro), were held in Belo Monte. The two last Kariri shamans (*pajés*) died in Canudos, and, with them, the secret of preparing *jurema* liquor, thus ending the festival.[80] A relatively high number of residents were blacks, which was somewhat unusual in the far reaches of the sertão, although blacks were a substantial element in the formation of the rural caboclo, at least in Ceará.[81] There were both descendants of fugitive slaves who had settled in the region earlier in the century, and slaves who had been emancipated in the years leading up to the formal abolition of slavery in 1888. In the early 1850s, the largest group of runaway slaves and

76. José Aras, *Sangue de irmãos* (Salvador, 1953), 159–160.

77. Testimony of Maria Guilhermina de Jesus, born in Canudos and a wounded survivor, in Odorico Tavares, *Bahia: Imagens da terra e do povo* (Rio de Janeiro, 1951), 272–274.

78. See Roberto Lyra, *Euclides da Cunha: Criminologista* (Rio de Janeiro, 1936), 11.

79. See Ivo Vannuchi, "Tipos étnicos e sociais de *Os sertões*," Adelino Brandão, ed., *Enciclopédia de estudos euclidianos* (Junaiai, 1982), I, 147–160.

80. Maria de Lourdes Bandeira, "Os kariris de Mirandela: Um grupo indígena integrado," *Estudos Baianos*, 6 (1972), 82–83. During the festival the participants danced to a *taquari*, a long flute.

81. See Billy Jaynes Chandler, "The Role of Negroes in the Ethnic Formation of Ceará: The Need for a Reappraisal," *Revista de Ciências Sociais*, 4:1 (1973), 31–43. Persons of "recognizable Negroid stock," either whole or partial, made up almost half of the population of Ceará in 1872.

their children lived in a cluster of about 30 houses along the banks of the seasonal Tapiranga River, fugitives from sugar *usinas* in Sergipe and Alagoas. Some had been ironworkers; others wood workers and mechanics. Conselheiro, who before 1888 had castigated slavery as an abomination, immediately attracted these and other blacks to his side, and they moved to Canudos when the city was established.[82] There at least one observer distinguished between the shacks constructed by caboclos and those built by former slaves. Another asserted that black women in Conselheiro's community dressed according to African custom: da Cunha speaks of the "outlandish topknots" in their hairstyles, in contrast to the "straight, smooth hair of the caboclas."[83]

The mestizos included the dozens of Brazilian categories of racial admixtures clustered around the mulatto grouping (mainly men and women from black-white pairings) and caboclos. Since racial categories in postimperial Brazil were to a degree as reflective of social status as of anything else, it is misleading to rely too heavily on official descriptions. In parts of the Northeast between 1868 and 1880, all baptized children of color who were not slaves were called *meia-branco*, or "part-white."[84] More commonly, free persons of high color would typically be classified as *negros*, or *prêtos*. Rural backlanders would usually be called mulattos. But a person of identical skin coloration and phenotype, perhaps a party to a fortunate marriage, would likely be called *pardo* (brown), or caboclo. In cases of highest social delicacy, such as some of the orphans rescued from Canudos after its destruction and carried to the coast where they were taken in by elite families, formal documents refer to them as *acoboclados*, or "caboclo-like," a term elevating them above others of the same skin color but of lower status.[85]

To da Cunha and the other eyewitnesses, all of Conselheiro's followers were pitiful or at best, in the case of the backlanders whose skills he so admired, contradictory, inconstant, and barbarous. The faithful were denied dignity for their beliefs and dismissed as fanatics. To be sure, backlanders continued to revere Conselheiro for years after his death: one

---

82. At least one chronicler claimed that some of the runaway slaves had been gun repairmen, and that they were used in Canudos to maintain the weaponry. See Aras, *Sangue de irmãos*, 5–6.

83. *RB*, 157. On the last years of slavery, see Eduardo Silva, "Por uma nova perspectiva das relações escravistas," Sociedade Brasileira de Pesquisa Histórica, *Anais da V Reunião* (São Paulo, 1985), 141–147.

84. Where this was done—for example, in [Alagoa de] Monteiro in Paraíba—one was either a *branco*, *meia-branco*, or *escravo* (slave). Courtesy of Linda Lewin.

85. Outsiders described Conselheiro as *acaboclado*. Da Cunha, at one point, called Conselheiro a "white gnostic." See Funchal Garcia, *Do litoral ao sertão*, 171. It is possible, of course, that those who besieged Canudos were more disposed to spare those with a more European appearance.

surviving *beato*, João Maria, later took with him Conselheiro's vision and used it as the basis for a new messianic community in southern Paraná, in the Contestado region.[86] But the poverty and exacting asceticism required as a condition of living in Canudos were taken by outsiders as a justification for withholding respect for the faithful, blaming them for their misfortune of having followed a raging lunatic. Even the "whites" who lived in Belo Monte, many of whom had been small property owners in the sertão who sold their assets to join Conselheiro's flock, wore "ragged garments without style" and were living amid "wretchedness and gloom."[87]

The woeful physical condition of the city and its inhabitants appalled visitors from the coast. It was later ascertained that the value of the northeastern peasant's diet had significantly declined over the period from 1870 to 1920, though since it was based on two nutritiously complementary foods, beans and manioc, it was actually better than the single-carbohydrate staple common in so many other parts of the world. Even in relatively good years, the rural diet fell deficient in calories, carbohydrates, animal fats, vitamins, thiamine, and protein. Men faced a life expectancy of 25.5 years at birth; women 28 years. Short of stature and ridden by debilitating diseases like ancilostomiasis, a blood infection causing weakness and apathy, the inhabitants of the rural hinterland seemed to outsiders to be subhuman. The poor suffered from Chagas disease, sleeping sickness, skin ulcerations, anemia, tuberculosis, malaria, leprosy, and were subject to outbreaks of bubonic plague.[88] That the visitors considered Canudos to be a "nucleus of maniacs" colored their impressions even further. Families relinquished most of their worldly possessions when they arrived. Men dressed themselves in dirty striped cotton trousers, roughhewn shirts, and uncured leather sandals. Women residents' clothing, ill-fitting shirts and blouse-like wrappings often so lacking in material that breasts and upper arms were left exposed, smelled from sweat and rancid oil.

The houses contained only sticks of furniture: neither beds nor tables, only wooden planks or hemp hammocks for sleeping, footstools, hampers

86. See Maurício Vinhas de Queiroz, *Messianismo e conflito social (A guerra sertaneja do Contestado, 1912–1916)* (Rio de Janeiro, 1966).

87. The baron of Jeremoabo himself commented on the presence of former property owners in Canudos.

88. See Jaime Reis, "Hunger in the Northeast: Some Historical Aspects," in *The Logic of Poverty: The Case of the Brazilian Northeast*, Simon Mitchell, ed. (London, 1981), 41–57. Also, see Reis's "The Abolition of Slavery and its Aftermath in Pernambuco (1880–1920)" (D. Phil. thesis, St. Antony's College, Oxford University, 1974). For data on army recruits in the late 1920s, see Arthur Lobo da Silva, "A antropologia do exército brasileiro," *Archivos do Museu Nacional*, 30 (1928), 9–300; for life expectancy, see Ludwig, *Brazil: A Handbook of Historical Statistics*, Table III–3.

made of wood or straw, leather bags or gourds to hold water. Cooking
was done over open fires made with sticks, in utensils handcrafted from
wood and scraps of tin. Consider the undisguised contempt in da Cunha's
description of a rough-hewn altar in the corner of one of the homes of
the faithful: "[It housed] atrociously carved saints and images, an objec-
tivization of the mestizo religion with its pronounced traces of idolatry:
proteiform and Africanized St. Anthonys with the gross appearance of
fetishes, and Blessed Virgins ugly as Megaeras."[89] In fact, life in any of the
wretched urban centers throughout the sertão proceeded on virtually the
identical scale of deprivation. If anything, Canudos boasted more urban
refinements than most of its neighbors: a legacy of misery afflicted the region, with whole towns depopulated by refugees fleeing hunger.[90] Houses
in Conselheiro's city, as everywhere else, were of mud and wattle construction, with solid roofs, but most were painted—a rarity for the sertão.
Three "neighborhoods" were painted mostly in grey; two in red. Some
houses were larger and contained several rooms, although none had doors
or windows, and most had only two rooms. There was only one street,
Campo Alegre, which divided the city in two, but there were winding
lanes and alleyways. Besides the houses and the two churches, there were
commercial establishments, warehouses, a *quartel* (barracks), armories,
and two cemeteries. The churches faced a central square, with the river
off to one side. Many houses had basements, as did the new church.

To the journalists sent to write about the war, Canudos seemed diaboli-
cally positioned to resist invasion. The truncated vegetation surrounding
the valley was exceedingly dense, frequently obscuring bends and dips in
the wandering, dirt trails. But the *sertanejos* had little trouble traveling in
and out. To the local population, Canudos was actually well connected to
neighboring towns. There were several trails in and out of the valley, and
the city was always well supplied with food, cattle, weapons, and anything
else it needed until the army sealed off the site in the final days of battle;
even pack drivers carried their wares into Canudos during all but the
height of fighting. Individual *jagunço* fighters were able to sneak through
the ring of troops and escape with relative ease, as many did when the
cause appeared lost.

Conselheiro surrounded himself with aides to whom he delegated
varying levels of authority. His armed lieutenants included Estevam,
"a burly, misshapen negro with a body tattooed by bullet and dagger
wounds"; "Shackle-Foot" Joaquim; "Crooked-Mouth" Raymundo of Itapi-

---

89. *RB*, 145. A less subjective description is offered by Dantas Barreto, *Destruição de
Canudos*, 4th ed. (Recife, 1912), 11–12, originally titled *Ultima expedição à Canudos*.
90. See *O Rio São Francisco e a Chapada Diamantina* (Salvador, 1938), 34, cited by
Rui Facó, *Cangaceiros*, 92.

curú, a "gallows-bird mountebank with a face twisted in a cruel grimace";
the agile-limbed "Kid Ostrich"; Quimquim de Coiqui, a "self-abnegating
religionist"; the "quack doctor," "Sturdy Manoel"; the "decrepit imam,
Old Macambira"; "Bear's Noodle"; "Peter the Invisible"; and others. That
some of the armed *jagunços* were deeply religious seemed to accentuate
their malevolence. There were Chiquinho and João da Matta, brothers
who "gave the impression of being a single individual as they say the beads
of the same rosary with the air of staunch believers," and "Pious Anthony,"
a "lean and seedy-looking mulatto, emaciated from fasting, half-sacristan,
half-soldier, the altar-boy." Anthony acted as a kind of religious policeman, according to da Cunha, "shrewdly working his way into homes and
ferreting out every nook of the village." Sharing the same predilection
was José Félix, the "Chatterbox," the guardian of the churches, Conselheiro's janitor and mayordomo, in charge of the pious women who served
Conselheiro and the other leaders.[91]

Conselheiro's lay political chieftain, known by the residents of Canudos
as the "commandante da rua" (street commander, or mayor), was João
Abbade. Frei Evangelista reported that the faithful called him *chefe do
povo*, the "people's chieftain." He commanded the Guarda Católica, Conselheiro's militia, and was a close friend of Antônio Vilanova, the most
prosperous merchant in Canudos; both lived in houses with tile roofs, a
mark of high status. Abbade had grown up in Tucano, on the other side
of the Ovó Mountains. He was tall, looked "like a priest," and was very
wily. Even his clothing differed from the other men, so that he stood
out in a crowd. His parents, of "good family" according to survivors, had
come from Pé de Serra. A story widely believed was that he committed
his first crime on the Tucano-Itapicurú road when he saw a man beating a
woman. The intervention led to murder, and he sought refuge in Canudos.
Still another version had him apprenticed to two local rifle-carrying bandits, João Geraldo and David. Abbade had led the *jagunço* forces against
the Bahian state police at Masseté in 1893, and then organized and commanded the Guarda Católica. His men obeyed him without question; he
was killed during one of the last days of fighting in Canudos.

According to one source, Pajeu, another trusted aide, was a former
private in the Pernambuco provincial militia who had deserted from the
region around Baixa Verde after committing several crimes. Da Cunha left
a description that is typical of the license he took in masterfully stirring
up images of primitivism:

> A full-blooded *cafuso* [half Indian, half African], he was endowed
> with an impulsive temperament which combined the tendencies

91. *RB*, 220–221.

of the lower races from which he sprang. He was the full-blown type of primitive fighter, fierce, fearless, and naïve, at once simple-minded and evil, brutal and infantile, valiant by instinct, a hero without being aware of the fact—in brief, a fine example of recessive atavism, with the retrograde form of a grim troglodyte, stalking upright here with the same intrepidity with which, ages ago, he had brandished a stone hatchet at the entrance to his cave.[92]

He had been born in Pajeu das Flores (Riacho do Navio), presumably the origin of the name by which he was known. In the last days before the end, he took command of the guerrilla resistance. Although most contemporary accounts cited his death in battle, he may well have escaped. Even current-day descriptions of Pajeu refer to him as Conselheiro's "negro ardiloso" (valiant black).

Other lieutenants included Zé Venâncio, wanted for 18 murders in Volta Grande and possibly a former member of the Volta Grande gang of *cangaceiros* in Lavras Diamantinas in the early 1890s. Venâncio ordered the destruction of nearby fazendas and smaller residences on the outskirts of Canudos so that they could not be used by approaching forces. But the most effective of all of the rebel fighters was Pedrão, who survived Canudos and died a half century later. Born and raised in Várzea de Ema, he joined Conselheiro after the itinerant preacher passed through the village in 1885. In 1893 he married Tibúrcia, a girl from a family in Soure which also had joined Conselheiro's minions. A brother was killed in Masseté. The vicar of Cumbe officiated at Pedrão's wedding, which was held in the old Canudos church. Of the couple's seven natural and ten adopted children, one, along with her mother, was wounded in the final round of fighting, but all survived and fled after taking personal leave of Conselheiro. In the early 1930s, Pedrão was recruited, along with other *cangaceiros*, by the interventor of Bahia, Captain Juracy Magalhães, to combat the bandit Lampião. Pedrão later migrated to the state of Piaui but returned to Várzea de Ema before his death; his funeral in 1958 was attended by hundreds.

One of Conselheiro's aides, Bernabé José de Carvalho, was related by marriage to Pedro Celeste, one of the major landowners in Bom Conselho. He was blond and had blue eyes and a heavy-set "Flemish" or "Dutch" countenance—the only male among Conselheiro's lieutenants to be listed as "white" in the documentation. Other leading figures of Canudos who

---

92. These and subsequent characterizations are based both on *RB* (159, for quotation on "Pious Anthony") and on eyewitness reports collected by Honório Vilanova cited by Macedo, *Memorial de Vilanova*; Aras, *Sangue de irmãos*; de Monte Marciano, *Relatório*; Benício, *O rei dos jagunços*; Calasans, *Quase biografias de jagunços (O séquito de Antônio Conselheiro)* (Salvador, 1986); and Barreto, *Destruição de Canudos*.

were related to important family clans on the outside included the merchants who plied their trade with the full cooperation of Conselheiro, and thereby assured the flow of supplies. One of them, Antônio da Motta, came to a bad end. The most affluent citizen of Canudos before Conselheiro's arrival on the basis of his goatskin business, he was invited to remain. After the first military expedition against Canudos in November 1896, however, he was anonymously accused of having leaked information to the state police. Condemned without a trial, he and his oldest sons were shot in broad daylight, supposedly in front of Antônio Conselheiro. His wife and remaining children escaped, taking refuge in the house of another merchant in the city and eventually fleeing through the sertão. His inventory was confiscated and his store looted.

Joaquim Macambira and Norberto das Baixas were two more local merchants and planters who had been welcomed to stay in Canudos. Both were caboclos, with large families. Macambira ran a dry goods store and farmed. Known locally as a peaceful man, he enjoyed good relations with political chieftains throughout the region, including Colonel João Evangelista Pereira de Melo in Joaseiro. One of his sons fought with the Guarda Católica and was killed attempting to disable one of the army cannons. Most of the rest of his family died in the final attack, although five of his children, one gravely injured, were taken to Salvador and ultimately resettled in the Bahian sertão. Army officials gave them special treatment because only one member of Macambira's family, his fallen son, had been a combatant. Norberto das Baixas, named after his fazenda, had held considerable influence in the region as well as in Bom Conselho, where he owned additional property. Much of his income came from importing wood from Bom Conselho to Canudos and its neighboring hamlets. Norberto fought with the Guarda Católica and fell in battle. Three daughters survived the final attack: two were taken away by soldiers, and a third, seven years old, was placed under the protection of the Comitê Patriótico in Salvador.

The most powerful merchant in Canudos, Antônio Francisco de Assunção [Vilanova], enjoyed more authority than anyone in the city except Conselheiro and João Abbade. Originally from Ceará, not only did he control the local economy but he consulted frequently with Abbade on political matters. His chits held the value of money, and he sat as a kind of justice of the peace. His tiled-roof house sat alongside the two churches. Leaving Ceará after the 1877 drought, he settled in Vilanova (today, Senhor do Bonfim) in Bahia and established his trading business. As early as 1873, a priest in Vilanova advised him to speak with Antônio Conselheiro about the possibility of supplying his followers, and when Canudos was established he moved not only his business but his extended family to the sertão. His brother, Honório, came with his lissome wife Pimpona, who was known for her elegance in dressing, and who therefore must have stood out among the Canudos women in their penitential poverty. Antônio himself was tall, bearded, and always dressed in suit and tie.

Vilanova quickly monopolized the lion's share of commerce in Canudos. Abbade took steps to favor him over the competition. One merchant, Jesuino Correio, was expelled; Antônio da Motta was killed. During the fighting he stockpiled and distributed arms and ammunition in his store and helped arrange for shipments of weapons. Just before the end, he calmly arranged for his family to leave, receiving personal permission from Conselheiro, who was near death. He rescued all of his relatives in small groups, burying four boxes of silver in the ground but carrying with him to Ceará, according to his brother Honório, three or four kilograms of broken gold and some jewelry. When he died, of natural causes, he was considered a rich man.

Men and women who did not join Conselheiro's sect also lived freely in the community. Conselheiro, who at one point in his life had taught children, established schools in Bom Jesus and Bom Conselho, and another in Canudos. The first one did not last long. The teacher who was hired under Conselheiro's direction proved to be an alcoholic, and was dismissed. Conselheiro directed the Canudos school himself, importing a teacher from Soure named Moreira who died shortly before the outbreak of war. Conselheiro then hired 22-year-old Maria Francisca de Vasconcelos, also from Soure. She had studied at the Escola Normal in Salvador, but when her family forbade her to marry a working-class youth, the couple fled to Soure and then took up residence in Conselheiro's Belo Monte. Her husband abandoned her before the conflict. No *beata*, Vasconcelos represented those Canudos residents attracted by the hope of egalitarian community.

Boys and girls attended school together daily, a fact which would have shocked traditionalists had it been known outside Canudos (and which contradicts Conselheiro's image as someone who abhorred "modern" practices). Each child paid a monthly tuition of 2,000 réis. There were several teachers. One escaped the final fighting and fled to Salvador, where she died in 1944. Fanatics or not, Conselheiro's followers were encouraged to educate their children in the formal manner, a privilege which virtually none of them would have had in the hamlets and villages of their birth.

Until the first military attack against Canudos, Conselheiro and his aides cooperated fully with the local police. When a fleeing murderer, "Black Marcos," appeared in the city, he was seized by Conselheiro's militia and turned over to the police in Monte Santo. He was tried and sentenced to prison in Salvador. The same courtesy did not always extend the other way. When men loyal to Conselheiro wandered away from Canudos and were arrested (for loitering, or on suspicion of being wanted for unnamed crimes), they were often pressured or manipulated into making formal statements against other members of Conselheiro's followers, providing an excuse for the police to enter Belo Monte and make further arrests.[93]

The Conflict

The decision to intervene with massive armed force was made after the relatively minor incident, mentioned above, in which a detachment of soldiers which had just made an exhausting march across desertlike terrain was caught by surprise at Uauá by Conselheiro's *jagunços*. The contingent retreated to Joaseiro under forced march. Fearing loss of face, the state government ordered a general mobilization and telegraphed Rio de Janeiro for assistance to put down the rebellious peasants.

The story of the four military campaigns against Canudos is as well known as it is terrible, and it will not be recounted here. The first expedition, in November 1896, involving 100 men under a lieutenant with instructions to capture Conselheiro, is the one that was intercepted by Conselheiro's *jagunços* and routed at Uauá. The second and third expeditions also failed; the latter, with 1,300 men, 16,000,000 rounds of ammunition, an artillery batallion, and a squadron of cavalry, was led by Coronel Moreira César, who died in the fighting. The fourth attack, which began in June 1897, garnered the resources of the entire Brazilian army, machine guns, Krupp field cannon, and tens of thousands of soldiers, many of them backlands *jagunços* pressed into uniform. Even so, Conselheiro's outnumbered forces waged effective defensive guerrilla war because they knew the terrain so intimately. Hundreds of soldiers deserted, but they were quickly replaced by fresh troops sent into battle. The final assault sent 5,000 armed men led by the commander of the Second Military District, General Artur Oscar de Andrade Guimarães, and watched personally by the minister of war, to encircle Canudos and starve it into submission. The great unpopularity of President Prudente de Morais and widespread anxiety stirred by the republican fears of a monarchist plot led to the decision that Canudos must be smashed without mercy.

The carnage was terrible. In later years, dozens of hastily buried corpses washed up during rains, some partially mummified in their blue

---

93. For example, the case of the "Negro Badulque," arrested as a spy for Conselheiro in Cumbe in Jan. 1895. Badulque's testimony led to the arrest and imprisonment of all of the male members of the Alves da Silva family in July 1897. In retribution, Badulque was later murdered. Justice prevailed inside and outside of Canudos.

uniforms striped in crimson.[94] In the end, more than a thousand federal troops were killed, with many more wounded or felled by rampant disease.[95] The telegraph brought reports of the fighting, filed daily by war correspondents, to the entire country. The most absurd rumors spread wildly and were believed. It was said that arms were arriving for Conselheiro from Argentina via Minas Gerais, and that foreign soldiers were being sent from the United States and also from Austria, to restore the monarchy.[96] True enough was the contention that the *sertanejos* were scattering through the backlands, attacking local towns and supply trains and enlarging the scope of the conflict. Stories of misappropriation of war supplies and treachery multiplied, too, as long as the fighting fared badly.

It was determined later that Antônio Conselheiro had died of dysentery on September 22, some two weeks before the final storming of the city. He was nearly 70, and he had been in failing health, although a photograph of his corpse suggests that he was not as emaciated as might have been expected. The battle had raged fiercely, led by the remaining *jagunço* fighters, parched, starving, and refusing to give up. On the day after the storming, all 5,200 houses were destroyed. Soldiers slit the throats of prisoners in camps in Canudos and in Queimadas, near Monte Santo. Conselheiro's body was exhumed, and the head removed by a knife thrust. It was later displayed on a pike, before delirious onlookers on the coast —"with carnival joy." Da Cunha's description of the end of the holy city is terrible and eloquent: "Canudos did not surrender. The only case of its kind in history, it held out to the last man. Conquered inch by inch, in the literal meaning of the words, it fell on October 5, toward dusk—when its last defenders fell, dying, every man of them. There were only four of them left: an old man, two other fully grown men, and a child, facing a furiously raging army of five thousand soldiers."[97]

What permitted observers and defenders of the republic to justify the massacre was the falsehood that Canudos had been rooted in crime and madness. Da Cunha himself would use the writings of the turn-of-the-century English psychiatrist Henry Maudsley to assert Conselheiro's madness. In Salvador, Conselheiro's personality was measured and evaluated by leading physicians and university professors. Among them, Raimundo

94. Nataniel Dantas, "De Canudos resta apenas a memória," *Cultura* (Brasília), Jan.–Mar. 1982, p. 38.

95. Data on casualties from the four military expeditions against Canudos are summarized in Neto et al., *Canudos: Subsídios*, 24–75.

96. *La Nación* (Buenos Aires), July 30, 1897; *A República*, Feb. 20, 1897, p. 1 and Feb. 22, 1897, p. 1.

97. *RB*, 475.

Nina Rodrigues stands out in the lucidity of his analysis and the force-fulness of his convictions. A professor of forensic medicine at the Bahian Medical School and himself one of the rare mulattos to attain such a high position at the time or later, Nina Rodrigues's conclusions reveal the think-ing of the elite not only about Conselheiro's mental state but also about the backlands population.

Published in the last month of the conflict, the title of Nina Rodrigues's article—"Epidemic of Insanity at Canudos"—is revealing. Conselheiro suffers from "chronic delirium," given to "progressive psychosis which re-flects the sociological conditions of his environment.[98] Nina Rodrigues's chronicle of Conselheiro's life is detailed, and includes several assertions which never appeared before or after in print: that he mistreated his wife; that she was raped by a policeman in Ipu before leaving him; that he had a violent side to his personality, at one point wounding his brother-in-law; that his frequent job changes represented instability and a "delirium of persecution." In Nina Rodrigues's narrative Conselheiro finds a "for-mula for his delirium" and an expression for his "megalomania" in railing against luxury and pleasure. He disrupts the "peaceful life of the agricul-tural population" of the backlands, advocating instead "errant living and communism." His arrest leads him to reveal publicly his paranoia; he be-gins to act like Christ, and becomes consumed with his "hallucinatory" vision.

The *jagunço*, Nina Rodrigues writes, is a "perfect type to be affected" because as a hybrid product of miscegenation he "suffers from the fusion of unequal races." He is not "any kind of mestizo." The recipient of "virile qualities from his savage Indian and negro ancestors," he lives a rudimen-tary but free life, in contrast to the mestizo on the coast, "degenerate and weak." He is "naturally a monarchist." Canudos's curse, the mulatto professor avers, results from the "fetishistic belief of the African deeply rooted in our population."[99] Nina Rodrigues's unshakable belief in biologic determinism permitted him to denigrate the results of miscegenation de-spite his own origins, and thereby to rationalize the elite's acceptance of the brutal suppression of the insurgents.[100]

98. Nina Rodrigues, "A locura epidemia de Canudos," *Revista Brazileira* (Salvador), Oct. 1897, pp. 129–218, esp. 130–141. For details of Conselheiro's early life he did rely on João Brígido's accounts to some degree.

99. See Nina Rodrigues, "O animismo fetichista dos negros bahianos," *Revista Bra-zileira*, Apr. 15–Sept. 4, 1896.

100. Examination of photographic portraits of distinguished *baianos* in the state geo-graphical and historical association suggests that perhaps two in ten members of the elite were visibly mulatto. They were never fully accepted, either socially or in terms of rec-ognition of their work. Nina Rodrigues's writings were only acknowledged in 1939 at the

However, even as a disciple of now-discredited French and Italian theories about crime and atavism, Nina Rodrigues showed a spark of originality. Far more than most other analysts, he acknowledged the impact of sociological factors on the behavior of Conselheiro and his followers. When Conselheiro's severed head was subject to medical examination, the professor of legal medicine registered surprise at the lack of evidence of degeneration, which adherents of the European theories expected.[101] The same result had occurred when he examined the skull of Lucas de Feira, a fugitive slave, who robbed and committed great numbers of crimes earlier in the nineteenth century. Finding the skull to have been entirely normal, Nina Rodrigues praised Lucas, saying that in Africa he would have been a great warrior but that, transported to Brazil and forcibly domesticated, he became a criminal for social reasons.[102] Canudos, therefore, was not unique, but was merely one among many expressions of *jagunço* bellicosity in the tradition of Chique-Chique, Andarahi, Cochó, Lençóes, Belmonte, Canavieiras, and Brejo-Grande, all Bahian towns and hamlets where violence had been provoked, and in "a thousand other localities" in Brazil. The difference, he noted, was that Canudos was the first conflict rooted in the monarchist convictions of the *sertanejo*, "too primitive in his social evolution" to be able to understand republican law. Conselheiro's crazed delirium of religious mission, he concluded, combined too naturally with the troublemaking instinct of the fanatical *jagunços*.[103]

The end of the battle on October 5, 1897 unleashed a storm of charges and recriminations. Opposition to President Prudente de Morais became more intense, led by his own vice-president. A month later Prudente narrowly escaped assassination; subsequently he used the event as a pretext for harsh repression against his enemies.[104] Bahian Rui Barbosa, in a speech written but never delivered, attacked the army's killing of its pris-

---

initiative of Afrânio Peixoto. Da Cunha's concluding sentence in *Os sertões*, lamenting that Brazil lacked a Maudsley, is ironic, since Nina Rodrigues had been following the same line of analysis in Salvador since 1897 (*RB*, 476).

101. He read, for example, the *Annales médico-psychologiques* (Paris); *Archives d'Anthropologie Criminelle* (Lyons); and *Archivo de Psiciatria, scienze penali ed antropologia criminale* (Turin). For a more modern treatment of the subject, see Artur Ramos, *Locura e crime* (Pôrto Alegre, 1937), esp. 78–122.

102. See Nina Rodrigues, *As collectividades anormaes* (Rio de Janeiro, 1939), esp. 16. Among the Europeans who influenced him in his notions about links between crime and racial types were Laségue, Falret, Sighele, Rossi, Le Bon, and Charcot.

103. Nina Rodrigues, *As collectividades anormaes*, 69–77. Nina Rodrigues omitted any consideration of political aspects of the *jagunço* lawlessness. In reality, most of the incidents he cited were instigated or led by local *coronéis*.

104. The would-be assassin, who did kill the minister of war, was described 50 years later by Pernambucan historian and diplomat José Maria Bello as "a young half-breed soldier from the North" (Bello, *A History of Modern Brazil*, 156).

oners and blamed "Brazilian indifference" for having not understood the realities of the backlands.[105] César Zama, a Bahian partisan of Luiz Vianna, published under a pseudonym a vehement attack on the way Conselheiro had been misunderstood and libeled.[106] But the overwhelming expression of opinion following Canudos's end was that of relief and acceptance of the hypothesis, laid out by da Cunha, of the irrevocable duality of Brazilian society between backlands and coast.

Since 1897, generations of writers on Brazil have used Canudos as evidence for their individual interpretations of Brazilian culture. Most have relied exclusively on da Cunha; many have distorted original meanings. An analysis published in 1903 compared Conselheiro's behavior to that of Mohammad, arguing that the backlanders, semisavages, were like desert Arabs, ready at any moment to join a religious leader of "superior energy."[107] Time did not diminish the practice of exaggeration. Conselheiro's followers were "a band of disgraceful creatures, convinced of their perdition," a scholar wrote in the staid journal of the Paulista Academy of Letters six decades later. Their behavior, he continued, represented "obstinate psycho-erotic infantilism, fixed among various provisional instincts of puerile lives."[108] Conselheiro fought all his life against the Church of Rome, another historian wrote, distorting the record to make his case that Conselheiro was a hero of socialism.[109]

Few critics acknowledged the long tradition of violence in the countryside, or the reasons why police and militia troops were as feared as outlaws in the small towns of the interior, but many borrowed da Cunha's morbid fascination with what he called the primitive tenacity of the backlanders without accepting his deep respect. The possibility that the individual decisions to join Conselheiro's followers may have been systemic, rooted in economic or psychological need, was disregarded. Certainly the physical conditions of deprivation in the interior were overlooked, even as intellectuals and journalists worked feverishly to close the books on the revolt and to dismiss the rebellion as an aberration caused by fanatics. Publicists

105. The speech was to have been delivered to the Senate on Nov. 6, 1897. It is published in *Obras completas de Rui Barbosa* (Rio de Janeiro, 1952–), XXIX, 183–187. Barbosa did deliver a speech in Salvador denying that Conselheiro had been trying to destroy the republic.

106. "Wolsey" (César Zama), *Libello republicano: Acompanhado de commentários sobre a campanha de Canudos* (Salvador, 1899).

107. José de Campos Novaes, "*Os sertões,*" *Revista do Centro de Ciências, Letras e Artes* (Campinas), 2:2 (1903), 45–55.

108. Octacílio de Carvalho Lopes, "*Os sertões*: Diagnose e denúncia," *Revista da Academia Paulista de Letras*, 24 (June 1967), 26–28.

109. Edgar Rodrigues, *Socialismo e sindicalismo no Brasil, 1675–1913* (Rio de Janeiro, 1969), 53.

for the republic regularly distanced themselves from the lower classes: in
data provided for a handbook for foreign travelers to Brazil it was shown
that the death rate in Brazilian cities compared favorably with the rate in
Europe, emphasizing that "the negro and the lower-class mulatto between
them account for some 75 percent of the mortality in Brazil."[110] Cultural
figures who borrowed da Cunha's racial pessimism included Monteiro Lo-
bato, Oliveira Vianna, and Paulo Prado.

Others selected the caboclo to symbolize freedom and anarchic indi-
vidualism, a substitution of the Indianist vogue of the nineteenth century.
Gilberto Freyre later acknowledged that his "lusotropical" interpretation
of Brazilian race mixture was strongly influenced by the positive side of
da Cunha's view of the backlander.[111] Still others, emphasizing the feudal
structure of backlands society and the class conflict underlying Canudos,
extolled the *sertanejos* as soldiers against latifundarism: in the words of
Rui Facó, "an unconscious but spontaneous rebellion against the monstru-
ous and secular oppression of semi-feudal latifundia."[112] But Canudos was
neither spontaneous nor a willful rebellion, and it is clear that Conselheiro
never advocated social revolution.[113]

Conselheiro well understood that the external world was changing,
and he warned that unless his precepts were followed disaster would result. The 1877 drought was followed by three harrowing years without
rain. By 1900, at least 300,000 northeasterners had fled to the Amazon
region, driven by drought and despair as well as drawn by the rubber
boom.[114] The arm of coastal government seemed to be inexorably penetrating the interior. The first major census, in 1872–74, enumerated all
citizens and asked questions about their occupations, race, and income.
The imposition of the metric system and decrees standardizing weights
and measures threatened the informal mechanisms of the *feira* market
system, and led to more than one hundred riots in the *agreste* region of
four northeastern provinces in 1874–75, the Quebra-Quilo revolts.[115] To

110. See David Brookshaw, *Race and Color in Brazilian Literature* (Metuchen, 1986),
52.

111. See the anarchist novel by Fábio Luz, *Na província* (Rio de Janeiro, 1902); author's
interview with Freyre, Recife, July 24, 1986. See also "Um pensador de raça," *Veja e Leia*
(São Paulo), July 29, 1987, pp. 84–85.

112. Rui Facó, *Cangaceiros*, 833; Edgar Rodrigues, *Socialismo e sindicalismo*, 54–55.

113. Della Cava makes this assertion (*Miracle at Joaseiro* [New York, 1970], 77) although
the main emphasis of his research on backlands religious movements has shown that they
were "part and parcel of a national social order," and not, as Pereira de Queiroz and others
have maintained, rooted in the geographical isolation of the sertão and therefore independent. See Pereira de Queiroz, *O campesinato brasileiro: Ensaios sobre civilização e grupos
rústicos no Brasil*, 2d ed. (Petrópolis, 1973), 321.

114. Rodolfo Teófilo, *História da sêca do Ceará (1877/1880)*, cited by Rui Facó, *Cangaceiros e fanáticos: Gênese e lutas* (Rio de Janeiro, 1963), 30.

115. See Roderick J. Barman, "The Brazilian Peasantry Reexamined: The Implications

officials, the leaderless revolts meant sedition; to small landowners and traders, the penetration of government into the backlands meant higher taxes, controls, and an increased threat of forced military induction.

The monarchy's ouster and the subsequent promulgation of the secular laws of the republic, especially the one legally recognizing only civil marriage and requiring state registry of deaths, shook devout Catholics.[116] Their simply expressed faith considered Emperor Pedro II a father figure and a kind of earthly saint ever since the renewal of the church in the 1870s and its conflict with the government. The world seemed to shake in its foundations. In France, the election of "progressive" Pope Leo XIII and the *ralliement* led to fears that the "real" pope had been kidnapped and imprisoned by the Masons in the cellar of the Vatican.[117] We know that Conselheiro railed against Masons, and that he bitterly opposed the secular republic for reasons that his backlands followers personally understood. As early as 1874–75, lower-class men and women, alarmed by rumors that the church had been taken over by evildoers, assaulted churches and destroyed books and furnishings in Recife and in Acarape and Quixeramobim in Ceará.[118] Conselheiro may well also have pointed out the high number of foreign priests sent to the backlands, objects of suspicion and distrust for their strange accents and unfamiliar ways. The strong emphasis among backlands Catholics on pilgrimages to seek personal intercession from the saints in exchange for *promessas* (vows) made it easier for residents of the region to leave their homes and to seek messianic intervention. Self-flagellation was another major element in backlands religious practice: if God brought suffering, hunger, disease, then one must pray harder and sacrifice more.[119] Families lived in terrible isolation, leading to submission in some but creating the strength for martyrdom in others.

If Conselheiro's settlement lasted nearly four years, it was due at least

of the Quebra-Quilo Revolt, 1874–75," *HAHR*, 57:3 (Aug. 1977), 401–424 and Armando Souto Maior, *Quebra-Quilos: Lutas sociais no outono do império* (Recife, 1978).

116. The late Joyce Riegelhaupt, working on the secularization of cemeteries in rural Portugal, observed that civil control tended to remove women from their traditional role of preparing bodies for burial and of organizing the funeral and wake. Courtesy of Linda Lewin.

117. On *De Rerum Novarum* and the new attitudes of the Catholic church toward republicanism and social change, see Harvey Goldberg, *The Life of Jean Jaurès* (Madison, 1962), 66–69; David Shapiro, "The Ralliement in the Politics of the 1890s," *St. Antony's Papers*, No. XIII, *The Right in France, 1890–1919* (London, 1962), 13–19, 48.

118. Eusébio de Souza, *História militar do Ceará* (Fortaleza, 1950), 293. Rui Facó notes that similar attacks occurred in Minas Gerais after the proclamation of the republic, acts he links to popular disillusionment with the new government.

119. See José Rafael de Menezes, *Sociologia do Nordeste* (Recife, 1985), 27–29. For a broader view of the psychological characteristics of rural Catholicism, see Pereira de Queiros, "Tambaú, cidade dos milagres," *Cultura, sociedade rural, sociedade urbana: Ensaios* (São Paulo, 1978), 135–143.

in part to the mere fact that during that time political fighting in Bahia had been stalemated, leaving Canudos in peace. For, inevitably, Canudos's sudden explosion in growth created dislocations. Because of the sertão's extremely low population density and corresponding lack of infrastructure, it placed an unprecedented strain on the surrounding area. The traditional system of agriculture and livestock raising in the parched backlands required landowners to exploit large numbers of sedentary manual laborers, either as squatters or for pitiful day wages. The presence of a docile lower class also anchored the political system of the new republic, based on control of the rural vote by local *coronéis*. Canudos abruptly challenged both systems.

From a moribund hamlet of a few hundred, Canudos grew to five thousand people in 1895 and tripled in size by 1896. The depletion of population in the surrounding region, mostly to the south and east, affected merchants and fazendeiros in direct proportion to the degree of outmigration from each município. The situation was made worse by the fact that once Canudos grew to the size of a small city, most transactions in Canudos were done with scrip rather than currency. This was not so much a result of Conselheiro's aversion to republican money—he was reputed to have once burned some of it in public as a symbolic gesture—as a consequence of Canudos's shortage of currency. Hide sales produced only minimal revenues, and there was no other source of income within the community. Conselheiro's flock did not leave their settlement to work outside as agricultural laborers, something permitted a generation later in Ceará by Padre Cícero as a pragmatic measure to keep neighboring overlords satisfied.[120] Conselheiro, more feared than Cícero and less knowledgeable about the political system, did not seem to acknowledge the regional dislocation caused by the staggering growth of his settlement. As a result, he virtually monopolized the local labor force, thereby directly threatening local landowners.

To be sure, isolation was not total. There was always commerce, as already noted, and even during the final armed struggle sympathizers linked to the Vianna faction of the PRF-Ba (including a Coronel Leitão in Santa Luzia, about whom little else is known) furnished materials, thus supplementing what Conselheiro's forces looted from military supply trains or took from dead and injured soldiers. There must have been still other channels of goods, especially given the political enmities in the state. If the picture of Conselheiro as a crazed fanatic isolated from reality is accurate, then his followers' ability to defend themselves against thousands of armed troops and heavy artillery defies logic. Cut off and completely

120. See della Cava, *Miracle at Joaseiro* and Pang, "Banditry and Messianism," 18.

surrounded for weeks, Canudos kept up defensive fire without stop until the end, with no shortage of functioning weapons or bullets.

The ability of the settlement to function as well as it did testifies to the organizational adeptness of Conselheiro and his aides. There was no transport or way to carry materials except by mule, and no medicines. On the road and in the trenches, soldiers and *jagunços* alike chewed the roots of shrubs. In Monte Santo, the major staging area for the government forces (and less than a day's march from Canudos), prices soared, to 2,500 réis for a dozen eggs and 4 milréis for a kilo of "old cheese, four to five times prices in the capital." Salaried full-time workers—a tiny elite within the lower-class population—earned from 30 to 55 milréis monthly.[121] In Canudos, 20 cows were slaughtered daily up to the end of the fighting, and the settlement raised large crops of manioc and beans. But Conselheiro's logistical miracle could only have occurred if his city was well connected to the regional economy and to regular sources of trade.

What can be said about the men and women who made Belo Monte their home? Even with a lower population than the figures usually cited, they did live crowded into a city whose river ran only intermittently, and their day-to-day existence must have been arduous. It is likely that the settlement reached its highest point of saturation in early 1897 but that many residents fled during the final months of battle—only a few hundred women and children were left when Canudos fell, and a maximum of a few thousand had died in the fighting.[122] Whatever the precise size of his flock, Conselheiro exercised immense personal influence over it, which Gilberto Freyre and others have attributed to the deep-seated residue of Sebastianism in the *sertanejo* population.[123] That one influence was probably secondary—it is doubtful that Canudos's residents consciously believed that King Sebastian would personally appear in the heavens— but certainly Conselheiro's appeal is consistent with our understanding of nineteenth-century backlands Catholic belief, not significantly changed from the sixteenth- and seventeenth-century Catholicism brought to Brazil by the Portuguese. Arguably more deeply felt than on the coast, it focused on the mystical state of the soul and the promise of salvation.

121. See Lelis Piedade's dispatch published Sept. 18, 1897 in the *Jornal de Notícias*; Angelina Nobre Rolim Garcez, "Aspectos econômicos," 24. On arms shipments, see Tristão de Alencar Araripe, *Expedições militares contra Canudos* (Rio de Janeiro, 1960); "Franciscanos nos Canudos/1897," *Revista Vozes*, 69:5 (June–July 1975), 387; Favila Nunes's dispatch, *Gazeta de Notícias*, Aug. 29, 1897, p. 1.

122. About 1,400 graves were exhumed by soldiers as part of their census of houses and occupants after Canudos fell.

123. Freyre, "Atualidade de Euclydes da Cunha: Conferência lida no Salão de Conferências da Biblioteca do Ministério das Relações Exteriores do Brasil, no dia 29 de outubro de 1940," 2d ed. (Rio de Janeiro, 1943), 21; Vamireh Chacon, *O humanismo brasileiro* (São Paulo, 1980), 139; Ribeiro, "Brazilian Messianic Movements," 58–59.

Ritual—the cult of the saints, festivities, novenas, and prayers—was a way to win the good graces of the supernatural world, the relationship of *do ut des:* giving in order to receive in kind. Rural culture was reflectively spiritualist, an environment in which saints and other rarefied beings interceded personally to overcome daily problems. Its culture typically blamed drought, crop failure, disease, and suffering on divine punishment. These beliefs legitimate institutions of hierarchy and exploitation, as Patricia R. Pessar has noted, but they also reinforce hope in messianic intervention.[124] For the citizens of Canudos, their world crashing in on them, religion filled the empty space separating the family from the rest of civil society. There was a near morbid concern with penitence and guilt. After Conselheiro's death, stories began to spread through the sertão that he had murdered not only his wife and mother but at least two others, and that his wandering, abstemious life was a divine punishment visited on him. For others, Conselheiro simply was a saint. He performed saintly works, and he spoke soothingly and gently to the people who came to watch him.[125] To the backlanders, after all, saints were not abstract but characteristically human, a palpable presence in family life. When he died, condemned by church as well as by state, his place in daily backlands religious practice was taken by devotions to the Holy Trinity, Santo Antônio, the cult of the Guardian Angel, Jesus Maria José, Senhor do Bonfim. This was perfectly understandable, given the chronic lack of priests and absence of formal religious training available to the rural population.[126]

The role of the Catholic church hierarchy in the affair represents a singular irony. Confronted by Conselheiro's orthodox but institutionally unsanctioned piety, it looked to the state to rid it of an impostor priest whose appeal threatened the hierarchy and its political power during a time of continued Ultramontanist pressure from Rome. Canudos occurred exactly at the time when church and state were formally separated—over

124. Pessar, "Unmasking the Politics of Religion," 257; Donald Warren, Jr., "Spirito-therapy in Rio de Janeiro around 1900," *Religião e Sociedade*, 12 (1985), 1; Consuelo Pondé de Sena, *Introdução ao estudo de uma comunidade do agreste bahiano: Itapicurú, 1830/ 1892* (Salvador, 1979), 142, 153–161; Pereira de Queiroz, *O campesinato brasileiro*, 72. Fredrick B. Pike speaks of a surge of personal (as opposed to institutional) spiritualism in Latin America from the late nineteenth century to the 1940s rooted in a belief that spiritual power rested in all individuals. To some extent this has always been a part of folk Catholicism in Brazil. See *The Politics of the Miraculous in Peru: Haya de la Torre and the Spiritualist Tradition* (Lincoln, 1986).

125. Interview, Desembargador Polybio Mendes da Silva, Itapicurú, with Consuelo Pondé de Sena, cited in her *Introdução ao estudo de uma comunidade*, 156. As a child, he was handed to Conselheiro, and kissed his hands. His family, in turn, offered wood from their *fazenda* to construct Conselheiro's new church at Vila Rica, today Crisópolis.

126. On "rustic Catholicism" in Brazil, see Pereira de Queiroz, *O campesinato brasileiro*, 72–99.

vehement church protests—as a result of positivist influence on the federal constitution of 1891. Hostile to his missionary emphasis on redemption and his stern demands for more, not less, observance of Catholic doctrine, in the end they turned their backs on a genuine expression of popular spirituality. A decade later, a similar thing happened when the national church hierarchy rejected opportunities to influence rising labor union militancy, opting instead to ally itself with the government and the industrialist elite.

Canudos touched political nerves as well. Local elites well remembered how quickly the fabric of authority fell apart when the rampaging Quebra-Quilo mobs threatened to invade major cities.[127] To partisans of the new republican government, the monarchist Conselheiro assumed omniscient proportions, even if in reality his personal powers were as modest as we know them to have been. Local conditions were in flux and economically strained, and national institutions (the armed forces, the civilian regime) untested. "In Brazil, where politics and institutions do not inspire confidence," read the headlines introducing a feature story on Canudos in the *Folha de São Paulo* some 80 years later, "Antônio Conselheiro attains new elements of meaning."[128]

The fact that the federal troops and state police forces sent to battle the Canudos *jagunços* were unprepared to fight underscores the republic's vulnerability. Many of the conscripts were peasants, hastily trained. In the midst of the final assault on Canudos, the commanding general requested 5,000 additional men, remarking bitterly that of the nearly 10,000 supplied so far only 2,600 had been found fit for service.[129] Boys were enlisted as young as 13. Some were used as servants; others actually fought. A number of youths of 14 died on the battlefield in the conflict.[130] Separated by a chasm of class and status from their officers, the troops were badly fed, miserably housed, and often were not paid, due to either inadequate appropriations or dishonest paymasters. Equipment was in disrepair.[131] Everyone near the front walked covered with dust in the more-than-40-degree (C°) heat of the day, since there was only enough water to drink,

127. Barman, "The Brazilian Peasantry Reexamined," 401.

128. "Cacaso" [Antônio Carlos de Brito], "O pesadelo no país de Canudos," *Folha de São Paulo*, July 5, 1987, p. 58. See also Nancy P. S. Naro, "Rio Studies Rio: Ongoing Research on the First Republic in Rio de Janeiro," *The Americas*, 44:2 (Oct. 1987), 429–440; Décio Saes, *A formação do estado burguês no Brasil (1888–1891)* (Rio de Janeiro, 1985).

129. Neto et al., *Canudos: Subsídios*, 69. The Bahian state police force in 1894 had only 1,812 men, and a high desertion rate.

130. Frei Pedro Sinzig, *Reminiscências de uma frade* (Rio de Janeiro, 1917), excerpted in *Revista Vozes*, 69:5 (June–July 1975), 384.

131. Correa Bittencourt, "Saúde pública," *Década republicana*, 2d ed. (Brasília, 1986), 228.

and that, a newspaper reporter described, was "the color of coffee with milk and with the taste of cattle urine."[132] The wounded were often bedded in the same improvised hospitals with patients carrying contagious disease; physicians were in such short supply that medical student volunteers were sent from Salvador.[133]

Not surprisingly, therefore, assignment to the front was considered a punishment. Captured deserters were sent to Canudos; soldiers arrested and convicted for military infractions were given prison terms which were suspended as long as the soldier fought. Since the foot soldiers were considered riff-raff anyway, they were at least permitted to take along their wives and any other women who joined them on the way. These were known as *vivandeiras:* more than two hundred followed the Saviget column from Sergipe. A few wives, some with small children, accompanied their soldier husbands all the way from the South of Brazil. Married men were charged for their wives' keep, although most of the women were expected to work, some as washerwomen or cooks, and others as medical aides at the front. One, a *gaúcha* named Busa, remained with the troops after her soldier companion was killed, and worked as a volunteer hospital aide at the front until she contracted smallpox and died.[134]

In August 1897, during the worst of the fighting, a citizens' committee was formed in Salvador to aid the victims. Unprecedented in Brazilian history, the "Comitê Patriótico" responded in part to the intense barrage of press coverage of the Canudos campaign, which intensified to its fullest extent at the onset of the fourth and last military campaign. Reporting ran the gamut from satire and ridicule, mostly directed against Conselheiro, to searching questions about the appropriateness of the brutality practiced against the *jagunços.* In the face of published reports that survivors were being forced into servitude and prostitution, the Bahian committee went into action.[135] Collection boxes were placed on every major street. The committee's president, Franz Wagner, was a Protestant. Other members included newspapermen, the owner of the music store, and some German

132. Dispatch published in *Jornal do Commércio* (Rio de Janeiro), Aug. 8, 1897, p. 3.
133. See "Apontamento de detalhes" files, 3rd Military District, Quartel General, Salvador, 1897. Career records of staff medical officers are stored at the Polícia Militar headquarters, Gabinete do Comando, Salvador (Corpo 376).
134. 3rd District, Quartel General, Salvador, Nov. 22, 1897, artigo 23 (p. 68) and artigo 25 (p. 100). A contingent of families was housed temporarily at 6th Military Region headquarters in Salvador on their way back from Canudos while their men awaited reassignment. Unaccustomed to this kind of surroundings, some of the women began to behave wildly, yelling, "dancing sambas, and making lewd advances to soldiers indiscriminately." The offenders were ordered evicted by the commanding officer.
135. See the Dec. 22, 1897 editorial in São Paulo's *Comércio de São Paulo,* "Diviserunt vestimenta mea," reproduced in Walnice Nogueira Galvão, *No calor da hora: A guerra de Canudos nos jornais,* 2d ed. (São Paulo, 1977), 103–105.

and Silesian priests from the Franciscan and Capuchin convents, recruited by Wagner. Only a few members of the city's leading families were represented, although there was a Barreto Filho and a Dias Lima Sobrinho, and local physicians were enlisted to help.[136] Outsiders (and working journalists) did most of the organizing work. Smaller committees were established in Queimadas and Alagoinhas to process women and children survivors left there by the retiring troops.

In late August, a delegation from the committee traveled by train and then wagon to the staging area in Cansação, to comfort the wounded, bury the dead, and carry medicine. A few children from villages en route who had been orphaned by attacks by Conselheiro's *jagunços* were taken by committee members back to Salvador, along with the more than one hundred surviving women and children found in Canudos, most of them wounded and weeping silently. In the days following the city's fall, the priests spent most of their time giving last rites and baptizing the "pagan" wounded. They were kept away from the prisoner encampments, but learned of "horrible cruelties" practiced against the survivors. Some were shot when they could not keep up with the forced march. Soldiers killed children by smashing their skulls against trees. Wounded *jagunços* were drawn and quartered, and burned.[137]

By mid-November, Lelis Piedade, the *Diário de Notícias* correspondent and secretary of the Comitê Patriótico who had brought news of the darker events of the battle to the public, affirmed that the committee had taken control, and that no child rescued from Canudos would any longer be taken by "orphanages, factories, or tutors" without all efforts to find living relations being first exhausted.[138] The committee's records confirm the varied nature of Canudos's population. Of the 146 survivors (16 women over the age of 20, and the rest children, mostly under 12 years old), 41 were described by committee interviewers as "white." In several cases, clarifying notations were added gratuitously: "white, blond, and of good family."[139] Even given the wide latitude in racial classification at the end of the nineteenth century—and the fact that captives of more European appearance were more likely to be spared—finding 28 percent of Canudos's survivors identified as white undermines the prevailing view of Conselheiro's followers as nothing but caboclo peasants.

136. See dispatch published in *O Comércio de São Paulo*, Dec. 22–24, 1897, reproduced in Galvão, *No calor da hora*, 496–510.

137. See "Franciscanos nos Canudos/1897," 394–398.

138. Lelis Piedade, "Declaração" in the name of Comitê Patriótico, Salvador, Nov. 17, 1897.

139. Of the 146 cases, only one such notation was added to the file of a nonwhite survivor.

We do not know, of course, how many more survivors escaped, or met ill fate at the hands of soldiers or others in the backlands. Even while the fighting continued, many soldiers had forcibly taken women and girls as concubines; whole families of children were put to work cleaning barracks and as servants. The records of several of the girls brought to Salvador by the committee indicate that they had been raped by soldiers, or beaten, or "abandoned to the streets." Nineteen were listed as gravely ill or wounded. Some annotations: a *mulata* of 15, described as having "left her parents dead at Canudos," with "land, a house, livestock, and benefactors" in Salgado. Or a caboclo, aged 10, "intelligent and alert, commended in the Canudos school for his vivacity, orphaned, of legitimate birth of parents from Genepapinho." The orphaned children were placed with relatives if they could be located, or entrusted to the care of volunteer families. Women who recovered from their wounds were first restricted to Salvador, where they worked as domestic servants, but after some time passed were permitted to return to the interior. To ensure that they would not be impeded during their journey back to the sertão, the citizens' committee issued safe conduct passes—with a photograph of Lelis Piedade so that illiterates would be able to recognize him and honor the document.

It is understandable that the Canudos conflict has lent itself to symbolism of dramatic proportions, for Conselheiro did at some point promise his followers salvation, even the Second Coming in the millenarian year 1900. But most of his preachments were not apocalyptic, only demanding personal morality and hard work and invoking spiritual protection from the corrupted secular world. That world, in the sertão, was also locked in economic crisis, as it had been to a greater or lesser degree for generations. Belo Monte was thus a place in which the faithful would lead disciplined lives according to Catholic precepts, removed not only from modern infamies but from hunger and want; yet it also seemed an environment of primitivism and audacity. What outsiders viewed as a rebellion was simply the collective statement by its inhabitants that they demanded the right to relocate to a place they considered a haven from an unfriendly world. In any case, Belo Monte had to be crushed because it upset the stability of the status quo in the sertão. It affected two major elements of rural oligarchical power: the docile labor system and the "herd vote" (*voto de cabresto*), the Old Republic's arrangement whereby rural bosses captured all of the votes under their control and delivered them in exchange for local power. Out-migration from all parts of the backlands to Canudos posed an immediate, real threat to the system. Had not the punitive expedition sent to meet Conselheiro been overcome at Masseté, there would have been less apparent justification for retaliation, but another pretext would have come sooner or later given the political realities of the day.

Educated Brazilians were easily terrified by the image of Conselheiro and his followers as renegades and savages because of the image of rural folk—even before the introduction of scientific racism—as primitive and prone to disorder. It is noteworthy that Conselheiro has not been remembered as an abolitionist, even by contemporaries (and later historians) seeking lessons of social injustice in the Canudos drama.

Referring to the Rodeador millenarian movement (1817–20), psychiatrist René Ribeiro notes that testimony from some of the members who were arrested revealed the "essential gentleness" of their conception of their holy crusade by which they sought to establish at Jerusalem the Kingdom of God on earth. A politically motivated uprising in the same region in 1817 hardly affected these religious folk and their dreamlike concept. Prayer and waiting for King Sebastian took precedence over militancy.[140] So, too, in Canudos. The holy city was a center of refuge, theocratically organized though pragmatically connected to the surrounding environment—an achievement that bespeaks considerable flexibility on the part of Conselheiro and his aides.

Neither Conselheiro's personal mannerisms nor the ways in which he comported himself were particularly unusual for the backlands. His coarse blue robe knotted at the waist by a cord was the standard garb not only for *beatos* in northeastern Brazil but of several religious orders throughout Latin America.[141] Vargas Llosa reminds us that missionaries in cassocks were more frequent visitors to backlands villages than urban priests dressed more conventionally, and thus the sight of Conselheiro was nothing extraordinary.[142] On the whole, furthermore, the inhabitants of Canudos were instrumentally rational, even if as individuals they displayed great personal courage in abandoning their former lives to enter Conselheiro's holy city. As Roderick J. Barman said of the peasantry at the time of the Quebra-Quilos, the backlanders were an "independent, aggressive group possessing a well-established way of life which they were capable of defending with concerted, effective action and without much regard for the wishes of those usually considered to be the dominant elements in rural society."[143] It is thus insufficient to dismiss Canudos and like movements as responses to anomie, or breakdowns of the traditional extended family owing to the rise of urbanization, the decline of paternalism, and other factors.[144] Nor was Belo Monte simply a kind of theater, as

140. Ribeiro, "Brazilian Messianic Movements," 65–66.

141. Nineteenth-century Augustinian monks in Cuba, for example, dressed in exactly the same clothing as Conselheiro. See John G. F. Wurdemann, *Notes on Cuba* (Boston, 1844), 22–23.

142. Vargas Llosa, *The War of the End of the World*, 3.

143. Barman, "The Brazilian Peasantry Reexamined," 404.

144. See, for example, Pereira de Queiroz, *O campesinato brasileiro*, 42–45, 59–63 and her "Messiahs in Brazil," *Past and Present*, 31 (July 1965), 62–86. Todd Alan Diacon evaluates

outsiders tended to regard it—a pathetic year-round version of the carnivalesque practice whereby the poor become rich and enact waking dreams of social inversion.

Before Canudos was attacked, most of its residents were too busy following Conselheiro's austere precepts of daily behavior to be crazed by end-of-the-world (or other) fantasies. Deprivation and Conselheiro's spellbinding explanations about the evilness of encroaching modern life brought them together, but they were not "fanatics" until circumstances united them in common defense against armed outside attack. After the bloodshed started, those who did not flee may well have capitulated to the mood of fiery prophesy and determination described by da Cunha. But it is the normal existence that Conselheiro established, even prosperous for a locality in the stricken sertão in the late nineteenth century, that the outsiders overlooked. Republican Brazil was too insecure and infested with factional warfare among its oligarchic factions to dismiss such pious folk without bloodshed.

---

the Pereira de Queiroz view in "Capitalists and Fanatics: Brazil's Contestado Rebellion, 1912–1916" (Ph.D. diss., University of Wisconsin, 1987), 381–384.

Index

Contributors

GEORGE REID ANDREWS received his Ph.D. from the University of Wisconsin-Madison and teaches at the University of Pittsburgh. The author of *The Afro-Argentines of Buenos Aires, 1800–1900*, he is currently writing a book on race relations in São Paulo, Brazil since the abolition of slavery.

HEBE MARIA MATTOS DE CASTRO is assistant professor of history at Universidade Federal Fluminense (Niterói, Rio de Janeiro, Brasil). She received her M.A. degree from that university in 1985, and is now working toward her Ph.D. with a research project on the formation of the rural labor force in south central Brazil after slavery. She is author of the book *Ao sul da história: Lavradores pobres na crise do trabalho escravo* (São Paulo, 1987), and is currently writing a book on relations between peasantry and slavery in Brazil.

SEYMOUR DRESCHER received his Ph.D. from the University of Wisconsin in 1960. He is a university professor at the University of Pittsburgh, and also is currently visiting professor at City University of New York. He is the author of several books, including *Econocide: British Slavery in the Era of Abolition* and *Capitalism and Antislavery: British Mobilization in Comparative Perspective*. He is currently working on *Processes of Popular Mobilization in Nineteenth-Century Europe*.

ROBERT M. LEVINE received his Ph.D. from Princeton University in 1967. He is chairman and professor of history at the University of Miami, Coral Gables. In addition to his continuing work on Canudos, he is studying relations between social classes in republican Brazil as well as the ways nineteenth- and early twentieth-century photographers interpreted reality and influenced the ways society came to see itself. This subject is treated in his original videotaped documentary, "Imágenes de Reinos," and his forthcoming monograph, *Images of History*.

REBECCA J. SCOTT is associate professor of history at the University of Michigan, Ann Arbor, and author of *Slave Emancipation in Cuba: The Transition to Free Labor, 1860–1899*. She is currently working on a comparative study of postemancipation society in sugar-producing regions of Brazil, Cuba, and Louisiana, focusing on the evolution of class relations in the countryside and their links to patterns of political mobilization. An essay of hers, "Comparing Emancipations," appeared in the Spring 1987 issue of the *Journal of Social History*.